D1000043

KINSEY, SEX AND FRAUD

The Indoctrination Of A People

AN INVESTIGATION INTO THE HUMAN
SEXUALITY RESEARCH OF ALFRED C. KINSEY,
WARDELL B. POMEROY, CLYDE E. MARTIN AND
PAUL H. GEBHARD

Authors: Dr. Judith A. Reisman and Edward W. Eichel

Editors: Dr. J. Gordon Muir and Dr. John H. Court

A Lochinvar-Huntington House Publication

Copyright © 1990 by Lochinvar Inc.

All rights reserved. No part of this book may be reproduced without permission from the publisher, except by a reviewer who may quote brief passages in a review; nor may any part of this book be reproduced, stored in a retrieval system or copied by mechanical, photocopying, recording or other means without permission from the publisher.

Distributed by Huntington House Publishers

P.O. Box 53788

Lafayette, Louisiana 70505

1-800-749-4009

Library of Congress Card Catalog Number 90-62974

ISBN 0-910311-20-X

Dedication

To the several hundred children who suffered inhumanely in the illegal sex experiments that constitute the basis for a significant portion of Dr. Alfred Kinsey's book *Sexual Behavior in the Human Male*. Many of these children will still be alive today.

It is also dedicated to those children who are being subjected to the kind of Kinseyan sex education curricula described in this book.

CONTENTS

PREFACE

This book is the result of a coincidental coming together of two people with diverse backgrounds whose professional work led them into the position of having to confront the sexuality research of Alfred C. Kinsey.

I first came across the work of Dr. Reisman when a friend (who has become an editor of this book) handed me a paper Reisman had presented at the Fifth World Congress of Sexology, Jerusalem, 1981. Her presentation was on the role of child abuse in Dr. Kinsey's research into the sexuality of children and the relationship of that research to the field of sexology, sex education and pornography. As a former practicing physician working in a medical research establishment, I was immediately aware that Dr. Reisman—if her facts were correct—was in possession of some shocking and astonishing information on a landmark piece of research—research which we all knew about but had never read. I began to study Kinsey's work. Dr. Reisman was on target. She began working on a book.

Shortly thereafter, I was contacted by Edward Eichel, a New York City psychotherapist, who had seen my name in a newspaper column describing Reisman's early work on Kinsey. Eichel was involved in his own research, which was touched by Kinsey's theories. He had studied Kinsey's impact on current trends in sex education and in academic sexology, an interest he had developed having come through the experience of a human sexuality program at New York University. Eichel's insights into Kinsey's influence on modern sex education and academic sexology were a perfect complement to Reisman's studies. Eichel began to cooperate with Reisman on the book project[1] and, with considerable help from many persons too numerous to mention, the present volume finally took shape.

Dr. J. Gordon Muir

President

Lochinvar Inc.

---

[1] Reisman's original book project, *Child Sexuality or Child Sexual Abuse: A Critical Analysis of the Kinsey Reports*, with D.F. Fink, 1985 (unpublished), has been extensively used as a key resource for the present volume.

FOREWORD

Forty years after is a good interval for assessing the value of a major research project. Freed from the climate and thinking of the time, we can ask different questions, and in different ways. Far removed from the original work, the original assumptions guiding data collection and interpretation can be challenged. With hindsight we can ask whether the apparent discoveries still stand the test of time. We can observe what has flowed from the findings and discern their value. And, freed from the constraints of personal contact with a distinguished investigator, one can establish more readily whether the reputation is warranted.

From their first appearance the Kinsey Reports were controversial, but this did not necessarily mean they were wrong. The sheer volume of data collected and reported was enough to ensure a reception in the academic community since nothing like it had ever been attempted before. A strong semblance of scientific reality flowed from the taxonomist turned student of human sexual behavior. An air of authenticity was created by claims of careful sampling techniques and massive sample numbers. Yet criticism arose at once, not only from those with moral views who expressed outrage, but also from among professional peers such as the medical profession and statisticians.

Nonetheless, there was a large body of professionals who wanted to believe the Kinsey findings and were ready to absorb his interpretations. The Kinsey Reports have become the starting point for subsequent sex research. The textbooks quote Kinsey's findings as if they were undisputed truth.

Voices of disquiet have been few and far between. Those who have raised methodological issues and challenged findings have largely addressed elements of the whole, though allegations of sample bias have been around for long enough to question everything that flows from the data.

At last we have a serious, scholarly and detailed critique of many elements of the Reports. The allegations are at best damaging, at worst awesome in the extent to which there appears to have been error, distortion and bias on such a grand scale that it cannot be dismissed as accidental. One cannot help being reminded of the Piltdown Man fraud, or the scandalous construction of data by Sir Cyril Burt relating to the inheritance of intelligence, which set back research for a generation, as it was only later revealed to be fabricated.

With Kinsey, the issues are more serious. Very basic questions such as the true nature of sexuality, the relationship between heterosexuality and homosexuality, and the sexual development of children are all addressed in an authoritative manner. His view of morality is superimposed on the data.

In this analysis by Reisman and Eichel, we see the fruit of those findings. Starting from uncertain data, reported with surprising levels of inaccuracy, generalizing well beyond the limits allowed by the inherent bias in the samples, Kinsey is shown to have spawned a whole movement dedicated to conveying a radical view of sexuality which is fast becoming the norm. To the advocates of homosexual liberation and pedophilia this presents no problems, but rather a springboard for advocacy.

By contrast, those who believe in the conservative values of home and family will recognize that the new sexology has a highly deceitful base. These authors have not commented from afar, but have carefully documented their sources for all to see. They have contacted those directly involved in the research, as far as this is possible, to ensure that their criticisms are adequately founded.

The result is both surprising and alarming. Perhaps we should not be surprised when we see the headway that has been made by gay activists and by pedophiles in shaping public opinion. Yet it is surprising that so many apparently responsible professionals can accept the Kinsey findings so uncritically even at a time when the STDs, and especially AIDS, are making the risks of promiscuity and anal sex so enormous.

We cannot afford to rest our understanding of human sexual response on false data. The implications are just too great to allow error to go unchallenged. Hence this expose of a standard research source is an invaluable document in beginning to determine the truth about human sexual behavior. We can reasonably assume that it is nothing like Kinsey proposed. Indeed it is time to demand answers to the blunt allegations posed in this book. Since a whole industry is now involved, an informed debate will be difficult to mount, but it must not be avoided. It is time to know the truth.

—Dr. John H. Court

Professor of Psychology and Director, The Psychological Center, Graduate School of Psychology, Fuller Theological Seminary, Pasadena, California.

ABOUT THE AUTHORS

Dr. Judith A. Reisman is president of The Institute for Media Education, a non-profit educational and research agency. Prior to receiving her Ph.D. in communications from Case Western Reserve University in 1980, Reisman enjoyed a successful career as a creative artist. During this period she was involved in projects that won several artistic awards (eg, the Dukane award, the Gold Camera award, the Silver Screen award and the Silver Plaque award).

In 1981, Dr. Reisman presented a paper on Kinsey's fraudulent child sexuality data at the Fifth World Congress of Sexology in Jerusalem. Her presentation, titled "The Scientist as Contributing Agent to Child Sexual Abuse: A Preliminary Consideration of Possible Ethics Violations," called for an investigation of the work of the Kinsey team and the Kinsey Institute. That paper forms much of the basis of the present book. Without hearing Reisman's lecture, leading U.S. sexologist John Money severely attacked Reisman (but not her facts), claiming that she was likely to set back sexology and sex education by 2,000 years.

Significantly, as a result of her subsequent related work, particularly her investigation under a Justice Department grant of "Images of Children, Crime and Violence in *Playboy, Penthouse* and *Hustler*," Dr. Reisman has been similarly violently attacked—notably by the staff of, writers for, and paid consultants to the named publications. Her Justice Department study has now been published under the same title by Huntington House, 1990. In press with the same publisher is Reisman's upcoming book *"Softporn" Plays Hardball: Targeting Children, Women and the Family*. Reisman's child pornography research has begun to be used as expert evidence in United States Supreme Court cases. It also was used as background and evidence in the 1990 child sexual abuse conviction of *Hustler* magazine's "Chester the Molester" cartoonist, Dwaine Tinsley.

It is, Reisman believes, important to note that her federally funded research effort was wrongfully gutted and subverted by her Washington, D.C., host academy, the American University (AU), while under the watch of past president Dr. Richard Berendzen. Dr. Berendzen was recently convicted of making obscene phone calls of a child-sexual-abuse nature, and, ironically, has been involved in the collection of child pornography. Dr. Reisman is currently in the process of seeking legal redress for grievances regarding AU's alteration of her child pornography research.

Dr. Reisman has been listed in *Who's Who in Sexology, Who's Who of Women, Who's Who in Education, International Who's Who in Education, Who's Who in Society, Personalities of America, Two Thousand Notable Americans*, to name only a few. She is a frequent invited speaker, TV talk show guest and contributor of articles to professional and popular journals.

Edward W. Eichel completed his Bachelor of Fine Arts degree at the School of the Chicago Art Institute in 1958 and was awarded the George and Isabella Brown traveling fellowship. He studied under Oskar Kokoschka at the artist's famous summer academy in Salzburg, practiced his art in Paris, and was a press artist at the Eichmann trial in Jerusalem. He was a recipient of a Louis Comfort Tiffany Foundation grant for painting in 1967. The Andy Warhol era—and subsequent anti-art movements—eroded Eichel's romance with the art world. He has since focused his energies on the scientific study of human sexuality.

Eichel currently is a psychotherapist in private practice in New York City. He received his Master's degree in the Human Sexuality, Marriage and Family Life Program at New York University. He has been a health educator in the CUNY (City University of New York) system, and with the Boys Club of America. His innovative research on sexual compatibility has been published in *Medical Sexology: The Third International Congress* (of the World Association of Sexology, 1980), the *Journal of Sex & Marital Therapy* (Summer 1988), *Medical Tribune* (German edition, January 27, 1989), and other publications. He coordinated symposia on male-female compatibility for professional conferences and observed the resistance and hostility to that kind of research by special interest groups dominating the human sexuality field. This reaction has led Eichel to his investigation of a hidden agenda in the field and to the connection of this agenda with the early Kinsey Reports.

Eichel is a member of the Society for the Scientific Study of Sex and the American Association of Sex Educators, Counselors and Therapists. He has been listed in the *International Who's Who in Sexology* and in *Who's Who in American Art*.

INTRODUCTION

THE SEXUALITY RESEARCH OF ALFRED C. KINSEY—40 YEARS LATER

Time for Accountability

Chapter Overview

No man in modern times has shaped public attitudes to, and perceptions of, human sexuality more than the late Alfred C. Kinsey. He advocated that all sexual behaviors considered deviant were normal, while polemicizing that exclusive heterosexuality was abnormal and a product of cultural inhibitions and societal conditioning. Beginning just over 40 years ago, he and his team of researchers presented the American people with "statistical data" showing that what they were supposedly doing sexually was more liberal, and more consistent with his own ideology, than anyone had believed possible. Put another way, Kinsey demonstrated with numbers that "normal" behavior was much more permissive than conventional wisdom had suspected.

Few people realized that the data he presented were not, as claimed, scientific. Nor were the data representative of societal norms. And it now is becoming clear that, in addition to being highly biased, Kinsey's results may have been fraudulent. For these reasons and because the foundation for some key Kinsey conclusions still accepted today as scientific fact is research conducted on human subjects illegally and against their will, it has become necessary to call on the scientific community to reexamine Dr. Kinsey's sex research effort.

*That is one purpose of this book. The importance of this issue is
underscored by the fact that Kinsey's conclusions have become, to some
extent, a self-fulfilling prophecy. They are the basis for much that is
taught in sex education and for an ongoing agenda to engineer public
attitudes about human sexuality.*

In 1948 and 1953 a two-part "cultural phenomenon" took place with
the publication of Dr. Alfred Kinsey's monumental works on, respec-
tively, male and female human sexuality (*Sexual Behavior in the
Human Male* by Alfred C. Kinsey, Wardell B. Pomeroy and Clyde E.
Martin [W.B. Saunders, Philadelphia, 1948] and *Sexual Behavior in the
Human Female* by Alfred C. Kinsey, Wardell B. Pomeroy, Clyde E.
Martin and Paul H. Gebhard [W.B. Saunders, Philadelphia, 1953]).
These books, which, contrary to expectations for scientific works,
quickly became national bestsellers, are customarily referred to as
Kinsey's *Male* and *Female Reports.* More than any other documents
in history, they have shaped Western society's beliefs and   understanding about what human sexuality is. They have defined what
people allegedly do sexually, thereby establishing what is allegedly
normal. Their impact on attitudes, subsequent developments in sexual
behavior, politics, law, sex education and even religion has been im-
mense though this is not generally realized by the public today.

WHAT KINSEY CLAIMED

What Kinsey claimed about "statistically common behavior" in the
United States population of the 1940s surprised most, shocked many
and delighted a number of others. It was assumed that his "scientific"
research among a sample of several thousand men and women could
be extrapolated to the U.S. population as a whole to provide an accurate
picture of national sexual behavior. Kinsey's findings were thus nothing short of stunning, but the most stunning finding of all went almost
unnoticed, except, it appears, by the FBI.

Even before the 1948 appearance of the Male Report, magazine and
newspaper articles proclaimed that a *scientific* study would reveal that:

- 85% of males in the U.S. have intercourse prior to marriage

- Nearly 70% have sex with prostitutes

- Between 30% and 45% of husbands have extramarital   intercourse

- 37% of all males have homosexual experiences between adolescence and old age

Writing in *Harper's*, Albert Deutsch exclaimed, "The Kinsey survey explodes traditional concepts of what is normal and abnormal,
natural and unnatural in sex behavior."

The Female Report in 1953 was almost anticlimactic by   comparison. However, despite Kinsey's protestations that his books were

presenting facts without moral interpretations, the "facts" of the Female Report continued the process begun in the male volume—"a persistent hammering at Judeo-Christian legal and moral codes," according to Albert Hobbs in *The American Journal of Psychiatry*. Stressed in the Female Report were data showing that premarital sexual intercourse was beneficial for women. This practice would help them adjust emotionally, sexually and socially. Avoidance of premarital intercourse was said to be a potential cause of damaging inhibitions that could persist for years after marriage.

However, the most profoundly shocking findings of both Kinsey Reports were almost totally ignored. These were Kinsey's conclusions on childhood sexuality. Kinsey's "scientific" "research" purported to prove that children were sexual beings, even from infancy, and that they could, and should, have pleasurable and beneficial sexual interaction with adult "partners" who could lead them into the proper techniques of fulfilling sexual activity.

The damage done to children from sexual relations with adults— what the public thought was molestation—was almost always, in Kinsey's view, the result of overreaction and hysteria by parents, schoolteachers, police, etc. But one aspect of Kinsey's research was completely missed by everyone. That was the criminal childhood sexuality *experimentation* which formed the basis of Kinsey's conclusions on childhood sexual potential. The results of these experiments are the basis for beliefs on childhood sexuality held and taught by academic sexologists today.

According to an article in *Esquire* magazine, Kinsey was the "Patron Saint of Sex," whose books set in motion "the first wave of the sexual revolution." They inspired the sexual philosophy of Hugh Hefner's *Playboy* Magazine—Hefner wrote in the first issue: "We believe . . . we are filling a publishing need only slightly less important than one just taken care of by the Kinsey Report." And, according to sexologist Morton Hunt, Kinsey was "the giant on whose shoulders all sex researchers since his time have stood."

John D'Emilio and Estelle B. Freedman, in their book *Intimate Matters: A History of Sexuality in America* (Harper & Row, 1988), noted that "the strongest assault on sexual reticence in the public realm emerged not from the pornographic fringe, nor from the popular culture, but from the respectable domain of science," with the publication of Kinsey's Male and Female Reports. By purporting to demonstrate a wide divergence between real sexual behavior and publicly espoused norms, the implication was that "cultural values surrounding sex needed revision." D'Emilio and Freedman observed that Kinsey's "scientific credentials" "gave legitimacy" to the way the media presented his findings and the way the public received them. They further noted that "The Kinsey studies, as much as pornography, shaped the context in which the Supreme Court responded to the obscenity issue."

One Kinsey legacy is the active and prominent Kinsey Institute for Research in Sex, Gender, and Reproduction—located on the Indiana

University campus. This institute is currently expanding its national role more than ever—entering biomedical research, initiating and participating in conferences, distributing syndicated sex advice columns and providing massive sex information resources on an international scale. [One recent Institute project was The Fourth Kinsey Symposium, *Aids and Sex: An Integrated Biomedical and Biobehavioral Approach*, where, among other things, the normalcy of heterosexual anal intercourse was suggested, even stressed (see chapter 7)].

If the legitimate pornography industry is, in a sense, another Kinsey legacy, then its leaders are clearly grateful. According to Christie Hefner, in the 1960s the Playboy Foundation became the major research sponsor of the Masters and Johnson Institute and made the initial grant to establish an Office of Research Services of the Sex Information and Education Council of the U.S. (SIECUS).[1] The latter organization is heavily involved in the incorporation of Kinsey's basic sexual philosophy into school sex education programs, as is later explained (see chapter 4).

In 1971, *Playboy*, according to the junior Hefner, "awarded a grant to establish a pilot program at the University of Minnesota" with the aim of "changing the attitudes of men and women medical students." This was necessary because "today's medical students and practicing physicians perpetuate arbitrary judgments about normal and abnormal sexuality . . . [and] are ignorant of the variety of possible human sexual expression." Hefner added that "the state of medical practice today [in 1987] is not much better than it was in 1971."

Another group grateful to Kinsey is the proliferating pedophile movement, which justifies its advocacy of adult sexual relations with children by quoting Kinsey's child sexuality findings. Tom O'Carroll, an active pedophile, chairperson of the international organization PIE (Pedophile Information Exchange) and author of *Paedophilia: The Radical Case* (Alyson Publications, 1980), cites Kinsey's research (correctly) as supporting the harmlessness of adult-child sexual interaction.

O'Carroll says,

A number of empirical studies have established some unassailable facts on the subject [of children as innate sexual beings]. *The most famous of these sources is of course the work of the biologist Alfred Kinsey and his coresearchers* which made almost as much impact in the early post-war years as Freud had in his time.

Perhaps the most striking of the Kinsey findings, as they concerned pre-adolescent children, relates to their capacity for sexual orgasm. "Orgasm has been observed in boys of every age from five months to adolescence," Kinsey wrote. Also, "Orgasm is in our records for a female babe of four months" [p. 36; emphasis added].

1   Christie Hefner, in the Foreword to *Sexuality and Medicine, Volume 11*, Earl E. Shelp (ed.), Reidel Publishing Co., 1987.

WHO WAS DR. KINSEY?

In his 1972 biography, *Dr. Kinsey and the Institute for Sex Research* (Harper & Row), Kinsey coworker and Male and Female Report co-author Wardell Pomeroy asks, "How was it possible for a sickly religious boy who grew up to be a serious college student with an obvious talent for biology and an abysmal ignorance of sex—how did this young man evolve into a world authority on sexual behavior who could be mentioned in the same breath with Freud?"

According to Pomeroy, Kinsey was a sickly child (rheumatic fever and rickets), brought up in a strictly religious atmosphere, who blossomed out in adolescence—becoming one of the first Eagle Scouts in the country (and later a scoutmaster)—before completing his college career with a D.Sc. in the biological sciences from Harvard.

Although he became "the world's foremost sex researcher," he was in his earlier years a "shy and lonely young man who had avidly pursued gall wasps instead of girls . . . ." Naive and unsophisticated about girls and sexuality, the reserved young Kinsey, "The boy who never had a girl" and whose boyhood had been a "sexually sterile world," married the first girl he had ever dated!

Pomeroy relates that Kinsey was a "complicated man who remained virtually unknown to the public." Even his Male and Female Reports were probably not well known *firsthand* to the public. Pomeroy describes him as the "most talked about and least read author of our time; the majority of people got their opinions of his work second hand." This certainly appears true of many scientists then and since and may explain how major problems with his research (described later) have been overlooked for 40 years.

Kinsey, who majored in taxonomy (the classification of animals and plants), spent his pre-sex-research years collecting gall wasps. He became the world's leading expert on this subject because of his avid, single-minded, driven approach to this painstakingly clerical task. As a young professor of zoology at Indiana University he developed the habit of talking to students about sex and helping them with their sexual problems—perhaps not a surprising activity for a biologist in the stuffy moral atmosphere of the period.

After 18 years at Indiana, Kinsey was chosen to be the coordinator of the university's new marriage course.[2] He quickly discovered that there was "no reliable body of statistics . . . on what people did sexually which might serve as a guide when people asked for the kind of advice he was expected to give." This was the starting point for Kinsey's great lifework. He began to do for sexual behavior statistics what he had done for gall wasps—he became a zealous, compulsive collector. He also, according to Pomeroy, began "to give expert advice [on sex]" despite the fact his "own knowledge . . . was rather recent."

---

2   In her forthcoming book *Softporn Plays Hardball* (in press, Huntington House Publishers), Dr. Judith Reisman challenges the official version, repeated here, that Dr. Kinsey was "chosen" for the university's new marriage course. Reisman argues that Dr. Kinsey maneuvered for many years to gain approval for this course.

Ironically, and perhaps significantly, one of the forces that propelled Kinsey into his sex research at Indiana was the fierce opposition from the local clergy to his Marriage Course lectures. This precipitated his choice between lecturing and field work in human sexuality. Hostility from the religious stuffed-shirts of his day, combined with his own loss of religious faith during his college student days and his reading of books on religion and culture, led Kinsey to be "indignant" about the effect of Judeo-Christian tradition on society.[3]

According to Pomeroy, Kinsey had also come to see a basic incongruity between science and religion and couldn't understand why all scientists didn't feel the same way. It is clear that he shared Pomeroy's view that Christians inherited an almost paranoid approach to sexual behavior from the Jews. Knowledge of this particular background is essential to an understanding of the subsequent difficulties Kinsey got himself into with statistics, experimental research and the attempt to undermine a system of morality without (he claimed) making moral judgments.

KINSEY'S PHILOSOPHY

Following his formative years in which Kinsey came to reject the tenets of Judeo-Christian morality, he clearly developed a viewpoint on human sexuality that considered animal sexual behavior as a model for human sexual behavior. His basic sexual philosophy has been well described in his own works and by one of his biographers, historian Paul Robinson. Kinsey's overall view of sex is probably best summed up by a statement in the Female Report:

> [C]onsidering the physiology of sexual response and the mammalian backgrounds of human behavior, it is not so difficult to explain why a *human animal* does a particular thing sexually. It is more *difficult to explain why each and every individual is not involved in every type of sexual activity* [p. 451; emphasis added].

To Kinsey, being involved in all types of sexual activity would represent freedom from the cultural conditioning which society imposes and which leads to artificial distinctions such as "right and wrong, licit and illicit, normal and abnormal, acceptable and unacceptable in our social organization" (Male Report, p. 678).

According to Robinson in his 1976 book *The Modernization of Sex* (Harper & Row),

> [Kinsey] believed that human fulfillment, in the sexual realm at least, lay in following the example of our mammalian forebears.... He evaluated every form of sexual activity in terms of its role in the sexual lives of the lower species, and *he frequently concluded that outlawed*

---

3   Two of Kinsey's four favorite books, according to Pomeroy, were *Man and His Gods*, by Homer Smith (1952), and *Sex Laws and Customs in Judaism*, by L.M. Epstein (1948). Pomeroy noted that "Kinsey knew a great deal about the Judeo-Christian tradition, and he was indignant about what it had done to our culture. He often cited the inaccuracies and paranoia in which he asserted it abounded. He was quite blunt in talking about this tradition and its effect on the sexual lives of people in our own time, and he backed up his opinions with a sound background of knowledge acquired not only from extensive reading but from numerous discussions with historians who were expert in the subject" (Pomeroy, 1972, p. 30).

sexual practices were entirely natural because they conformed to "basic mammalian patterns." . . . [He] even sought to invest [sexual relations between humans and animals] with a certain dignity by suggesting they could achieve a psychological intensity comparable to that in exclusively human sexual relations [pp. 55, 56; emphasis added].

A few pages later, Robinson noted that Kinsey strongly implied

. . . all orgasms were equal, regardless of how one came by them, and that there were accordingly no grounds for placing heterosexual intercourse in a privileged position [p. 59].

Kinsey, Pomeroy, Martin and Gebhard claim in Hoch and Zubin's 1949 work, *Psychosexual Development in Health and Disease* (Grune & Stratton), that this mechanical, stimulus-response explanation of human sexuality is biologically programmed for both young and old:

[W]e suggest that sexuality, in its basic biologic origins, is *a capacity to respond to any sufficient stimulus.* It is simply a picture of physiologic response and psychologic conditioning in terms that are known to the biologist and psychologist. *This is the picture of sexual response in the child and in most other younger mammals.* For a few uninhibited adults, sex continues to remain sex, however they have it [p. 27; emphasis added].

This of course is the Kinsey principle of "outlet sex"—sex is sex any way you have it, the only difference in quality for some people being the effect of "inhibitions." [It should be noted that the Kinsey authors included the *child* in this description of sexual response as an ability to react to a sufficient stimulus.] As Robinson saw it, the notion of "outlet sex" enabled Kinsey to relegate marital heterosexual intercourse to an inferior place in the sexual spectrum:

The notion of *outlet*, for all its apparent innocence, performed important critical services for Kinsey. Principal among these was the demotion of heterosexual intercourse to merely one among a democratic roster of six possible forms of sexual release (the six, in order of their treatment in the Male volume, were masturbation, nocturnal emissions, heterosexual petting, heterosexual intercourse, homosexual relations, and intercourse with animals of other species). . . . marital intercourse, was even more rudely confined to a single chapter toward the back of the book, where it received about one third the attention devoted to homosexual relations. . . . a remarkable feat of sexual leveling . . . *the fundamental categories of his analysis clearly worked to undermine the traditional sexual order* [Robinson, 1976, pp. 58, 59; emphasis added].

Robinson here points out a basic truth about the presentation of Kinsey's work: it was designed "to undermine the traditional sexual order." Of course, there is nothing wrong with trying to change the traditional sexual order if sound scientific research shows it to be unfounded.

Some have dismissed critics of Kinsey's work as "moralists." However, careful review shows that Kinsey's own position on sexuality was a moral one— he had his own moral agenda. The Kinsey Reports,

Robinson tells us, "were informed by a set of *values* and intellectual preferences that, taken together, could be said to constitute an *ideology*" (Robinson, 1976, p. 49; emphasis added). Robinson added:

> ... in undermining established categories of sexual wisdom. ....Kinsey assigned [prominence] to masturbation and homosexuality, both of which were objects of his partiality. ...[He had a] tendency to conceive of the ideal sexual universe according to a homoerotic model [*ibid*. pp. 54, 64, 70].

Wardell Pomeroy states in his Kinsey biography that some of Kinsey's best friends were scientists like himself who, in one way or another, were part of his "grand scheme" (Pomeroy, 1972, p. 155).[4] Kinsey's research was in fact the scientific base which Kinsey and colleagues hoped to use in their effort to change society's traditional moral values. The specific tactics for implementing the "grand scheme" are examined in later chapters.

Essentially, Kinsey initiated a two-part strategy. First, he advocated the establishment of bisexuality as the "balanced" sexual orientation for normal uninhibited people. In effect, this would encourage heterosexuals to have homosexual experiences. This was the basic step in obliterating the existing heterosexual norm of sexuality with its traditional protective family structure, values and conventional sexual behavior (spousal heterosexual intercourse implied). This would open the way for the second and more-difficult-to-implement step—creating a society in which children would be instructed in both early peer sex and "cross-generational" sex (adult sex with children).

KINSEY'S RESEARCH

Between the years of 1938 and 1963 (seven years after Kinsey's death), the Kinsey research team took the "sex histories" of about 18,000 persons. In his Male (1948) and Female (1953) Reports Kinsey used data from just over 5,000 of the male sample and almost 6,000 of the female sample. Somewhere and sometime in the course of the project, Kinsey appears to have directed experimental sex research on several hundred children aged 2 months to almost 15 years. These children were orally and manually stimulated to orgasm by a group of nine sex offenders, some of whom were "technically trained" (if they were not child sex offenders before, they were after the experiments). These orgasm tests on children constituted Kinsey's experimental child sex research database!

By presenting his male and female interview data in the form of numerous tables depicting the frequencies of various sexual activities, Kinsey provided a picture of what people were supposedly doing sexually in 1940s society. Kinsey co-author Wardell Pomeroy, writing in Forleo and Pasini's 1980 book *Medical Sexology* (PSG Publishing Co.), explained it this way:

---

4   Pomeroy elsewhere in his book says that the "grand scheme" or "design" was in its "simplest terms" to find out what people did sexually (p.4). As will later become apparent, it was to provide a statistical base for a new morality.

By shifting to a scientific methodology that largely involved frequency counts and cross-tabulations with basic variables [Kinsey] implicitly and explicitly reinforced the view that what is *done* is normal. Nowhere in the Kinsey reports is there the idea of "normal" in the moral sense, although there *is* the recognition that ideas about normal sexuality do not correspond with statistically common behavior [p. 76; author's emphasis].

It was Kinsey who established in the public awareness what "statistically common behavior" was. And this was far removed from what anyone had ever imagined. Moreover, this revelatory behavior gradually came to be seen as normal. Psychologists Zimbardo, Ebbeson and Maslach, writing in their 1977 book *Influencing Attitudes and Changing Behavior* (Addison-Wesley), described the effect of this new sexual knowledge (of what people in society purportedly did sexually) on society itself:

> [T]he results of the Kinsey surveys on sexual behavior of the American male and female *established, to some degree, social standards of what was acceptable common practice* [p. 89; emphasis added].

The problem with Kinsey's "statistically common behavior" (or statistical morality), however, is that it was defined by using data from a sample of interviewees that was unrepresentative of society—that contained, in the case of the male sample, for example, a high percentage of prisoners and sex offenders. Present and former prison inmates made up as much as 25% of the group of men Kinsey used to find out what "normal" male sexual behavior was!

The entire make-up of Kinsey's samples was such as to undermine the credibility of his research findings (see chapters 1 and 2). His conclusions on sexual behavior in society, it turns out, corresponded more closely with his philosophy of what that behavior should be than with what it actually was. If even some of the information we now have of Kinsey's research methods had come out 40 years ago, the Kinsey team would have become scientific pariahs instead of instant celebrities.

What was the ultimate goal of Kinsey's research? It appears to have been dual. The first part was, as noted, to change society's view of what "normal" human sexuality was. The second was to establish himself as the world's foremost sex researcher. Both parts of this goal have been achieved, *temporarily*. And the achieving of part two has placed a stamp of authority on the "rightness" of part one.

Information very recently unearthed from the archives of the University of Akron adds to our understanding of the lengths to which Kinsey was prepared to go, and the level of deceit he was prepared to practice, in order to realize his ambition. When confronted with evidence from an expert that there was bias toward unconventional sexual behavior among the subjects who volunteered for his sex research, Kinsey ended his professional relationship with this individual and, in a clear breach of scientific ethics, deliberately ignored and concealed the information. The expert was the late and noted psychologist Dr. Abraham Maslow. The full story is recounted in chapter 6.

Even Kinsey's coworkers were chosen, apparently, with a particular set of results in mind. Pomeroy's qualifications for directing the evolution of human sexuality (by being part of the Kinsey team) were recognized by Kinsey himself (Pomeroy, 1972, p. 98). At a scientific conference in 1983, Pomeroy related that Kinsey had hired him on the basis of his personal sex history, deducing that he "had not picked up all the taboos, and the inhibitions, and the guilts that. . .[his] colleagues had . . . " (Eastern Regional Conference of the Society for the Scientific Study of Sex, Philadelphia, April 17, 1983).

Pomeroy mentioned Kinsey's hiring stipulations in his biography, where he relates that "no one could have come to work for Kinsey without giving his [sex] history first. It was a condition of employment, which a few employees in the lower echelons resented" (Pomeroy, 1972, p. 461). Elsewhere Pomeroy recounted that Kinsey refused to hire an applicant for a research staff position because the person believed "extramarital intercourse harmful to marriage, homosexuality abnormal, and animal contacts ludicrous."[5]

What Kinsey and this handpicked staff concluded from illegal and even violent sexual experimentation on child subjects was that the orgasmic potential of *infants* and children was scientifically established for the first time. This "research" on infants and children has been translated into the "widely recognized" *fact* of infant and childhood sexuality, as is explained in modern college human sexuality texts, eg, Crooks and Baur's *Our Sexuality* (Benjamin/Cummings Publishing Co., 1983):

> However, *with the widespread circulation of the research findings of Alfred Kinsey and other distinguished investigators, the false assumption that childhood is a period of sexual dormancy is gradually eroding.* In fact, it is now widely recognized that *infants of both sexes are born with the capacity for sexual pleasure* and response [p. 410; emphasis added].

Later chapters (especially chapter 1) examine the methods by which Kinsey's child sexuality "findings" were obtained.

KINSEY'S INFLUENCE

Kinsey's conclusions on human sexuality have to some extent become a self-fulfilling prophecy through "the sexual revolution" that they helped inspire. Also, mechanisms are now in place to ensure the continuation of this process. New developments in sex education, for example, are leading to the exposure of more and more children to the teaching that heterosexuality is merely one "option" in a range of acceptable sexual behaviors.

Today, in many school systems children learn the "Kinsey scale," a seven-point numerical rating system in which bisexuality occupies a middle "balanced" position between heterosexuality (0) and

5   Brecher R. Brecher E (eds.), *An Analysis of Human Sexual Response*, Andre Deutsch, 1967, p. 117.

homosexuality (6). They learn that Kinsey established that 10% of American males are "normally" homosexual. In the Los Angeles school district, for example, a program was introduced in 1984 called "Project 10" (after Kinsey)—a gay and lesbian counseling service for youth. Described in the publication *United Teacher* as "a model for school districts throughout the United States," this program offers books featuring stories on homosexual lovemaking (claimed to be written by children) and is an attempt to help children "accept" their homosexuality, as well as their sexual potential.[6]

Parts of Kinsey's "prophecy" have, of course, remained unfulfilled. Most members of the public have never heard of cross-generational sex. And despite Kinsey's claim that adult-child sex can be beneficial to children that is, if the police would just leave everybody alone (their interference "disturbs" children)—most members of the public are still likely to disagree with Kinsey on this point. But the process of continuing to educate society toward full acceptance of what Kinsey said was good for it, and "natural" to boot, is proceeding quietly.

In this regard, influential figures in today's sex education establishment who share Kinsey's views on childhood sexuality are beginning to broach the subject of the legitimacy of adult-child sex. Consider, for example, the article "Sex Education in the Future" in the *Journal of Sex Education and Therapy* (Spring/Summer 1985), by SIECUS co-founder Dr. Lester Kirkendall of Oregon State University and Dr. Roger Libby of the University of Massachusetts. In this, they predict that sex education programs of the future "will probe sexual expression . . . with same-sex [partners]" and "even across . . . generational lines." They proclaim that with "a diminished sense of guilt. . . . these patterns will become legitimate" and "[t]he emphasis on . . . normality and abnormality will be much diminished with these future trends."

The loosening up of restrictions on adult/child sex is just one of the goals of several influential sex educators and their academic mentors. In the case of "sex across generational lines," the "scientific" basis for the merit of these developments is Kinsey's experimental research among children—conducted by sex offenders—in the 1940s.

In the chapters to follow we will examine Kinsey's research and conclusions, *particularly with respect to children*. In addition, we will look closely at the type of people who formed the "samples" from which Kinsey got his information, and the persons involved in his child sex experiments. It will become increasingly clear that many of Kinsey's conclusions derived from his male and female samples are invalid because of the flagrantly unrepresentative group of "interviewees" he used. With respect to Kinsey's experimental child sex research, it will become obvious that this involved the actual perpetration of illegal and sometimes violent sex acts on children—*perhaps* (as we surmise) prospectively arranged. Surviving Kinsey colleagues are invited to respond.

6   See Appendix D for an account of Project 10 in action.

Lately, the error of some other of Kinsey's conclusions is beginning to show up. According to Kinsey's results, 10% of white American males are "more or less exclusively homosexual" (ie, near the right end of Kinsey's "scale") for at least three years between the ages of 16 and 55; 8% are "exclusively homosexual" (6 on the "scale") for the same period; and 4% are exclusively homosexual throughout their lives (Male Report, p. 651). These data have been used by the Centers for Disease Control and others (including the New York City Department of Health) to prepare forecasts of AIDS-virus infection rates (since the early spread of AIDS has been largely among the homosexual population).

According to Bruce Lambert in *The New York Times* (July 19, 20, 1988), the estimate of the number of homosexual/bisexual men in New York City, which was based on Kinsey's 1948 data, has had to be revised downward (based on observations of the spread of AIDS) from 500,000 to 100,000—a massive reduction, by any measure. And on a national level, the Federal Government's estimate—first made in 1986—of up to 1.5 million Americans infected with the AIDS virus, based largely on Kinsey's data, may have to be revised downward to 1 million or less, four years later!

Kinsey's statistics on the prevalence of homosexuality in society have been grossly in error, which would probably be no surprise to Kinsey—he knew the bias he was building into his research. He even presented his homosexuality numbers deceptively, counting as "adult" homosexual experience the isolated same-sex experimentation of adolescent heterosexual males. More recently, published surveys of male sexual behavior have indicated that the occurrence of exclusive homosexuality has been significantly overestimated (see chapter 6).

WHY THIS BOOK

There are now so many indications of serious error and irregularity in Kinsey's human sexuality research, even upon a superficial examination, that it became necessary for this book to be written. In fact the whole notion of Kinsey's sex studies being considered "science" will have to be re-evaluated. This is a vitally important social issue in view of Kinsey's conclusions on childhood sexuality (chapters 1 and 2)—accepted in academic sexology as scientific fact—and the pervasiveness of his theories in current sex education and AIDS education programs (chapters 4 and 5). If Kinsey's science is flawed, then today's children are among his prime victims, which is ironic in a way because children also were the prime victims in the live sex experiments which took place in the 1940s and which form the basis of many Kinsey conclusions.

It is Kinsey's work which established the notion of "normal" childhood sexual desire. This "scientific" fact about children provides justification for pedophiles and a "scientific" basis for the children-can-enjoy-sex-with-peers (then with adults) movement that clearly exists within the sexology and sex education establishments today. Children are victims here also because they are not in a position to take part in the debate over the scientific evidence for their own sexuality. They are not in a position to analyze Kinsey's research data that are used to argue the case that they can benefit from, and have a *right* to, sex with adults. The debate also is being directed to some extent by those who, while seeming to champion "children's rights," are on record as desiring legal sanction for adult sex with children.

Some readers will doubt that things have come to this pass. Society, they would argue, could never look approvingly on adults having sexual access to children. This is not necessarily a valid assumption. One requirement necessary for legitimization of adult-child sexual activity has been met with Kinsey's "demonstration" that children can and should have active sex lives. Steps toward meeting the other requirement have just recently (1988) begun to be discussed openly, with the proposition from a "nationally recognized expert on sex offenders" that "pedophilia . . . may be a sexual orientation rather than a sexual deviation." The comparison, in this sense, to homosexuality is *beginning* to be made (*Behavior Today,* December 5, 1988, p. 5; see also chapter 7).

Whether or not Kinsey's research could stand close scientific examination was never an issue in 1940s America. It had all the required attributes for that period: it was a *major* project, it was headed by a *scientist* and it had *never been done before.* Perhaps most impressive of all, it dealt with large numbers of "facts" that *seemed* to have been handled in a *statistically* proper way. Co-researcher Wardell Pomeroy described it this way:

> No research in human behavior on so broad a scale had previously been attempted. Along with this, one has to consider the peculiarly American trait of counting noses. If this project had been undertaken in Europe or Asia it might never have attracted any attention or even succeeded, but in America we like to count things. As a result, the research was done and it accomplished the primary objective of making such investigation acceptable [Pomeroy, 1972, p. 466].

Thus a new view of sexual behavior was presented in the form of numbers and brought forth to an awed American public. One of the early Kinsey reviewers caught on to this. Physician and author Iago Galdston wrote in his critique of the Female Report, "So Noble an Effort Corrupted,"

> Kinsey of course does not "advocate" libertinism. He doesn't advocate anything. He allows his figures to do that for him. But *his figures are like puppets, and he pulls the strings* [In Geddes DP: *An Analysis of the Kinsey Reports on Sexual Behavior in the Human Male and Female,* Mentor Books, 1954, p. 47].

The scale of Kinsey's sex research was matched by the pretentiousness of its presentation. His book titles imply that sexual behavior for all peoples is being defined, when, in fact, as Kinsey contemporary Ashley Montagu of Rutgers University astutely noted, "These books deal with the sexual behavior of a very limited branch of humanity, namely the American variety, and a small segment of that variety at that" (*ibid.,* p. 127).

Kinsey's Male and Female Reports did not, however, get the scrutiny of experts in the "hard" sciences that might have demolished their credibility at the time. Practically all of his advisors and scientific readers were "behavioral scientists" who knew very little about scientific procedures themselves. What Kinsey presented was *scientism*,[7] as opposed to science. As such, it was not recognized or acknowledged by those also involved in its practice.

Since Kinsey's work was misconstrued as "science," serious error has been allowed to masquerade as fact for 40 years in our understanding of perhaps the most important area of human behavior. The ready acceptance of this "science"— though it overturned cherished values—is partly explained by Amherst professor Benjamin DeMott in a March 1980 *Psychology Today* article describing attempts to weaken the incest taboo:

> [It is believed that] the history of mankind is properly understood as a progress from dark restricting superstition to reasoned liberating enlightenment. [It is also believed that] since moral and spiritual versions of the human condition come to us from the past, they're necessarily infected with superstition, whereas *scientific versions of our condition are myth-free* [pp. 11, 12; emphasis added].

A further reason for a second look at the work of Dr. Kinsey and colleagues is the disturbing fact that major social conclusions are based on a body of research that involved the use of experimentation on human subjects *against their will*. This actuality somehow escaped the notice of reviewers at the time. There remains therefore an obligation to the principle of scientific integrity, as well as a responsibility to the pursuit of truth in science, to reexamine the research of Kinsey and colleagues and the circumstances under which it was carried out.

THE ISSUE OF FRAUD

It will become clear from subsequent chapters that the issue of fraud in Kinsey's research is one that now has to be faced squarely by scientists and lay persons alike. The critical importance of this is that many influential figures in sex education are "true believers" in a philosophy of human sexuality shaped by Dr. Kinsey and his co-authors. And the Kinsey team's research conclusions provide a scientific basis for, among other things, the acceptability of early childhood sexual activity and adult sexual relations with consenting children. Just as Hugh Hefner, according to author Thomas Weyr,[8] found in Kinsey's work "demonstrable evidence" to undergird his *Playboy* philosophy, so does today's sex education establishment find in Kinsey the justification for teaching the normalcy of homosexuality, bisexuality—and much more.

If Kinsey's research is seriously flawed or fraudulent, a whole house of cards collapses. Could a research project of this magnitude and importance be bungled or even rigged and no one notice for 40 years? Even in the 1970s and '80s, when scientific research has been

---

7   Defined as the application of quasi-scientific methods to unsuitable subjects.
8   *Reaching for Paradise: The Playboy Vision of America*, Times Books, 1987, p. 11.

scrutinized and peer-reviewed more stringently before publication than ever was the case with the Kinsey team's work, it has now been discovered that intentional misrepresentation in science is not an isolated aberration (Editorial, *British Medical Journal* 296:376, 1988). This was highlighted not too long ago by the fraud conviction of medical researcher Stephen Bruening, "who published some 50 articles based on fraudulent data on the use of psychoactive drugs in mentally retarded patients" (*ibid.*). [Perhaps as disturbing as some of the recent fraud exposes has been the reluctance of authorities to investigate when presented with reasonable grounds for suspicion. Despite this and recent publicity, however, it is likely that fraud in science still is unusual.]

Breuning's data impacted public health policy nationally. Kinsey's data have impacted public morality and the understanding of human sexuality internationally. There is good evidence that Kinsey's research was designed to provide a scientific base for his preexisting radical sexual ideology: his coworkers were chosen *for* their bias; biased samples were *knowingly* used; unwarranted conclusions were drawn from data presented; methods are sometimes obscured, sometimes flawed; some data are contradictory; there is a prior history of deception in other scientific endeavors; Kinsey has dissembled in the medical literature; Kinsey co-authors have knowingly misrepresented their data in subsequent publications; criminal experimentation has been the prime source of Kinsey's childhood sexuality data; and then there is the Maslow affair, which reveals Kinsey as a man on the way to a scientific conclusion regardless of the evidence.

If even only some of the above are correct, then Kinsey's research results clearly are false. Normally in a major project in an important area of research, false conclusions would sooner or later be detected. As Daniel Koshland, editor of *Science*, has pointed out, "You may falsify an important finding, but then it will surely form the basis for subsequent experiments and become exposed" (*Science* 235:141, 1987). However, *the Kinsey research never has been replicated*, and even an attempt to "clean up" the data was suspiciously botched. False conclusions in science can be an honest mistake, but outright deception is quite another matter. In the case of Kinsey's sex research, there is strong (we believe compelling) evidence of fraud, which would make this research the most egregious example of scientific deception in this century.

This brings us to an interesting situation. With the exception of Dr. Kinsey, all of the scientists involved in the creation of the Kinsey research findings are alive and functioning as influential scholars, writers, lecturers, experts on national and international panels and commissions, courtroom witnesses, and academic luminaries in the sexology and sex education fields. What will now happen? Will scientific peers have the courage to investigate this landmark work of 40 years ago? If they do not, the public will be entitled to know why. Here is what *should* happen when there is even a *suspicion* of fraud in scientific research:

[O]nce *suspected* or detected, fraud needs *intensive investigation* with publicity given to the results and retraction in the journals concerned and in the bibliographical databases [Stephen Lock, Editor, *British Medical Journal*, February 6, 1988, p. 377; emphasis added].

The argument for investigation is even more powerful when data have been derived from the abuse of human subjects—in this case children. Can the reader begin to imagine what such an investigation could mean for society and its understanding of human sexuality and values?

CHAPTER ONE

MALE CHILD
SEXUALITY

Dr. Judith A. Reisman and Dr. J. Gordon Muir

Chapter Overview

This chapter deals mainly with Kinsey's child sexuality statistics, first presented to the world in chapter 5 of his 1948 Male Report. Included in this Kinsey Report is the first—and only—body of experimental data ever obtained purporting to demonstrate that infants and children—preadolescents in general—could enjoy and benefit from sexual activity, particularly with adults. This is the body of proof relied upon by segments of the academic sexology world—and the pedophile movement—for their contention that children are sexual beings. This, and many other Kinsey concepts, are now an integral part of modern sex education curricula.

Kinsey's information about childhood sexuality was allegedly obtained by the same process as all his 1948 adult male sexuality statistics, namely, from 5,300 male interviewees, including 212 preadolescents. His landmark experimental data on childhood sexual response reportedly came from the "histories" and "records" of those interviewees— especially from nine members (some "technically trained")—who had manually and orally masturbated some of several hundred infants and children (2 months to 15 years old) in efforts to elicit "orgasm."

Kinsey revealed little about the exact composition of his total male interviewee sample, which should have been representative of the population of the United States. It is now clear that it contained inappropriate numbers of sex offenders, pedophiles and exhibitionists, and a significant portion of it (perhaps 25%) consisted of prison inmates. Even those persons who volunteered for Kinsey's research were shown to have been biased toward the sexually unconventional. Kinsey knew this but concealed the evidence. Yet, from his research on this skewed sample, Kinsey defined "normal" male sexuality—and his definition was largely accepted as valid.

Kinsey's interview population was deliberately biased. In this chapter Kinsey's personal bias is also examined. Both are important because Kinsey's findings established to some extent social standards of what was acceptable behavior. The massive publicity and uncritical acceptance that characterized the launch of Kinsey's books probably set off "the first wave of the sexual revolution." According to sexologist Morton Hunt, Kinsey became "the giant on whose shoulders all sex researchers since his time have stood." His philosophy was that designations of right and wrong, licit and illicit, acceptable and unacceptable in human sexual behavior were culturally imposed, artificial distinctions. Kinsey made it clear that all sexual activity—including adult sexual relations with children—was "natural," and therefore normal. Some activities were, however, unjustly stigmatized because of "societal restraints" and "inhibitions," he claimed.

Kinsey's concept of sexuality as a natural continuum from birth to death, and as a continuum embracing heterosexuality, bisexuality and homosexuality (a concept embodied in the "Kinsey Scale"), is now almost universally accepted by academic sexologists. It is widely taught in parochial, private and public school sex education courses and is used in popular programs such as On Being Gay *and* About Your Sexuality.

However, Kinsey's research, on which all this is based, lacks scientific validity. Moreover, the claimed methodology for the child sex experiments Kinsey describes is inaccurate—some of what is purported to be "history" is clearly prospective research or the work of sex criminals (or else it is false). Sadly, it took 40 years for the facts to be reported. What is sadder is the possibility that Kinsey and his team were themselves directly involved in acts of dubious legality in the course of this research.

SUSPENSION OF DISBELIEF

In order to take seriously the story that unfolds in the pages ahead, the average reader will have to practice what English poet Coleridge referred to as "that willing suspension of disbelief." Using common sense as a guide, it will at first be difficult to fathom that a major piece of science from a famous scientist could come out of a research project so brazenly bizarre. When it is fully realized what Kinsey and his team did, it will also be difficult to understand why most of the academics and experts familiar with this research haven't said something over the years.

Perhaps, as we so recently have seen with communist leaders in Eastern Europe, there now will come some sudden conversions on the part of Kinsey true believers. It will be interesting to see who is prepared to defend his research, his methods and his conclusions.

What follows is largely an examination of the male child sexuality data presented in chapter 5 of Kinsey's 1948 Male Report (*Sexual Behavior in the Human Male*), authored by Alfred Kinsey, Clyde Martin and Wardell Pomeroy. Chapter 5 of the Male Report is titled "Early Sexual Growth and Activity" and is of profound importance in that it presents the only experimental data ever obtained purporting to demonstrate that humans can partake of and enjoy sexual activity from infancy (more generally, *all* humans have the ability to respond sexually to *any* sufficient stimulus).

As Wardell Pomeroy wrote many years later:

[It was] Sigmund Freud whose genius introduced the idea of *childhood sexuality*—that children are sexual beings was an idea never considered before—*an idea that forever affected our conception of human sexual development and thoughts about sex education* (In Forleo and Pasini: *Medical Sexology*, PSG Publishing, Co., 1980, p. 76; emphasis added).

The *idea* may have been Freud's, but it was the work of the Kinsey team that attempted to demonstrate the *reality*, providing the first scientific data to support the claim that children can both desire and benefit from genital sex with adults.

THE MALE SAMPLE

For their collection of male child sexuality statistics, the Kinsey team used their three standard research methods: 1) adolescent and adult recall interviews; 2) child interviews; 3) actual observation of children in "orgasm" under experimental conditions. In contrast to the Kinsey female research, where the experimental technique was reportedly employed on only seven small girls, the male child research involved recorded measurements of the sexual stimulation of *hundreds* of boys—ranging in age from 2 months to nearly 15 years.

The Kinsey team's child sex data came from both the children and the adults who comprised the total sample for Kinsey's 1948 Male Report. Basically, these data are claimed to prove that children are "orgasmic." To the Kinsey team this meant children normally belonged in a continuum of sexuality stretching from birth to death and, in its fullest expression, embracing *all* types of sexual activity—same-gender, cross-gender and cross-species (sex with animals). The Kinsey child sex experiments demonstrated the validity of "outlet sex" and applied it to children.

According to sexual historian Paul Robinson, the concept of "outlet sex" served a purpose for Kinsey:

The notion of outlet, for all its apparent innocence, performed important critical services for Kinsey . . . demot[ing] heterosexual intercourse to merely one among a democratic roster of six possible forms of sexual release (the six, in order of their treatment in the Male volume, were masturbation, nocturnal emissions, heterosexual petting, heterosexual intercourse, homosexual relations, and intercourse with animals of other species). . . . marital intercourse, was even more rudely confined to a single chapter toward the back of the book, where it received about one third the attention devoted to homosexual relations. . . . a remarkable feat of sexual leveling . . . *the fundamental categories of his analysis clearly worked to undermine the traditional sexual order* [Robinson, *The Modernization of Sex*, Harper & Row, 1976, pp. 58, 59; emphasis added].

The Kinsey notions of "outlet sex" and childhood orgasmic potential were allegedly developed from "interviews" with approximately 5,300 males and from sex experiments on several hundred infants and children, the exact number being unknown.

PROBLEMS WITH THE MALE SAMPLE

The Kinsey team actually started with a sample of 6,300, but 1,000 black males (16%) were removed from the evaluation process for reasons not adequately explained. It appears that 212 interviews were conducted with adolescent boys (see Male Report, p. 165).

The adult male sample consisted largely of people who *volunteered* to be interviewed by Kinsey and his team. When volunteers are used in studies of human sexuality, problems of *bias* can be expected. Although he was warned by an expert that the bias introduced by using volunteers was likely to affect the type of information he got from his interviewees, Kinsey chose to ignore the expert's advice and all but ignored this whole issue in his published work.

There is an important principle involved in the selection of participants for sexuality studies—it is Maslow's principle of *volunteer bias*. Essentially, psychologist Abraham Maslow had shown long before the publication of Kinsey's work that, because of the intimate nature of sexuality research, the normal process of enlisting volunteers results in an overselection of persons who tend to exhibit (and take delight in admitting) unconventional behavior—ie, the percentage reporting "disapproved" behavior (eg, promiscuity, homosexuality) is inflated.

Maslow personally demonstrated to the Kinsey team that this would apply to *their* volunteer group. Kinsey ignored Maslow's findings, refused to correct for the error predicted for his own sample and deceitfully claimed in his Male Report that it was not known how this factor could have affected his results. Abraham Maslow, the expert on the subject of how volunteers can skew the results of sex surveys, gave Kinsey notice—and evidence—of the effect on his own research. But Kinsey withheld the evidence, even as he wrote in his first book that "how [volunteering] affects a sexual history is not yet clear" (Male Report, p. 103). This story is told in more detail in chapter 6.

Lewis M. Terman of Stanford University, who in 1948 wrote one of the best researched critiques of Kinsey's Male Report, enlisted the aid of statistician Quinn McNemar in analyzing Kinsey's male sexuality data. Interestingly, McNemar, who is unlikely to have known of Maslow's criticisms, came to the same conclusion about volunteering, solely from internal evidence in the Kinsey data. As Terman put it, "[McNemar's calculations] confirm the suspicion that willingness to volunteer is associated with greater than average sexual activity. And since the volunteers account for about three-fourths of the 5,300 males reported upon in this volume, it follows that Kinsey's figures, in all probability, give an exaggerated notion of the amount of sexual activity in the general population" (Terman LM. "Kinsey's 'Sexual Behavior in the Human Male': Some Comments and Criticisms." *Psychological Bulletin* 45:443-459, 1948).

An additional problem with Kinsey's male sample, noted by Terman, is that "many" of the volunteers were actually seeking advice in connection with their personal problems—eg, looking for information on such topics as "[what are the] harmful effects from 'excessive' sexual activity?" (Male Report, p. 37). Terman also objected to Kinsey's "burden of denial" strategy in questions to his male sample. Kinsey described this technique as follows:

> The interviewer should not make it easy for a subject to deny his participation in any form of sexual activity. . . . We always assume that everyone has engaged in every type of activity. Consequently we always begin by asking *when* they first engaged in such activity [Male Report, p. 53; emphasis in original].

At the outset, these criticisms would suggest a research team that was less than careful about ensuring an absence of bias in their survey results. However, important as they are, these defects have become overshadowed by subsequent information that has come to light about the composition of Kinsey's male interviewees. This group was so overtly unrepresentative of society, then or now, that the fact that a group of "scientists" defined the "normal" sexual behaviors of U.S. males from this sample is astonishing in retrospect. However, that is what happened. And by doing so largely unchallenged, the Kinsey team, through the mass of statistics presented in their Male Report, had the effect of legitimizing a broad spectrum of illegal and/or unhealthy sexual behaviors such as sodomy and promiscuity. Though largely unrecognized, or unacknowledged, Kinsey's research can also be used to legitimize adult sexual relations with children.

As noted previously, Kinsey set in motion "the first wave of the sexual revolution." What was not said was that the wave was generated by highly questionable statistics. But then, as Paul Robinson suggested, Kinsey had an ideology and values, and his sex data were *meant* to bring tabooed activities under the same conceptual roof as marital relations and in the process render them innocuous (Robinson, 1976, p. 118).

Incomplete Information

The Kinsey team gave only fragmentary demographic information on the subjects they interviewed. It is possible, of course, that they failed to realize the importance of such data, or else neglected to take full advantage of the information available to them in interviews. However, as more is learned about who some of the Kinsey team's subjects really were, a willingness to believe in the researchers' good intentions, but lack of expertise, gives way to a reasonable suspicion of a more devious motive for excluding such detail. According to Gershon Legman, former bibliographer of erotica at the Kinsey Institute, Kinsey purposely obscured his "real activity" under a "cloud of statistical hokum" in order not to detract from his "propagandistic purpose" of "respectabilizing homosexuality and certain sexual perversions" (see below).[1]

Heavy Reliance on Prison Inmates/Sex Offenders

Although he was ostensibly attempting to find out what average American males were doing sexually, Kinsey included an extravagant percentage of prison inmates and sex offenders in his interview sample. This inevitably would distort his findings. Terman objected to the use of this population, noting that "Kinsey [had] data on more than 1,200 persons who [were] convicted of sex offenses" (Terman, *ibid.*). Terman did not know how many of these persons were included in Kinsey's 5,300 male sample, but it turns out that perhaps most of them were. In his 1972 book *Dr. Kinsey and the Institute for Sex Research* (Harper & Row), Pomeroy described the efforts of the Kinsey team to interview prison inmates:

> We went to the [prison] records and got lists of the inmates who were in for various kinds of sex offenses. If the list was short for some offenses—as in incest, for example—we took the history of everybody on it. If it was a long list, as for statutory rape, we might take the history of every fifth or tenth man. Then we cut the pie another way. We would go to a particular prison workshop and get the history of every man in the group, whether he was a sex offender or not [pp. 202, 203].

Kinsey claims that he sought out "volunteers" by getting introductions from persons he befriended, whether prison inmate "kingpins" or leaders of homosexual groups (Male Report, pp. 38-40). Clearly this is not a process that would lead to a representative group of American men. Terman complained about this aspect of Kinsey's male sample:

> The author lists (p. 39) 32 groups of "contact" persons numbering "many hundred" in all, who helped in obtaining volunteers. Seven of these 32 were delinquent groups: male prostitutes, female prostitutes, bootleggers, gamblers, pimps, prison inmates, thieves and hold-up men. These presumably would have brought in others of their kind, but in what numbers they did so we are not told [Terman, *ibid.*].

How many prison inmates were in Kinsey's male sample? While our calculation follows, it will be instructive to note what is said on this subject by members of the Kinsey team. Pomeroy stated,

> By 1946, [Kinsey], Gebhard and I had interviewed about 1,400 convicted sex offenders in penal institutions scattered over a dozen states [Pomeroy, 1972, p. 208].

1   In support of Legman's conclusion is Kinsey's effort to mislead readers of a reputable medical journal about his intentions and his data concerning the study of homosexuality. Seven years before the publication of his Male Report, Kinsey wrote in the *Journal of Clinical Endocrinology* (vol. 1, pp. 424-428, 1941) that it was important in the study of homosexuality to use subjects who were not from select, biased groups such as are found in prisons. Kinsey implied his own study—then underway—was not doing this. The irony of this article will become apparent in the pages ahead.

Kinsey claimed to have "gotten such records from something between 35 and 85 percent of the inmates of every [prison] institution in which we have worked" (Male Report, p. 129).

In their 1965 book *Sex Offenders: An Analysis of Types* (Harper & Row), Gebhard, Gagnon, Pomeroy and Christenson assert that between 1940 and 1945 they collected the histories of 37% of a white Indiana prison population of 888 and 38% of 1,356 white sex offenders (pp. 18, 27). The question remains: How many prison inmates were there in Kinsey's 5,300 male sample? Neither Kinsey nor co-authors have ever revealed this. Pomeroy disclosed in his 1972 book, *Dr. Kinsey and the Institute for Sex Research*, that the concealment of "the exact figures" was quite purposeful—to avoid disputes about the nature of the sample (pp. 292, 293). Our calculations suggest the prison inmate figure was considerable, possibly a quarter of the total male interviewee population.

In a telephone conversation, January 24, 1988, John Gagnon told author E. Eichel that "44% of all the prisoners" in the Kinsey male sample had had "homosexual" experience in prison. He said that this 44% "equalled a third among the rest of the [non-college] population." This means that the total prison population was about three quarters of the non-college population. A clue to the relative sizes of Kinsey's college and non-college subgroups—the only published information, as far as we know—is contained in an article in *Time* magazine, August 24, 1953, p. 51 (author unknown). Here it is stated that 63% of Kinsey's sample was college educated.[2] If this is correct, it means that 37% were non-college educated. Since about 75% of these were prisoners, the prison group would have been about a quarter of the whole sample!

This calculation is not out of line with a statement by Gebhard in his 1979 book, *The Kinsey Data: Marginal Tabulations of the 1938-1963 Interviews Conducted by the Institute for Sex Research* (W.B. Saunders Co.), where he indicates that about a quarter to a third of the non-college group (ie, the non-prisoner portion) could have been high school students (p. 9). This is particularly interesting because, in a telephone conversation between E. Eichel and Paul Gebhard on January 23, 1988, Gebhard stated that *there was only one high school included in the study and that it was "aberrant"* because of an unusually high percentage of homosexual experience among the students.

So here is a truly remarkable situation for a study of national male sexual behavior: up to a quarter of the study sample were prisoners (44% of whom had had homosexual experience in prison, and perhaps even more had experience out of prison—see below) and most, if not all, of the high school students, were from a group that was "aberrant" because of an unusually high percentage of boys with homosexual experience![3]

---

2   From an analysis of Table 81, p. 336, and the clinical tables in the Male Report (chapter 23), Hobbs and Lambert deduced the similar figure of 64% for the college-educated group (Hobbs AH, Lambert RD. An evaluation of "Sexual Behavior in the Human Male." *American Journal of Psychiatry* 104:758, 1948).

3   This "aberrant" high school is further discussed in chapter 6.

This helps to explain why Kinsey's homosexuality statistics—
which in the last 40 years have been taken to apply to the U.S. male
population—are open to question. Confirmation of possible error is
now beginning to appear in projections for the spread of AIDS that have
been based on the Kinsey data. Further confirmation also has recently
appeared in the results of two smaller sex surveys published in 1989.
The relevance of AIDS incidence and the more recent sex survey data
to the understanding of possible error in the Kinsey team's conclusions
about the prevalence of homosexuality in American men is more fully
discussed in chapter 6.

Corroborating evidence for an abnormally high representation of
prisoners/ex-inmates in Kinsey's male sample (and an abnormally high
incidence of homosexuality) comes from former Kinsey Institute staff
member John Gagnon in his 1977 book *Human Sexualities* (Scott,
Foresman & Co.). Here Gagnon states in a footnote,

> . . . it appears that there were about 1300 men in the Kinsey Report of
> 1948 with educations of twelve years or less. *Somewhere between
> 900 and 1000 of these cases had had some prison experience.* An
> examination of a later study of the Institute for Sex Research, publish-
> ed in *Sex Offenders* (1965), shows that twenty-six percent of men in
> the control group in that study (men with no prison experience and
> less than college educations) had had a homosexual experience by age
> twenty, compared to *fifty percent of the men with prison experience
> (not as sex offenders) having had homosexual experiences outside of
> prison* [p. 253; emphasis added].

These figures begin to explain the prevalence of homosexuality that
was *assumed* for the U.S. population after publication of Kinsey's Male
Report. (For further discussion of Kinsey's homosexuality data, see
chapter 6.)

"Statistical Hokum"

It was noted above that Kinsey purposely obscured certain information that would be damaging to the credibility of his results. A
former member of the Kinsey Institute staff, Gershon Legman, un-
charitably described Kinsey's data handling as "statistical hokum"
designed to disguise his real purpose. Two of the more perceptive of
the early reviewers of the Male Report, sociologists Albert Hobbs and
Richard Lambert of the sociology department of the University of
Pennsylvania, pointed out that Kinsey's methods lent themselves to
covering up "selectivity" in his sample (Hobbs AH, Lambert RD. "An
evaluation of 'Sexual Behavior in the Human Male.'" *American Journal of Psychiatry* 104:758, 1948).

Hobbs and Lambert observed, for example, that the Kinsey authors
seemed *purposely* to ignore the limitations of their own sample in order
"to compound any possible errors in almost any way which will increase
the apparent incidence of [homosexuality]." One of the ways this was
done was by the use of the highly misleading "accumulative incidence"
technique, which, as Hobbs points out, "is the basis for most of the
generalizations regarding sexual behavior of the entire male population
of the United States." Implicit in the use of this technique is the

assumption that there has been absolutely no change in sexual beliefs or practices during the 40 or more years over which the technique is applied. As an illustration of how this method of data tabulation can be highly misleading, it will serve a purpose to quote the following passage from Hobbs and Lambert's paper:

> The [accumulative incidence] technique used for expansion of the data is, briefly, to treat each case as if it were an additional case falling within each previous age group or previous experienced category. Thus, a man who was 45 at the time of the interview would provide a case for each age group previous to that, and if he was married at the time of interview would constitute a case for the single tabulations in the years before he was married. The authors attempt to justify this technique upon the basis of evidence as to the persistency of sexual patterns from generation to generation, assuming that a man who was 15 years of age 30 years ago can be counted in the calculations as though he were, 15, 16, 17 . . . . 45 years of age today.

This *"accumulative incidence technique" is the basis for most of the generalizations regarding sexual behavior of the entire male population of the United States.* It can be applied with least danger of error to determine if given individuals have engaged in specific acts once during their lifetime. However, since most people engage in multitudinous types of behavior, many of which are mutually contradictory, information about any one type is of little value in describing actual social relationships or patterns of behavior. Most people were infantile when they were infants, childish when they were children and adolescent when they were in their teens, and such a technique would demonstrate these facts with reasonable accuracy. It could be used to demonstrate that 100% of the population is "selfish" (has engaged in selfish behavior), but it would also show that 100% of the population is "unselfish."

With this technique one could demonstrate that well over 50% of the adult male white population is "exclusively unemployed" (have been unemployed for at least three years) and that over 90% is "exclusively employed," according to the same criteria. Thus the technique has serious limitations if it is used as a basis for attempts to describe human behavior rather than to enumerate specific acts.

To ascertain the number in any age group who are engaging in the specified activity ("active incidence"), use of the accumulative incidence technique would presumably necessitate a high degree of representativeness for all significant factors within the given age group, and persistence of the type of activity from time of first incidence to time of report. *Since the data from one age category are included in others, the age categories are not independent and cannot be designated as random samples. Comparison of one age group with another necessitates a degree of representativeness which is not present* [emphasis added].

Statistical Reviews

It is remarkable that in all the many hundreds of reviews of Kinsey's Male Report that appeared within a short time of publication no one, apart from Hobbs and Lambert, saw the importance of Kinsey's mistake in using the accumulative incidence technique to compute occurrence rates of sexual behavior.

This may in part be explained by the fact that statisticians who reviewed the book were not alert to the unsuitability of this method for studying some aspects of sexual behavior.

Setting aside consideration of the accumulative incidence technique, however, statistical experts found sufficient other problems in Kinsey's Male Report to independently cast serious doubt on his results.

One authoritative review was that published in 1953 by statisticians William G. Cochran, Frederick Mosteller and John Tukey ("Statistical Problems of the Kinsey Report." *Journal of the American Statistical Association* 48:673-716, 1953). This is recommended reading for those who wish to do a little research on their own. When considering the comments of Cochran and colleagues—some of which are repeated below—it should be borne in mind that they did not know the full degree of the prisoner/sex-offender bias in Kinsey's sample.

Cochran *et al.* noted that the Kinsey team operated on the "assumption that everyone has engaged in all types of [sexual] activity . . . [which] seems . . . likely to encourage exaggeration by the respondents." As experts on sampling, they pointed out that Kinsey had made no effort to measure the effect of volunteering. They seem not to have known that Kinsey had been *warned* by Maslow about the biasing effect of volunteering in sex studies *but knowingly ignored this effect.*

Some of the main problems pointed out by Cochran and colleagues were:

1. "[T]he present results must be regarded as subject to systematic errors of unknown magnitude due to selective sampling (via volunteering and the like)."

2. "[T]he 'sampled populations' are startlingly different from the composition of the U.S. white male population. . . . The inference from [Kinsey's] sample to the (reported) behavior of all U.S. white males contains a large gap which can be spanned only by expert judgment."

3. "[T]he author who values his reputation for objectivity will take pains to warn the reader, frequently repetitiously, whenever an unsubstantiated conclusion is being presented, and will choose his words with the greatest care. [Kinsey, Pomeroy and Martin] did not do this."

4. There was "substantial discussion" of social and legal attitudes about sexual behavior "*not* based on evidence presented . . ." (emphasis in original).

According to these reviewers, the inability to relate Kinsey's data accurately to the U.S. population was because of sampling deficiencies—"no use of randomization" and "the absence of any orderly sampling plan." They noted that Kinsey reported having some 100% samples (a substitute for randomization; Male Report, p. 93). Kinsey claimed this for about one quarter of his male interviewees (Male Report, p. 95). However, they were not to know what Paul Gebhard would reveal about 30 years later—"The term '100%' [was] actually a misnomer . . ." (Gebhard and Johnson, 1979, p 11). This latter information is important, not so much from a statistical point of view, but for what it reveals about the element of misrepresentation.

Disproportions in the Male Sample

Just how unrepresentative Kinsey's male sample was of the United States population was never fully understood by his reviewers. The extent of overrepresentation of present or former prison inmates, for example, was not known. The high prisoner/sex offender content of Kinsey's interviewees may be the most devastating disproportion discovered in his research population, but it was not the only one. And there is a strong suspicion he used a high number of male prostitutes (see next section).

Although the Kinsey authors tried to disguise some of the worst aspects of their sample, disturbing fragments of information are scattered throughout their writing. On page 544 of the Male Report there is mention of 6,000 marital histories and nearly 3,000 divorce histories. These presumably are among the 12,000 histories collected for males and females at that time, but, as Lewis Terman pointed out, a sample where divorce histories are half as numerous as marital histories is no basis for a sexual behavior census in the 1940s.

Probably by design, the numbers of persons in the various contributing groups of Kinsey's sample are almost never stated. Additionally, there is what Lewis Terman called "one of the most puzzling omissions in the book . . . the author's failure to give the complete age distribution of his subjects at the time they were interviewed." Thus there is the unacceptable situation of equal weight being given to reports from distant memory and reports of current activity.

Hobbs and Lambert in their 1948 article (*ibid.*) made an attempt to figure out some of the disproportions in the male sample. Their figures for these imbalances were *approximations* "because of the unconscious or deliberate failure of the authors to include the actual numbers of cases involved in the various categories." The more notable examples were:

1. Sixty-four percent of the Kinsey sample were college-educated, versus 12% of the U.S. male population.

2. Seventy-eight percent of the sample 20 years of age or older were single, versus 30% in the population.

3. "Widowed or divorced" persons constituted 20% of Kinsey's married population aged between 20 and 50, but only 3% of the equivalent U.S. population.

4. The "widowed or divorced" made up 55% of Kinsey's married sample between ages 30 and 50 who never attended high school, but only 4% of the population.

5. Eighty percent of Kinsey's sample were "inactive" Protestants, Catholics or Jews, who did not attend church regularly or take part in church activities.

Terman noted the contrast between what Kinsey actually did and the advertising circular for the Male Report stating that the interviews were "conducted with full regard for the latest refinements in public opinion polling methods"!

MORE ON THE "INTERVIEWEES"

Monumental conclusions on human sexuality have been drawn from the data the Kinsey team obtained from their "interviewees." In addition to the concepts of "outlet sex" and child sexuality, Kinsey derived the now widely used and accepted Kinsey Scale (grading an individual's "orientation" from fully heterosexual [0] to fully homosexual [6]) from data obtained in his interviews. Teaching the "Kinsey Scale"—ie, the equality of homosexuality, bisexuality and heterosexuality—is now an integral part of many junior and senior high school sex education courses. [This subject is discussed more fully in chapters 4 and 5.]

Included in Kinsey's data are, he claimed, *"the histories of persons with specifically sadistic or masochistic experience*, the accumulation of correspondence, drawings, scrapbooks, collections of photographs, and other documentary materials, the accumulation of a considerable library of published and amateur writing, *and a study of prison cases of individuals who have been convicted of sex crimes involving the use of force"* (Female Report, pp. 88, 89; emphasis added).

Kinsey obtained the "[sexual] histories" of an unknown number of his sample through "contacts," who included "clinical psychologists," "ne'er-do-wells" and "underworld" figures (Male Report, pp. 38-40, 75; Christenson CV, *Kinsey: A Biography*, Indiana University Press, 1971, p. 117). According to Kinsey, when he attempted to secure histories in a specific community he would devote endless hours to establishing rapport with his contacts:

> In securing histories through personal introductions, it is initially most important to identify these key individuals, win their friendship, and develop their interest in the research. Days and weeks and even some years may be spent in acquiring the first acquaintances in a community. . . . If it is a prison population, the oldest timer, the leading wolf, the kingpin in the inmate commonwealth, or the girl who is the chief trouble-maker for the administration must be won before one can go very far in securing the histories of other inmates. . . . If it is the underworld, we may look for the man with the longest FBI record and the smallest number of convictions, and set out to win him. To get the initial introductions, it is necessary to become acquainted with someone who knows someone who knows the person we want to meet. Contacts may develop from the most unexpected sources. . . . The number of persons who can provide introductions has continually spread until now, *in the present study, we have a network of connections that could put us into almost any group with which we wished to work, anywhere in the country.* . . . In many cases we have developed friendships which are based upon mutual respect and upon our common interest in the success of this project. . . . Among more poorly educated groups, and among such minority groups as rural populations, Negroes, segregated Jewish populations, homosexual groups, penal institutional inmates, the underworld, etc., the community . . .

is particularly dependent upon the advice of their leaders in deciding whether they should cooperate [Male Report, pp. 39, 40; emphasis added].

Kinsey made the artless claim that "The greatly disturbed type of person who goes to psychiatric clinics has been *relatively rare* in our sample" (Male Report, p. 37; emphasis added). However, he seems to have believed that "psychopathic" individuals were as valuable a source of sexual information as the "well-adjusted":

> There has not even been a distinction between those whom the psychiatrist would consider sexually well-adjusted persons and those whom he would regard as neurotic, psychotic or at least psychopathic personalities [Male Report, pp. 7-8].

A number of histories from "persons who are professionally involved in sexual activities (as prostitutes, pimps, exhibitionists, etc.) . . ." were obtained in exchange for payment (Male Report, pp. 40, 41). Concerning male prostitutes another fascinating fragment of information comes from one sentence in the Male Report (p. 216) that says "several hundred male prostitutes contributed their histories." If there were a bare minimum of 200 and all the histories were used, this group would amount to 3.8% of the male sample. They could have been an even greater percentage of the sample used to provide homosexuality statistics (see chapter 6).

Kinsey clearly set out to obtain—or did not try to avoid—a high percentage of sexually promiscuous persons in his sample. His chief concern over this appears to have been that reviewers would find out how many there were (Pomeroy, 1972, pp. 292, 293). Had these people emerged in the course of random sampling, their numbers would have been significant and revealing. The fact that Kinsey sought them out in bars, clinics and prisons severely compromises the results of his study.

Unlike Kinsey, it appears that his co-researchers, Gebhard, Pomeroy and Martin, were sensitive to the "mistake" of including so many prisoners in the population of males on which the book *Sexual Behavior in the Human Male* was based. Kinsey disagreed with them and overruled them on this point. However, during preparation of their second volume, *Sexual Behavior in the Human Female*, Kinsey's colleagues demonstrated to him that there was a "substantial difference" in the sexual behavior of prison and nonprison females. Kinsey was prevailed upon to omit females with prison experience from his Female Report.

CHILD SEX EXPERIMENTS

Fortuitously for the Kinsey team, among their interviewees were a group of men who had data on hand from what seem to have been identically designed genital stimulation experiments on children—data obtained by "actual observation" and "timed with second hand or stopwatch" (Male Report, chapter 5). By further good fortune, some of these men were "technically trained." Thus, it is implied by Kinsey, their observations on the results of homosexual masturbation of young boys (sometimes, he claims, for 24 hours at a time), ranging in age from 2 months to 15 years, are a valid and meaningful way to learn about childhood sexuality. It seems extraordinary that this assumption on Kinsey's part was never challenged from the very beginning by the media and by those scientists competent to evaluate his work.

Kinsey's data on the nature and frequency of orgasm in children came, allegedly, from a combination of recall information from interviews and the technical information from the "trained" observers:

> Our several thousand histories have included considerable detail on the nature of orgasm; and these data, *together with the records supplied by some older subjects who have had sexual contacts with younger boys,* provide material for describing the different sorts of reactions which may occur. . . . [T]he data supplied by adult observers for 196 pre-adolescent boys are the sources of the percentage figures indicating the frequency of each type of orgasm among such young males [Male Report, p. 160; emphasis added].

The identity of these 196 boys is never made clear, which is another astonishing omission in this research project. Elsewhere, Kinsey recorded that 200 boys between 1 and 14 years were observed in orgasm (Male Report, p. 175) and that "actual observations" of "climax" were made on 206 males between 5 months and 14 years (Male Report, p. 176).

As with Kinsey's female child data (chapter 2), different numbers can be applied in different places to the same things, without any attempt at explanation. The number of boys observed under experimental sexual stimulation appears to have been at least 317 and was possibly considerably more. Kinsey's failure to acknowledge the need for a full accounting of his child subjects, however, and the scientific community's failure to demand an explanation of the child "orgasm" techniques is quite remarkable.

Not much is known either about the "older subjects" whose illegal activity with these boys constitutes Kinsey's landmark experimental child sexuality data. In their Male Report, the Kinsey authors tell us almost nothing, except:

> Better data on pre-adolescent climax come from the histories of *adult males who have had sexual contacts with younger boys* and who, with their adult backgrounds, are able to recognize and interpret the boys' experiences. Unfortunately, not all of the subjects with such contacts in their histories were questioned on this point of pre-adolescent reactions; *but 9 of our adult male subjects have observed such orgasm. Some of these adults are technically trained persons* who have kept diaries or other records, which have been put at our disposal; and from them we have secured information on 317 pre-adolescents who were either observed in self-masturbation, or who were observed in contacts with other boys or older adults [Male Report, pp. 166, 177; emphasis added].

It is documented then that nine pedophiles (some "technically trained") were at the core of Kinsey's child sex experiments. In a 1981 response to an inquiry from J. Reisman, former Kinsey coworker Paul Gebhard, then-director of the Kinsey Institute, elaborated:

Since sexual experimentation with human infants and children is illegal, we have had to depend upon other sources of data . . . [including] homosexual males interested in older, but still prepubertal, children. *One was a man who had numerous sexual contacts with male and female infants and children and, being of a scientific bent, kept detailed records of each encounter.* Some of these sources have added to their written or verbal reports, photographs and, in a few instances, cinema. We have never attempted follow-up studies because it was either impossible or too expensive. The techniques involved were self-masturbation by the child, child-child sex play, *and adult-child contacts—chiefly manual or oral* [Letter: Gebhard to Reisman, March 11, 1981; emphasis added. Full text in Appendix B].

Here, for the first time, 33 years after publication of Kinsey's Male Report, it is stated that orogenital stimulation of the male children was one of the research techniques. The "man who had numerous sexual contacts" may be the bizarre sexual polymorph (one of the "technically trained"?) identified by Kinsey co-author, Pomeroy, in his 1972 book, . *Dr. Kinsey and the Institute for Sex Research:*

The longest history we ever took was done . . . by Kinsey and me. . . . When we got the record . . . it astounded even us, who had heard everything. This man had had homosexual relations with 600 preadolescent males, heterosexual relations with 200 preadolescent females[4] intercourse with countless adults of both sexes, with animals of many species, and besides had employed elaborate techniques of masturbation . . . . *[O]f thirty three family members he had had sexual contacts with seventeen. His grandmother introduced him to heterosexual intercourse, and his first homosexual experience was with his father* [p. 122; emphasis added].

Attention is drawn to this Kinsey research source because, astoundingly, according to Pomeroy, the data he provided "was *the basis for a fair part of Chapter Five in the Male volume, concerning child sexuality. Because of these elaborate records we were able to get data on the behavior of many children . . . ." (ibid.* p. 122; emphasis added). Pomeroy also noted the apparent harmlessness of this sex offender, who may have remained at large and active for many years:

[He] was sixty-three years old, quiet, soft-spoken, self-effacing—a rather unobtrusive fellow [*ibid.*].

Specific questions in Reisman's 1981 letter to the Kinsey Institute regarding the identity, training and current location of Kinsey's child sex experimenters were ignored in Paul Gebhard's reply (see Appendix B).

---

4   Curiously, in spite of this and other sex offender data on rape in their possession, the Kinsey team virtually ignored this subject in the entirety of their human sexuality research (see chapter 2).

COMPROMISED RESEARCH

At this point, readers familiar with the process of research in human subjects could reasonably consider Kinsey's entire male sexuality data worthless, based on what already is known of the interviewees, tabulation methods and the "sex experimenters." More probably, most readers are wondering if what they have been reading could possibly be true. It is, and it will be necessary to continue with that "suspension of disbelief." The stretching of credibility has only just begun. Certainly, today, no researchers trained in the biological sciences could accept that Kinsey's statistics on male sexual behavior apply to the U.S. population of his day—that is, if they were familiar with the methods by which these numbers were gathered.

Recently, however, public health authorities *have* used Kinsey's data on the prevalence of homosexuality as the basis for projections of the expected numbers of AIDS cases and AIDS-virus-infected individuals. Already, in the New York area, this has resulted in a considerable overestimate of the homosexually-mediated spread of these conditions. And nationally, the Federal Government's 1986 estimate of up to 1.5 million people infected with the AIDS virus—also based largely on Kinsey data—has had to be cut by a half million or more! Thus, although the medical experts who have relied on Kinsey's homosexuality figures for disease forecasting have apparently never studied the methods Kinsey used in his research, they are beginning to discover error—by backing into it (see chapter 6).

Despite proof that Kinsey's work is seriously compromised, a full analysis is critical because an examination of Kinsey's child-sex-experiment results makes clear there are more weighty questions to answer, such as: 1) were the child-sex-experiment data really provided retrospectively by interviewees possessing identical sets of experimental measurements, and 2) was Kinsey himself (and/or his coworkers) more directly involved in this research than the public has been led to believe?

PERSONAL BIAS

There is a clear bias in the way the Kinsey team presented their male and female (chapter 2) child sexuality data. This should be no surprise considering what is known of Kinsey's sampling methods. It could almost be predicted from sample composition and the sources of child sexuality information that Kinsey would find in favor of children having the capacity to lead active sex lives among themselves and with adults. As a result of Kinsey's later female child sex research, Kinsey and team would reach predictable conclusions of great import on child molestation and incest.

As pointed out by historian Paul Robinson, Kinsey's bias suggests a motive for the Male Report: " . . . the fundamental categories of his analysis clearly worked to undermine the traditional sexual order" (Robinson, 1976, p. 59).

Also noted earlier were Kinsey's clear views that every type of sexual activity is normal (ie, heterosexuality is *not* the norm), so-called "outlawed" practices are "entirely natural," and basic human sexuality is the "capacity to respond to any . . . stimulus."

Kinsey equated natural human sexuality with the animal model. According to Pomeroy, Kinsey and colleagues concluded from their direct studies of both human and animal behavior that "the human animal was even more mammalian than we had thought" (Pomeroy, 1972, p. 186). Ashley Montagu, chairman of the department of anthropology at Rutgers University noted in a 1954 critique that Kinsey suffered "very badly" from the "fallacy" that any behavior is normal if it has a biological basis. This, of course, could apply to robbery or murder, not just sex, as British anthropologist Geoffrey Gorer observed. Author and psychiatrist Iago Galdston felt that this biological materialism took Kinsey out of touch with social reality.[5] Certainly, Kinsey's reliance on the child sex experiments described below as a source of information on human sexuality indicates that this renowned scientist was out of touch with reality in other ways.

Kinsey's preset views on child sexuality are strongly suggested by his use of prison inmate/sex offender experience and records as if these could provide knowledge of a normal population. Looking to sexual molesters for information on childhood sexuality is like drawing conclusions on the sexuality of adult females from the testimony of rapists. Kinsey's bias, furthermore, was clearly revealed by his approach to the criminal element among his sample. According to Pomeroy, the Kinsey team took pains to reassure offenders of their feeling that all sex was normal and of their ability to share the offenders' satisfactions and frustrations (Pomeroy, Flax and Wheeler, *Taking a Sex History: Interviewing and Recording*, The Free Press, 1972, p. 6).

The Kinsey authors describe two diverse views on sexual behavior in society: The "upper-social-level" view, which is flawed because it deals with "right and wrong" and makes decisions on the basis of "morality"; and the "lower-social-level view," which is "natural"—like premarital intercourse—and therefore not hypocritical. Kinsey's sympathies lie with the "lower-level *boy* or *girl*" who has sexual relations and then becomes a victim of "unrealistic sex laws." He seems to think sex offenders are also victimized by parole boards "because they are judged by the standards of the upper level community" (Male Report, pp. 384, 385, 391, 393; emphasis added).

Although the sexual experimentation documented in Kinsey's Male Report involved only male children, the Kinsey team interpreted the results as supporting their view that willingness to use any sexual outlet (what some have called, in the non-Freudian sense, pansexuality) is the desired, natural and "uninhibited" form of human sexual expression. Looking again at the Kinsey authors' definition of human sexuality in *Psychosexual Development in Health and Disease*, this becomes quite clear:

5   See: Geddes DP (ed.), *An Analysis of the Kinsey Reports on Sexual Behavior in the Human Male and Female*, Mentor Books, 1954; Himelhoch J, Fava SF (eds.), *Sexual Behavior in American Society: An Appraisal of the First Two Kinsey Reports*, W.W. Norton and Co., 1955.

[W]e suggest that sexuality, in its basic biologic origins, is *a capacity to respond to any sufficient stimulus.* It is simply *a picture of physiologic response and psychologic conditioning* ... [In Hoch and Zubin: *Psychosexual Development in Health and Disease*, Grune & Stratton, 1949, p. 27; emphasis added].

One of the strongest accusations of bias in Kinsey's research comes from Gershon Legman, the original bibliographer for Kinsey's erotica collection at the Kinsey Institute. In his 1964 work *The Horn Book* (University Books), Legman described the Kinsey Reports as "pure propaganda" and an attempt to "respectabilize ... sexual perversions":

> Kinsey's real activity has been generally misunderstood, owing to the cloud of statistical hokum and tendentiously "weighted" population-samplings in which the propagandistic purpose of his first, and only influential work, on the "Human Male" was disguised. ... Kinsey's not-very-secret intention was to "respectabilize" homosexuality and certain sexual perversions. ... [He] did not hesitate to extrapolate his utterly inadequate and inconclusive samplings . . . to the whole population of the United States, not to say the world. ... This is pure propaganda, and is ridiculously far from the mathematical or statistical science pretended. ... Kinsey's "Reports" were and are accepted as a sort of abstruse mathematical gospel that "validates," as normal human acts and states, the specific abnormality of homosexuality and a whole theory of wildcat pansexuality of entirely anti-social effect [pp. 125, 126; emphasis added].

According to Legman, Kinsey sought to prove his own "fantasy" that sexual perversions do not exist (*ibid.*).

Despite the evidence of a moral agenda, Alan Gregg of the Rockefeller Foundation wrote in the Preface to the Male Report that Dr. Kinsey presented his work "without moral bias or prejudice."

It is appropriate at this point to look at the "sexual response in the child" that the Kinsey team claim to have documented.

THE "CHILD SEXUALITY" DATA

These data purportedly came from two sources: memories of persons interviewed and "[b]etter data on preadolescent climax ... from the histories of adult males who have had sexual contacts with younger boys and who, with their adult backgrounds, are able to recognize and interpret the boy's experience." This latter source apparently consisted mainly of the "technically trained persons" and Pomeroy's "quiet, soft-spoken, self-effacing" sex offender, who started his sex life with his grandmother (or possibly his father). Despite these bizarre sources, the Kinsey team applied their conclusions to "the population as a whole" (Male Report, p. 178). One of the major conclusions was that

> [it is] certain that many infant males and younger boys are capable of orgasm, and *it is probable that half or more of the boys in an uninhibited society could reach climax by the time they were three or four years of age*, and that nearly all of them could experience such a climax three to five years before the onset of adolescence [Male Report, p. 178; emphasis added].

Kinsey added,

The most remarkable aspect of the pre-adolescent population is its capacity to achieve repeated orgasm in limited periods of time [Male Report, p. 179].

The Kinsey team's record of infant and child orgasmic potential was presented in tables 30 through 34 of the Male Report. Data from Kinsey's "First Preadolescent Orgasm" table (Table 30) are presented below. Very little information was given on the origin of these numbers, but that is a characteristic of Kinsey's research.

First Preadolescent Orgasm
(From Male Report , Table 30, p. 175)

AGE	DATA FROM PRESENT STUDY	DATA FROM OTHER SUBJECTS	TOTAL CASES	% OF TOTAL
1	–	12	12	2.5
2	–	8	8	1.6
3	2	7	9	1.8
4	–	12	12	2.5
5	5	9	14	2.9
6	15	19	34	7.0
7	21	17	38	7.8
8	27	21	48	9.9
9	24	26	50	10.3
10	56	26	82	16.8
11	54	22	76	15.6
12	51	23	74	15.2
13	15	9	24	4.9
14	3	3	6	1.2
15	–	–	–	–
TOTAL	273	214	487	100.0
MEAN AGE	10.40	8.51	9.57	
MEDIAN AGE	9.77	8.10	9.23	

The following explanatory note was provided:

All data based on *memory* of older subjects, *except* in the column entitled "data from other subjects." In the latter case, original data gathered by certain of our subjects were made available for use in the present volume. Of the 214 cases so reported, all but 14 were *subsequently observed* in orgasm [Male Report, p. 175; emphasis added].

This table is an unscientific mixture of data from memory, from observation, and from memory plus subsequent observation—all without further explanation. The "certain subjects" and their methods of "gathering data" are not described; nor are the circumstances of the repeat observations in 200 of the children.

The next table, titled "Preadolescent Experience in Orgasm" (Table 31), listed the ages at which individuals among a group of 317 children "reached climax." Part of this tabulation is reproduced below.

Preadolescent Experience In Orgasm
[From Male Report, Table 31, p. 176]

AGE WHEN OBSERVED	TOTAL POPULATION	CASES NOT REACHING CLIMAX	CASES REACHING CLIMAX	PERCENT OF EACH AGE REACHING CLIMAX
2 mths.	1	1	0	
3 mths.	2	2	0	
4 mths.	1	1	0	
5 mths.	2	1	1	
8 mths.	2	1	1	
9 mths.	1	1	0	
10 mths.	4	1	3	
11 mths.	3	1	2	
12 mths.	12	10	2	
Up to 1yr.	28	19	9	32.1
Up to 2 yr.	22	11	11	
Up to 3 yr.	9	2	7	
Up to 4 yr.	12	5	7	57.1
Up to 5 yr.	6	3	3	
Up to 6 yr.	12	5	7	
Up to 7 yr.	17	8	9	
Up to 8 yr.	26	12	14	63.4
Up to 9 yr.	29	10	19	
Up to 10 yr.	28	6	22	
Up to 11 yr.	34	9	25	
Up to 12 yr.	46	7	39	80.0
Up to 13 yr.	35	7	28	
Up to 14 yr.	11	5	6	
Up to 15 yr.	2	2	0	
TOTAL	317	111	206	65.0

The above data are remarkable. The Kinsey team claim here that "orgasm" was "observed" in an infant of 5 months. Perhaps more staggering is that attempts were made to produce orgasms in babies of 2, 3 and 4 months! These efforts apparently failed. The relationship of the 317 boys to the 273, 214 (and 200) boys of the previous table is not explained, which is unsatisfactory. These data allegedly are from "actual observation," though this has been implied to mean from details of observations provided to the Kinsey team during interviews. However, with reference to this table, the Kinsey authors said:

In 5 cases of young pre-adolescents, *observations were continued over periods of months or years*, until the individuals were old enough *to make it certain that true orgasm was involved* [Male Report, p. 177; emphasis added].

This is one of the first indications that the child sex abuse statistics are more than just after-the-fact recall. It contrasts also, in that respect, with Gebhard's letter to Reisman, in which he states that "[w]e have never attempted any follow up studies . . . ." The implication of the above passage is that the Kinsey team had interviewees who did follow-up studies on the children they molested.

The main conclusion drawn from these child-abuse data was that most preadolescents can experience orgasm—in those who cannot, there is probably a psychological problem:

The observers emphasize that there are some of these pre-adolescent boys (estimated by one observer as less than one quarter of the cases), who *fail to reach climax even under prolonged varied and repeated stimulation*; but even in these young boys, *this probably represents psychologic blockage more often than physiologic incapacity* [Male Report, p. 178; emphasis added].

The Kinsey team generalized these data to conclude that *in an* uninhibited society the majority of boys could be having orgasms by 3 or 4 years of age:

In the population as a whole, a much smaller percentage of the boys experience orgasm at any early age, because few of them find themselves in circumstances that test their capacities; but the positive record on these boys who did have the opportunity makes it certain that many infant males and younger boys are capable of orgasm, and *it is probable that half or more of the boys in an uninhibited society could reach climax by the time they were three or four years of age, and that nearly all of them could experience such a climax three to five years before the onset of adolescence* [Male Report, p. 178; emphasis added].

Another remarkable data table is the one detailing "speed of preadolescent orgasm" (Table 32). This is reproduced, in part, below.

Speed Of Preadolescent Orgasm
[From Male Report, Table 32, p. 178]

TIME	CASES TIMED	PERCENT OF POPULATION
Up to 10 sec.	12	6.4
10 sec. to 1 min.	46	24.5
1 to 2 min.	40	21.3
2 to 3 min.	23	12.2
3 to 5 min.	33	17.5
5 to 10 min.	23	12.2
Over 10 min.	11	5.9
TOTAL	188	100.0

The Kinsey authors here inform the reader that the mean time to climax was 3.02 minutes and the median time 1.91 minutes. The children were "five months of age to adolescence" and "observations [were] timed with second hand or stopwatch" (Male Report, p. 178).

Further information from the text indicates that

. . . two two-year-olds [came] to climax in less than 10 seconds, and there are two-year-olds who may take 10 or 20 minutes or more [Male Report, pp. 178, 179].

The Kinsey team must have realized it would be a matter of some scientific (as well as legal) interest to know what kind of "interviewees" these were whose records provided stopwatch data on the number of seconds it took to stimulate 2-year-olds (or 5-month-olds) to orgasm.

Kinsey's fourth child sex data table (Table 33) presented the number of alleged "orgasms" achieved among 182 preadolescent boys and the time between "orgasms" recorded in 64 preadolescent boys. The means were 3.72 orgasms and 6.28 minutes, respectively. Remarkably, three children required less than 10 seconds, and 15 children 11 to 15 seconds, between orgasms. Again, the Kinsey team generalized sweepingly from these assault findings to the sexual capacities of American children:

[T]he most remarkable aspect of *the pre-adolescent population* is its capacity to achieve repeated orgasm in limited periods of time. This capacity definitely exceeds the ability of teenage boys who, in turn, are much more capable than any older males [Male Report, p. 179; emphasis added].

In their final table of male child sex experiment data (Table 34 in the Male Report) the Kinsey team claimed to demonstrate that

[e]ven *the youngest males, as young as 5 months in age, are capable of such repeated reactions [orgasms].* Typical cases are shown in Table 34. *The maximum observed was 26 climaxes in 24 hours* [in a 4-year-old and a 13-year-old], and the report indicates that still more might have been possible in the same period of time [Male Report, p. 180; emphasis added].

The following data, according to Dr. Kinsey and colleagues, "substantiate" the "view of sexuality as a component that is present in the human animal from earliest infancy . . ."—one of the most extraordinary claims in the "scientific" literature, considering its source.

Examples of Multiple Orgasm In Preadolescent Males
(Male Report, Table 34, p. 180)

AGE	NO OF. ORGASMS	TIME INVOLVED	AGE	NO OF ORGASMS	TIME INVOLVED
5 mon.	3	?	11 yr.	11	1 hr.
11 mon.	10	1 hr.	11 yr.	19	1 hr.
11 mon.	14	38 min.	12 yr.	7	3 hr.
2 yr.	[7]	9 min.	12 yr.	[3]	3 min.
	[11]	65 min.		[9]	2 hr.
2.5 yr.	4	2 min.	12 yr.	12	2 hr.
4 yr.	6	5 min.	12 yr.	15	1 hr.
4 yr.	17	10 hr.	13 yr.	7	24 min.
4 yr.	26	24 hr.	13 yr.	8	2.5 hr.
7 yr.	7	3 hr.	13 yr.	9	8 hr.
8 yr.	8	2 hr.		[3]	70 sec.
9 yr.	7	68 min.	13 yr.	[11]	8 hr.
10 yr.	9	52 min.		[26]	24 hr.
10 yr.	14	24 hr.	14 yr.	11	4 hr.

This table is purported to document "typical cases" of the orgasmic potential of male infants and children. By any reasonable definition of child abuse, these children were being sexually assaulted. These data may be the only example in Western science where egregious abuse of human subjects has been presented as "scientific" by scientists wishing to be taken seriously. Why this material was not rejected out of hand and why there was no call for an explanation at the time of publication is discussed later in this chapter.

Inexplicably, the total number of children tested is unclear. Some, it appears from the table, may have been tested more than once. It is also unexplained why the number of "orgasms" for the 5-month infant is recorded but not the time involved.

These data tables represent another of the most remarkable claims in scientific literature—namely, that the figures came from the *"histories . . .* of our adult male subjects who have observed such orgasm."

Kinsey made the further amazing claim that these data—obtained by interviewing pedophiles and sex offenders who had all secured identically precise measurements from *illegal* experimentation on children—help illustrate "the sexual history of the human male" (Male Report, p. 182).

It is suggested that readers with access to the Male Report carefully examine pages 160 and 161 for its description of the tests conducted on children. Here Kinsey documents six types of preadolescent orgasm from these "histories": Four of these involved pain or tension of some kind, such as

Extreme tension with violent convulsion . . . gasping, eyes staring . . . mouth distorted, sometimes with tongue protruding . . . whole body or parts of it spasmodically twitching . . . throbs or violent jerking of the penis . . . groaning, sobbing, or more violent cries . . . masochistic reactions . . . more or less frenzied movements . . . extreme trembling, collapse, loss of color, and sometimes fainting of subject . . . pained or frightened . . . will fight away from the *partner* and may make violent attempts to avoid climax, *although they derive definite pleasure from the situation* [Male Report, p. 161; emphasis added].

The use of the euphemism "partner" and the notion of "pleasure" derived from the assaultive situation anticipate Kinsey's 1953 conclusion of female children benefitting from sexual interaction with adults (chapter 2). For male infants and children, Kinsey put it this way:

[T]here are cases of *infants under a year of age who have learned the advantage of specific manipulation,* sometimes as a result of being so manipulated by older persons. . . . When an older person provides the more specific sort of manipulation which is usual among adults, the same child may be much aroused, and in a high proportion of the cases may be brought to actual orgasm [Male Report, p. 501; emphasis added].

Ignoring the fact that no reputable scientist would be using data from the above-described experiments, no reputable scientist would be content to leave these children without some kind of follow-up. Paul Gebhard's response to Reisman's written question on this point was that follow-up studies would have been "either impossible or too expensive" (see Appendix B).

A PEDIATRIC OPINION

The question of how the infant and child orgasmic sex experiments were actually performed has been discussed with a number of professionals in a variety of medical and psychological disciplines. Apart from the general view that such testing procedures would be unthinkable, illegal and inhumane, there was a consensus that a significant number of the children would have had to be forcibly held down. It was also uniformly agreed that the emotional trauma involved could have been extremely serious, perhaps even fatal in some cases. The following letter from Baltimore pediatrician, Lester H. Caplan, M.D., F.A.C.P., was typical of the reaction of medical professionals:

Dear Dr. Reisman:

I have done a review of your paper . . . based on an examination of the Kinsey data and its effects . . . upon . . . the child, and I have come to the following conclusions:

1. That the data were not the norm—rather data taken from abnormal sexual activities, by sex criminals and the like.

2. Unnatural stimulation was used by the researchers to get results.

3. The frequencies and the number of orgasms in 24 hours were not natural nor the mean.

4. *One person could not do this to so many children— These children had to be held down or subject to strapping down, otherwise they would not respond willingly* [emphasis added].

KINSEY CONCLUSIONS

The Kinsey team gave the impression that they had clearly established—for the first time—the orgasmic potential of infants and children (Male Report, p. 175). From interviews with young children and adults, and observations by "parents" and "other subjects," they additionally concluded that genital play and exploration among very young children were commoner than believed (Male Report, p. 163). However, according to Kinsey, the inhibitory effect of "social values" came into play early on in children's lives, with culturally acquired reactions to "the mysterious," "the forbidden" and "the socially dangerous" (Male Report, p. 164).

That preadolescent sex play did not continue unabated in many children was considered a product of "cultural restraints" and "community attitudes." However, "lower social level boys," freer of such restraints, had a better chance of continuing sexual activity without a break, more like the "pre-adolescent sex play in the anthropoids, [which] is abundant and continues into adult performance (Bingham 1928)" (Male Report, pp. 167, 174).

The interviews and sex experiments were, in Kinsey's opinion, "an important substantiation of the Freudian view of sexuality as a component that is present in the human animal from earliest infancy . . ." (Male Report, p. 180). But Kinsey believed he had disproved Freud's theory of a sexually latent period in adolescence:

> [The data do not] show any necessity for a sexually latent or dormant period in the late adolescent years, except as such inactivity results from parental or social repressions of the growing child [Male Report, p. 180].

The child sex experiments reported by Kinsey were a key to "proving" this. Such experiments had never been done before, and quoting Moore (1943), Kinsey pointed out: "the memory of the adult [does not] reach back to those early years so that he can tell us whether or not it is really true that in infancy and early childhood he experienced specific sexual excitement, and that this was repressed and became latent, as Freud maintained" (Male Report, p. 181). So Kinsey claimed to have established two things: 1) the beginnings of erotic sexuality in infancy, and 2) the myth of Freud's latency period, except as a function of social repression. With his child sex data, Kinsey had debunked the popular view that "although the child is capable of a tender personal love, it is of a non-erotic character and has nothing to do with the beginnings of sexuality" (Male Report, p. 181).

The Kinsey team's research data—from the memories of adult males and the memories or records of pedophiles' experiments on male children—are largely homosexual data. Kinsey clearly believed that enjoyment of such activities was also hindered by the prevailing "social taboos." He held that "younger pre-adolescents" needed the help of older "more experienced persons" to "discover masturbatory techniques that are sexually effective." Without such assistance, "younger adolescents" attempting "homosexual play" were limited to "contacts [that] are still very incidental and casual and without any recognition of the emotional possibilities of such experience" (Male Report, p. 170). (This, incidentally, is a rare Kinsey reference to "emotion" in sexual activity.)

Kinsey clearly perceived masturbation of children by adults as preparation for adult homosexual relationships. He conjectured that if children could learn elaborate enough masturbation techniques—preferably from experienced adults—the "incidental" and "casual" type of sexual exploration that is common among adolescents could be turned into a truly homosexual experience. Kinsey termed this an "emotional possibility." Without such training, children were likely to pass on from incidental experiences to exclusive heterosexual relationships.

Kinsey felt that social conditioning inhibited older males from such involvement: "The anatomy and functional capacities of male genitalia interest the younger boy to a degree that is not appreciated by older males who have become heterosexually conditioned and who are continuously on the defensive against reactions which might be interpreted as homosexual" (Male Report, p. 168).

A repressive society, in Kinsey's view, was responsible for the inhibition of the full expression of all types of sexual activity in "the human animal." This view achieved fuller expression in his 1953 Female Report, where, readers will notice, Kinsey took pains to express the harmlessness, and even benefits, to female children of sexual contact with adults (chapter 2).

THE KINSEY IMPACT

Kinseyan views on childhood sexuality, and human sexuality in general, have—by constant repetition over the past four decades—become incorporated as givens into modern sexology's corpus of knowledge. The net result is that some—but not yet all—of Kinsey's findings have become self-fulfilling prophecies. Sexual taboos still remain at the beginning of the 1990s, but most of these, too, are at odds with true Kinseyan philosophy. The era of "AIDS education," however, has become a rare opportunity for the promotion of the more socially sensitive tenets of the Kinsey philosophy. [See chapter 4 for a full discussion.]

As noted earlier, psychologists Zimbardo, Ebbeson and Maslach, wrote in their 1977 book, *Influencing Attitudes and Changing Behavior* (Addison-Wesley), that

> The results of the Kinsey surveys on the sexual behavior of the American male and female established, to some degree, social standards of what was acceptable common practice [p. 89].

Today, at the end of the 1980s, Kinseyan philosophy has been given new life as the basis of a new wave of sex education programs finding sudden funding, staffing and popularity in the rush to provide "AIDS education." Further attitude shifts and behavioral changes should be expected to result.

The effort to educate the American public in the unscientific concept of Kinsey-type childhood sexuality is ongoing. (This too will be driven by the perceived need to educate children in "safe-sex" practices—the "health" imperative being, for some at least, a useful mechanism for implementing education in the total Kinseyan philosophy.) Crooks and Baur's 1983 college human sexuality text, *Our Sexuality* (Benjamin/Cummings Publishing Co.)—a typical example of such works—cites the Kinsey team's findings on child sexuality as applicable to today's children:

> In many Western societies, including the United States, it has been traditional to view childhood as a time when sexuality remains unexpressed and adolescence as a time when sexuality needs to be restrained. . . . However, with the widespread circulation of the research findings of Alfred Kinsey and other distinguished investigators, the false assumption that childhood is a period of sexual dormancy is gradually eroding. In fact, it is now widely recognized that infants of both sexes are born with the capacity for sexual pleasure and response.
>
> *Signs of sexual arousal in infants and children, such as penile erection, vaginal lubrication, and pelvic thrusting, are often misinterpreted or unacknowledged.* However, careful observers may note these indications of sexuality in the very young. In some cases, both male and female infants have been observed experiencing what appears to be an orgasm. The infant, of course, cannot offer spoken confirmation of the sexual nature of such reactions. . . . *The following two quotations [from Kinsey's Male and Female Reports] are offered as evidence for this conclusion* [p. 410; emphasis added].

Actually, the "misinterpretation" of certain physiological reactions in infants and children is entirely the authors'. The placing of a sexual connotation on these reflexive nervous and vascular reactions is done with reference to Kinsey's data, which come from hurtful, unethical, illegal and, consequently, invalid research.

But the acceptance of infant and childhood sexuality is powerfully entrenched in sexology circles. The "given" factor can be clearly seen in statements from Mary Calderone (past president and co-founder, with Lester Kirkendall, of SIECUS). Speaking before the 1980 annual meeting of the Association of Planned Parenthood Physicians, Dr. Calderone reportedly explained that providing today's society "very broadly and deeply with awareness of the vital importance of infant and childhood sexuality" is now the primary goal of SIECUS (*Ob.Gyn.News*, December 1, 1980, p. 10). In 1983, Calderone wrote of the child's sexual capacities that

> [these should] be developed—in the same way as the child's inborn human capacity to talk or to walk, and that [*the parents'*] *role should relate only to teaching the child the appropriateness of privacy, place, and person—in a word socialization* [*SIECUS Report*, May-July 1983, p. 9; emphasis added].

Today, SIECUS personnel view the AIDS era as an opportunity to advance their view of human sexuality—"A time of rare opportunity," according to Dr. Ann Welbourne-Moglia, former executive director of SIECUS, writing in the January-February 1987 *SIECUS Report*. Welbourne-Moglia stated that "to prevent and educate about AIDS it is essential to be able to communicate and teach about sexuality in general" (*SIECUS Report*, January-February 1987, p. 15). This is undoubtedly true. But theories of sexuality that are being taught in such programs are generally Kinseyan in type (see chapter 4).

In fact, the Kinsey research has done more than just influence the content of modern sex education. That is only the thin end of a much longer wedge. Kinsey's childhood sexuality research approximates to a pedophile's charter. Pedophiles believe their "love of children" is socially beneficial. As justification for their position, they rely on academic and scientific works (see Lanning and Burgess, "Child Pornography and Sex Rings," *FBI Law Enforcement Bulletin*, January 1984). An example of this is Tom O'Carroll's effort in his book *Paedophilia: The Radical Case* (quoted in Introduction) to establish a scientific basis for adult-child sexual relationships. O'Carroll often referred to the Kinsey Reports and their influence on his becoming a pedophile.

The impact of Kinsey's homosexuality statistics on the early and modern gay activist movements is discussed in later chapters.

KINSEY REVERED

In sexology circles, Kinsey and his findings still are revered. Writing in the December 1983 *Esquire*, Stanley Elkin described Kinsey as "The Patron Saint" of sex, the man responsible for "the first wave of the sexual revolution." Hugh Hefner has described in the first issue of *Playboy* how he drew inspiration from Kinsey's sex research. Morton Hunt, hired by The Playboy Foundation to try to update the Kinsey studies, wrote of Kinsey in *Sexual Behavior in the 1970s* (Playboy Press, 1974) that he was sexology's patriarch:

> The debt this book owes to the late Dr. Alfred C. Kinsey is beyond the scope of acknowledgment; he was *the giant on whose shoulders all sex researchers since his time have stood.* Those who participated in the present project used his data, his thoughts and his words every day until we supposed them our own [In "Acknowledgements"; emphasis added].

Hefner, it is claimed, was particularly dazzled by Kinsey. As Thomas Weyr put it, "Hefner recognized Kinsey as the incontrovertible word of the new God based on the new holy writ—demonstrable evidence [concerning human sexuality]" (*Reaching for Paradise: The Playboy Vision of America*, Times Books, 1978, p. 11).

It is likely that in the world of sexology many professionals subscribe to Kinsey's views on childhood sexuality, but they are very careful how they articulate this concept. John Leo described the situation insightfully in a 1981 *Time* magazine article subheaded, "Some researchers openly argue that 'anything goes' for children":

The idea [of young children conducting a full sex life] is rarely presented directly—most of the researchers, doctors and counselors who believe it have the wit to keep a low profile and tuck the idea away neatly in a longer, more conventional speech or article. The suggestion comes wrapped in the pieties of feminism (children, like women, have the right to control their own bodies) and the children's rights movement (children have rights *versus* their parents). According to the argument, children are sexual beings who need to develop skills early in life [*Time*, September 7, 1981, p. 69].

Leo cited as "anything goes" proponents Mary Calderone of SIECUS, sexologist John Money of Johns Hopkins and Kinsey co-author Wardell Pomeroy. [See also the *Time* article "Attacking the Last Taboo" (Appendix C) and chapter 7 for more information on how sex researchers are currently "chipping away" at the adult-child sex prohibition.]

BEYOND CHILDHOOD SEXUALITY

While Kinsey held that all sex was natural, he argued that the narrow limits prescribed by society were unnatural. Virginity before marriage and sex exclusively within marriage were limited and therefore unnatural—thus, in a sense, immoral.

Both childhood sexual activity and *all* sexual activity were regarded by Kinsey as normal. In fact he regarded some forms (eg, bisexuality) as superior in that more variety was offered. Parents already may be familiar with their children being taught the "Kinsey Scale," that humans are essentially bisexual—not "naturally" exclusively homo or heterosexual—and that each sexual choice is equally good.

Sex education now is rapidly progressing beyond the peripheral tenets of the Kinseyan philosophy. Texts are cropping up in some schools suggesting that monogamy and fidelity are "abnormal," selfish habits. Others speak well of bestiality.

One contemporary sex education text, *Boys and Sex* (Pelican Books, 1981), by Kinsey co-author Wardell Pomeroy, suggests the naturalness of sex between adolescents and animals:

What would happen if a boy had intercourse with an animal? About one out of five boys who live on farms or else visit one during summer vacation have intercourse, or attempt it with animals . . . ponies, calves, sheep, pigs, even chickens or ducks. Dogs are also commonly used, but cats rarely. . . . [Some] build a strong emotional attachment to a particular animal . . . *a loving sexual relationship with an animal* and . . . . felt good about their behavior until they got to college, where they learned for the first time that what they had done was "abnormal." Then they were upset and thought of themselves as some kind of monster [pp. 134, 135; emphasis added].

The implication, again, appears to be that negative "societal inhibitions" come into play to interfere with these normal sexual proclivities of youth.

Approval of "loving sexual relationships" with animals does, in fact, fall within the Kinsey doctrine. This is a natural extension of the philosophy of "outlet sex." With such a doctrine there are no limits.

RESEARCH WITHOUT LIMITS

Did a philosophy of "sex without limits" drive a team of dedicated researchers to conduct "unlimited" sex experiments—beyond the pale of what was morally or ethically acceptable, and legally permissible? There is evidence that this indeed is what happened—almost compelling evidence.

It will be important to bear in mind the "assault" aspect of Kinsey's research—for masturbating infants and children, some of whom were weeping, screaming, convulsing and fainting, and in some cases for 24 hours at a time, is serious assault.

The previously cited letter from Gebhard to Reisman admits that sexual experimentation of this kind is illegal. Also, John Gagnon, a former project director at the Kinsey Institute, wrote of the Kinsey child sex experiments that

> . . . much of [Kinsey's] information comes from adults who were in active sexual contact with . . . boys and who were interested in producing orgasms in them. *A less neutral observer than Kinsey would have described these events as sex crimes*, since they involved sexual contact between adults and children [*Human Sexualities*, p. 84; emphasis added].

While Kinsey's own descriptions indicate *child abuse* rather than *contact*, nowhere in his two major reports does Kinsey acknowledge that the experimental data he is presenting come from criminal activity. Also, nowhere does Kinsey provide a credible account of how this precisely measured information was obtained.

HISTORICAL RECALL

According to Kinsey and co-authors, the child sex experiment data came from the "*histories* of adult males who have had sexual contacts with younger boys and who, with their adult backgrounds, are able to recognize and interpret the boy's experiences" (Male Report, pp. 176, 177; emphasis added). It is simply not believable that the data, reproduced from the Male Report earlier in this chapter, could have been derived in this way—even if all of these histories were from "technically trained persons" (Male Report, p. 177). There are some insurmountable problems with this explanation of how the research was done.

First, how does one recruit a team of pre-trained individuals (who are also sex offenders) who have precise stopwatch data obtained under identical research conditions? Secondly, how does a lone adult manually or orally masturbate a young child for up to 24 hours and simultaneously keep exact records of what is happening? Thirdly—assuming the first two scenarios are possible—can pedophiles make unemotional and objective "observations" while involved in such "work"? The first two scenarios clearly are far-fetched. Kinsey, himself, has attempted to address the problem of the third:

[C]linical records or case history data . . . constitute secondhand reports which depend for their validity upon the capacity of the individual to observe his or her own activity, and upon his or her ability to analyze the physical and psychologic bases of these activities . . . . This difficulty is particularly acute in the study of sexual behavior because *the participant in a sexual relationship becomes physiologically incapacitated as an observer.* Sexual arousal reduces one's capacities . . . [however, our] observations were made in every instance by scientifically trained observers [Female Report, p. 570; emphasis added].

One implication of this statement is that some of the "trained observers" were not directly involved but part of a team whose goal was purely scientific (see below).

One of the principal supporting indications that the Kinsey child sex research was not carried out as implied in the Male Report is the lack of replication in the 40 years since publication. In recent times it would be easier—theoretically—to recruit a team such as Kinsey's. It has never been done, to our knowledge.

There are other problems with Kinsey's historical recall explanation—for example, until recently, it seems, pedophiles were loath to involve themselves with infants and very young children (O'Carroll, 1980, p. 58)—but these are incidental to the implausibility of this putative research method.

DIRECTED RESEARCH (?)

Kinsey stated in his Male Report that he complied with the requirement that "writers . . . test their theories . . . by empirical study and statistical procedures" (Male Report, p. 181). Taking this description of his methodology together with the implied third-party role of his "observers" and the statement (noted earlier) that some observations "were continued over periods of months or years until the individuals were old enough to make it certain that true orgasm was involved" (Male Report, p. 177), there is a hint that prospective, directed research was involved here.

This is the only plausible way Kinsey's experimental child sex data could have been obtained—unless it was fabricated. Since Kinsey in his Reports—and associates in their later works—often leave clues to the deciphering of some aspects of the research methodology, are there any further clues to the possibility of this being *the* methodology? It should be noted, first, that such a methodology would have involved planned, illegal sexual abuse of human subjects—and a subsequent cover-up. The clues are there.

Retake Histories

It is alleged that the Kinsey team conducted "retakes" from 162 of their interviewees, and that the average time lapse between the first and second interviews was 3.2 years (Male Report, p. 121). Kinsey claimed

that "Retakes, of course, cover activities which had not been engaged
in until after the time of the original history" (*ibid.*). Writing in the
American Sociological Review in 1949, one critic noted the following:

> No indication is given of the circumstances under which the subjects
> of this test were procured for re-take histories . . . . There is some
> evidence that marked sexual activity in certain outlets was a selective
> factor for participation in the test. The incidence of homosexual
> experience in this group is almost 50 percent, which is considerably
> higher than the incidence reported for the population at large from
> which the group was drawn [Wallin P. "An appraisal of Some
> Methodological Aspects of the Kinsey Report." *American Sociologi-
> cal Review* 14: 197-210, 1949].

If some degree of "training" took place at the *first* interview, it now
becomes understandable that Kinsey could claim some kind of
methodological standardization or consistency for the subsequent research collected at the "retake." This, of course, would implicate
Kinsey and his team in promoting, and perhaps participating in, the
criminal activity.

Sperm Collecting

There is some indication that Kinsey was directly involved in the
intricacies of measuring clitoral sizes in his black female sample. As
Pomeroy explained in 1972, this may have been a forerunner:

> This observation of anatomical differences [in clitoral size]—and it
> typified the kind of research Kinsey knew would be attacked if it was
> known— *was the first step toward observing actual behavior*
> [Pomeroy, 1972, p. 173; emphasis added].

Sperm collecting may have been the next, and final, step. Pomeroy
places Kinsey directly in the activity of collecting sperm from "early
adolescents":

> Kinsey discussed the subject of male fertility with Dr. Frank K.
> Shuttleworth of the Institute of Child Welfare, University of Califor-
> nia at Berkeley. *He [Kinsey] believed that students in the field had
> all been "too prudish" to make an actual investigation of sperm count
> in early-adolescent males. [Kinsey's] own research for the Male
> volume had produced some material, but not enough.* [Kinsey] could
> report, however, that *there were mature sperm even in the first
> ejaculation,* although he did not yet have any actual counts [Pomeroy,
> 1972, p. 315; emphasis added].

Back in 1948, in his Male Report, Kinsey refers only to an "important body of data from certain of our subjects who have *observed first
ejaculation* in a list of several hundred boys" (Male Report, p. 185;
emphasis added).

Pomeroy implies that microscopic examination of seminal fluid
took place ("mature" sperm). This suggests a prospectively planned
procedure. Were the Kinsey team close by for these events, or did they
arrange for technicians to be on hand?

A History of Deception

If Pomeroy is to be believed, there is a history of deception associated with some of Kinsey's other research projects. To assist in his study of *adult* sexual behavior, Kinsey hired a professional cinematographer "with the idea of recording [on film] what he hoped to observe" (Pomeroy, 1972, p. 173). This was risky business in the 1940s. Pomeroy explained:

In spite of the importance Kinsey attached to what our cameras were recording, he was constantly apprehensive about this aspect of the research, and fearful of the possible consequences of discovery. Unquestionably, he had every right to be worried. If it had become publicly known, there is little reason to believe the Institute would have survived the publicity. *But no one outside the inner circle knew about this phase of our work. We did not talk about it to anyone, and the filming was mentioned only once in the books we compiled—a single cryptic reference in the Female volume* [Pomeroy, 1972, p. 186; emphasis added].

This movie-making was conducted on the premises of Indiana University, but Kinsey purposefully misled the University authorities about what he was doing. According to Pomeroy,

Kinsey told them, truthfully, that he wanted to photograph animal behavior, *but he did not add that he included humans in this category* [Pomeroy, 1972, p. 174; emphasis added].

It was only after the acceptance of Masters and Johnson's adult sexual experimentation work that Pomeroy publicly acknowledged Kinsey's activity in this area. Prior to this time, it was represented as the work of "observers." A similar misrepresentation may yet apply to Kinsey's child sex experiments. In other words, this may have been planned *prospective* research, with the Kinsey team either directly or indirectly involved. In the opinion of this book's authors, that is exactly how part of Kinsey's child sexuality research took place.

In support of this view are the following facts:

1. Kinsey did indeed conduct "experiments" at the Institute, during which he and his team "observed" various kinds of deviant behavior. Perhaps the most notorious is the performance put on by a homosexual sadist and a masochist whom Kinsey had recruited from Chicago and New York City. So fascinated was he with the possibility of filming the cruelty of the one and the receptivity of the other that he paid their fares to Bloomington and had his photographer film them in action. Similar film footage was obtained of other sex couples, usually male homosexuals. Kinsey's own team observed such performances and took notes. Some of the variables they recorded (eg, time to climax and number of climaxes) were precisely those studied in the experiments on infants and children (Pomeroy, 1972, pp. 172-187).

2. Kinsey's description of the children's "observers" as "our adult male subjects" does not at all exclude his own team members from this role. Each member of Kinsey's staff had had to give his own sex history

before recruitment, and thus, technically, activities of Kinsey's team members became part of his collection of "histories."

3. Kinsey, according to Pomeroy, was the type of person who needed to see things for himself. Pomeroy gave the example of orgasm in the female rabbit. Because he had not personally witnessed this event, Kinsey had difficulty in accepting its reality, even on the strength of testimony from a distinguished scientist (Pomeroy, 1972, pp. 184, 185). How then did Kinsey testify to the actuality of orgasm in a 5-month-old infant from the mere "history" of a sex offender?

According to Kinsey biographer C.V. Christenson, Kinsey made it clear back in 1940 in an address to the National Association of Biology Teachers that the resolution of the nature of erotic arousal lay in the laboratory and science classroom (Christenson, 1971, p. 211). In his Male Report, Kinsey repeats this view (p. 157). Pomeroy noted Kinsey's "determination to go further in his work than anyone had done before" (Pomeroy, 1972, p. 195). In another insight he states that Kinsey "would have done business with the devil himself" (Pomeroy, 1972, p. 198).

One further, remote possibility may be advanced to explain Kinsey's experimental child sex data. It may not be Kinsey's work at all. We are told by Pomeroy in his 1972 Kinsey biography that Kinsey interviewed a disproportionate number of social scientists, some of whom may have volunteered the results of their own surreptitious, illegal studies. There clearly are professionals capable of such experimentation (eg, Mengele) without the slightest twinge of conscience. However, it is highly unlikely that Kinsey would have known enough such persons who all had the same notes from identical experiments to provide such a large body of precisely measured information. It is certainly more likely that the "some" who witnessed such activity and "kept . . . records" were a team of researchers, composed of observers and men who had "contacts" with infants and very small children.

Before leaving this subject, it should be noted that other examples reveal Kinsey to be quite practiced in the art of deception. As pointed out earlier, in 1941, when his research was well underway, Kinsey told readers of the *Journal of Clinical Endocrinology* that studies of homosexual behavior were biased by being conducted on prison populations and other select groups. He went on to hold out his own data as "providing a fair basis for estimating the frequency of [homosexuality] in our American population as a whole . . . ," when he knew full well that his own sample was invalid for the same reasons.[6]

AN UNETHICAL PHILOSOPHY OF RESEARCH

As noted, John Gagnon made the point that a *less neutral observer* than Kinsey would have described the child sex experiments of Kinsey's Male Report as "sex crimes."

---

6   Another oft-repeated Kinsey fable was his story that the Vatican had an extensive pornography and erotica collection, as big or bigger than the Kinsey Institute's. Believed by the press and repeated in books, the lie was finally laid to rest last year (see *Fidelity* magazine, April 1989).

Thus it is surprising that no reviewers in 1948 challenged or questioned the methods of this aspect of the Kinsey team's work. Surprising because in 1946 there had been considerable publicity given to the trial at Nuremberg of 20 Third Reich doctors for inflicting unnecessary suffering and injury in experiments on human subjects.

The Nazi defendants were found to have corrupted the ethics of science by repeatedly and deliberately violating their subjects' rights. Out of this case came the Nuremberg code—a list of principles to provide moral, ethical and legal standards for the conduct of research on human subjects. (See *A History and Theory of Informed Consent*, by Ruth R. Faden and Tom L. Beauchamp, Oxford University Press, 1986, p. 155.)

Also during the 1940s, The American Psychological Association had been concerned with the general question of professional ethics. In 1951 a draft of that body's position on the use of human research subjects was published in the *American Psychologist*. One of the principles expounded was that where the danger of serious aftereffects exists "research should not be conducted unless the subjects are fully informed of this possibility and volunteer nevertheless" (cited in Faden and Beauchamp, 1986, p. 169).

However, Kinsey's highly detailed child sex experiment data, obtained apparently without parental and certainly without "informed" subject consent and involving clear abuse of infants and children, elicited no comment whatever with respect to how this research was conducted. Reviewers evidently took at face value the claim that they were reading "historical recall"—or they did not pay close attention—when they encountered passages in the Male Report describing extreme cruelty to child subjects, such as the already-quoted description of the emotional and physiological responses to adult-induced orgasm in 196 boys:

> Extreme tension with violent convulsion . . . mouth distorted . . . tongue protruding . . . spasmodically twitching . . . eyes staring . . . hands grasping . . . throbs or violent jerking of the penis . . . sobbing or more violent cries, sometimes with an abundance of tears (especially among younger children) . . . will fight away from the *partner* and may make violent attempts to avoid climax, *although they derive definite pleasure from the situation* . . . [Male Report, p. 161; emphasis added].

The incongruous use of the word "pleasure" in this context was not explained by the authors. It presumably was considered a scientifically accurate observation by the "partners." No reviewers have commented on this passage.

From the above and similar experiments comes the received "scientific" knowledge that, as Kinsey put it, "sexuality [is] a component that is present in *the human animal* from earliest infancy" (Male Report, p. 180; emphasis added).

It was from the just-described experiments that the scientific world first learned that orgasm in male infants and children "is, except for the

lack of an ejaculation, a striking duplicate of orgasm in an older adult."
The nature of this orgasm was described in some detail:

> . . . the behavior involves a series of gradual physiologic changes, the
> development of rhythmic body movements with distinct penis throbs
> and pelvic thrusts, an obvious change in sensory capacities, a final
> tension of muscles, especially of the abdomen, hips, and back, a
> sudden release with convulsions, including rhythmic anal contrac-
> tions—followed by the disappearance of all symptoms. . . . It may be
> some time before an erection can be induced again after such an
> experience [Male Report, p. 177].

Observations from separate histories are unlikely to have provided
specific, clinical, difficult-to-recognize details such as the presence and
type of "anal contractions" in an infant who is being masturbated
presumably for the pleasure of the participating sex offender. No
reviewers asked the obvious question: "How could this have been done
other than by directed, prospective research by individuals who knew
what they were looking for?" We asked Dr. Albert Hobbs, a 1948
Kinsey reviewer, why he had not questioned the nature of the Kinsey
child sex research. His response was that in concentrating on other
aspects of Kinsey's work, such as statistical methods, he had not noticed
the problem.

Kinsey's research conclusions on childhood sexuality, based on
hideously unethical experiments on children, have been accepted as
"fact" and repeatedly referred to in reputable textbooks and scientific
journals for 40 years. This perhaps is better understood in light of what
William Seidelman observed in 1989 in the *International Journal of
Health Services* in an article titled "Mengele Medicus: Medicine's Nazi
Heritage." Two of Nazi medicine's most infamous experimenters,
Otmar von Verschuer (experimentation on human twins) and Ernst
Rudin (eugenic sterilization of humans), "continue to be referred to in
the medical scientific literature without critical reference to . . . the
context of their work. Each man has been cited at least 20 separate
times in the past 10 years in some of the leading modern medical
journals." In other words, the original nature of some of their work has
been forgotten.

In Kinsey's case, however, there should be no debate about using
the results of unethical experiments. The "science" was as bad as the
ethics.

THE UNETHICAL RESEARCH MIND

By whatever means Kinsey's child sex research was accomplished,
it was the work of sex offenders capable of criminal acts—possibly
offenders with an interest in science since such meticulous care in
recording results was evident. On the other hand, *scientists are capable
of criminal thoughts and acts*, and the Kinsey team, according to one
of their number, may have fallen into this category.

In the 1977 book *Ethical Issues in Sex Therapy and Research*
(Masters, Johnson and Kolodny [eds.]; Little, Brown & Co.), Kinsey
co-author (of the Female Report) Dr. Paul Gebhard makes some very

frank statements about how the Kinsey team dealt with some of the ethical issues *they* confronted. Gebhard's comments go some way toward clarifying the entire Kinsey research philosophy.

It was Gebhard's view that "Each researcher must establish his or her own ethical hierarchy and decide as problems present themselves whether the ultimate good resulting from the research or therapy supersedes a particular ethic" (Masters, Johnson and Kolodny, 1977, p. 14). Concerning the nature and sources of information for the Kinsey Reports, Gebhard had this to say:

> We have always insisted on maintaining confidentiality, even at the cost of thereby becoming amoral at best and criminal at worst. Examples of amorality are our refusal to inform a wife that her husband has just confessed to us he has an active venereal disease, and our refusal to tell parents that their child is involved in seriously deviant behavior [*ibid.*, p. 13; emphasis added].

The matter of the husband and wife, though certainly not the child, would possibly be handled the same way by some researchers today. But Gebhard went on to give an example of outright "criminality":

> An example of criminality [in the Kinsey research] is our refusal to cooperate with authorities in apprehending a pedophile we had interviewed *who was being sought for a sex murder* [*ibid.*, p. 13; emphasis added].

It is assumed that the murder victim in this case was a child. It is not impossible that before he/she died, information of a sexual nature was obtained by the killer that subsequently appeared as part of Kinsey's child sexuality tables.

In another illustration, Gebhard recounted the story of Wardell Pomeroy being told by a prison interviewee that he intended to stab another prison inmate to death with a "file which had been turned into a ten-inch knife." Pomeroy did not know that the prisoners were just testing him. He discussed his dilemma with other members of the Kinsey team. If he told the authorities about the knife, he might save a life. If he said nothing,

> . . . someone might get stabbed. We decided that the man might get stabbed anyway. . . . We kept perfectly quiet. . . . *[I]n order to facilitate the research, we had to literally gamble with someone's life* [*ibid.*, p. 18; emphasis added].

This type of philosophy was rationalized by Gebhard as "ow[ing] . . . allegiance to science . . . [and not] to any one society" (*ibid.*, p. 19). Confidentiality was more important than life itself:

> We would keep confidentiality even if life itself were at issue. We simply would not break confidentiality for any reason whatsoever. So, in many ways, we are rather amoral, but we simply set ourselves to one side and say, "We are scientists and observers, and we are not willing to get involved in this thing one way or another" [*ibid.*, p. 17].

The contrast of the above position with the *New England Journal of Medicine's* approach to research ethics is quite staggering. The *Journal* will not even publish reports of unethical research, regardless of their scientific merit. Dr. Marcia Angell of the Journal staff wrote, "Only if the work was properly conducted, with full attention to the rights of human subjects, are we willing to consider it further." She added, "Knowledge, although important, may be less important to a decent society than the way it is obtained" (Editorial, *New England Journal of Medicine*, May 17, 1990, pp. 1462-1464).

Ashley Montagu, in his 1954 review of the Kinsey Reports, wrote of the dangerous desire of some social scientists to *know at all costs*, as if they were dispassionately examining machinery. Without the benefit of the later Gebhard exposition of the Kinsey team's research philosophy, Montagu hinted then that Kinsey was guilty of "scientomania":

> The desire to know can, in many cases, become like dipsomania, a "scientomania," in which the victim loses control of himself, and becomes controlled by the intoxicating potations of knowledge to which he has become addicted. I am afraid this has happened to many scientists, with results that are at this stage in the history of humanity almost too frightful to contemplate ["A Most Important Book, But . . .," by Ashley Montagu. In Geddes DP: *An Analysis of the Kinsey Reports on the Sexual Behavior of the Human Male and Female*, Mentor Books, 1954, p. 124].

Only the survivors of the Kinsey era at Bloomington can say exactly how the Kinsey research philosophy was applied in practice in the gathering of the child sex experiment data for the Male Report. It is important for society to know in the interests of truth in science and, more importantly, because crimes may have been involved that should be a matter of public record.

THE FRAUD TABOO

Although scathing in some of their criticisms, none of Kinsey's reviewers went so far as to suggest actual fraud. They thought Kinsey was an honest scientist sincerely attempting objective research. They assumed Kinsey was part of the same honor system they were. This is the system that enables science to move forward so rapidly. As the editor of *Science* wrote in a January 9, 1987, editorial, "the entire procedure of publishing and advancing knowledge is based on trust—that the literature reports accurate measurements of actual experiments. If each researcher had to go back and repeat the literature, the enormously productive rush of modern science would slow to a snail's pace."

However, 40 years after Kinsey, when the damaging effects of his work are so apparent and when a clear and unmistakable agenda, based on his results, has been identified and documented (see later chapters), the honor system has to be set aside. Kinsey's work was never replicated, and an attempt to "clean up" his data (which may have shown how unrepresentative his sample was) "failed"—on purpose, it appears (chapter 6). And today there is the unacceptable situation that those teaching and writing about this most important area of human existence are expected, as objective scientists themselves, to believe Kinsey's findings.

We will not be as reticent as Kinsey's earlier critics. Based on what we now know of just the Kinsey team's male sexuality research, we believe the case for the investigation of fraud is very strong.

According to the Committee on the Conduct of Science of the National Academy of Sciences, fraud in science can encompass a wide spectrum of behaviors, but the "acid test of scientific fraud is the intention to deceive . . . ."[7] That Kinsey's work is incriminated by this test is beyond question. A formal investigation of the research of Kinsey and his team is justified, and a reappraisal of the effects of this research—on sex education, for example—requires to be undertaken.

It may be that the stimulus for all this will have to come from the grass-roots level.

---

7   *On Being a Scientist*, National Academy Press, Washington, D.C., 1989.

CHAPTER TWO

FEMALE CHILD SEXUALITY

Dr. Judith A. Reisman and Deborah Fink[1]

Chapter Overview

This chapter examines some findings on female sexuality presented by the Kinsey team in their 1953 Female Report. These data—derived from interviews of over 5,900 women—were presented to the public five years after Kinsey's data on male sexuality (chapter 1).

Kinsey and his co-authors examined a non-random sample of subjects who were totally unrepresentative of American women, but the title of their published research, Sexual Behavior in the Human Female, *gave the clear impression that their findings on sexual behavior applied to the entire female population of the United States. That is how the information was presented, and that is how it was perceived by the media and, thus, by society. Perhaps best remembered is Kinsey's conclusion (not supported by his own data) that premarital intercourse helps women with subsequent marital adjustment.*

The most serious and important of Kinsey's findings, however, which were almost totally overlooked or ignored at the time, concern female child sexuality. Kinsey reached the following conclusions on this subject—conclusions which, though startling, are quietly shared by leading sexologists today:

1. Adult-child sexual contacts are not likely "to do the female child any appreciable harm if the child's parents do not become disturbed."

2. Adult male sexual contacts with female children are unlikely to cause physical *harm. There were* "few instances of vaginal bleeding [resulting from such contacts] which, however, did not appear to do any appreciable damage." *There is a need for the public to learn to recognize when physical sexual contacts between adult males and female children are harmless.*

---

1   Deborah Fink is coordinator for the first international graduate degree program in child protection, being developed at George Mason University, Virginia

3. *Any harm to the child from adult-child sexual activity is usually the fault of inappropriate response from a sexually repressed society.* "Some of the more experienced students of juvenile problems have come to believe that the emotional reactions of the parents, police officers, and other adults who discover that the child has had such a [sexual] contact, may disturb the child more seriously than the sexual contacts themselves."

The Kinsey team reported that adult sexual activity with preadolescent females—even in the hostile environment of a 1940s society that became inappropriately "disturbed" by such activity—could "contribute favorably to their later socio-sexual development."

Today, the public and the media are generally unaware of these Kinsey conclusions, and academic sexologists are usually very careful in referring to them—having the "wit," as John Leo [formerly] of Time magazine put it, "to keep a low profile" on the subject of sex with children.

Kinsey gathered an unknown amount of incest data in his female research and today his two leading co-authors are making conflicting claims about this material. According to Wardell Pomeroy, in a sex-industry publication, "we [found] many beautiful and mutually satisfying relationships between fathers and daughters." According to Paul Gebhard, in a letter to one of us (J.R.), incest received almost no mention because there were "too few cases." And each author has erroneously claimed that a "random sample" or "cross section" of the population was studied.

Another intriguing Kinsey research puzzle is the alleged observation of orgasm in seven female children less than 4 years old. No information about the identity of these children or their "observers" has ever been revealed.

PREDICTABLE CONCLUSIONS

This chapter chiefly addresses the Kinsey team's (Kinsey, Clyde Martin, Wardell Pomeroy and Paul Gebhard) data and conclusions on female child sexuality. The material was presented in chapter 4 of their 1953 Female Report (*Sexual Behavior in the Human Female*) under the title "Preadolescent Sexual Development." More recent statements on female child sexuality made by members of the Kinsey team also are examined.

Two principal areas of Kinsey's female child sexuality research are analyzed: 1) preadolescent sexual response and orgasm, and 2) preadolescent contacts with adult males.

For their data on these aspects of female sexuality, the Kinsey team relied on the three research methods described in the previous chapter: 1) the method of recall in interviews with adults and adolescents; 2) interviews with children; 3) direct observation of, and experimentation upon, children.

Following from the information presented in the previous chapter, it will not come as a total surprise that two clear conclusions are deduced by the Kinsey team from their research on women: 1) female children are capable of sexual response from a very early age, and 2) the use of this sexual ability, either with peers or with adult "partners," is not harmful but actually can assist healthy development. The Kinsey authors are so intent that the reader believe them about this subject that they repeatedly, and unscientifically, assert that their conclusions "must" be so or are "certain," when, in fact, no valid evidence is presented.

According to the Kinsey authors,

> ... it is *certain* ... that there are children, both female and male, who are quite capable of true sexual response [Female Report, p. 103; emphasis added]

And although they could interpret this response by age 3 in only a very small percentage of cases,

> This, however, *must* represent only a portion of those children who were responding at that age . . . [Female Report, p. 103; emphasis added]

Benefits from early sexual activity—and harm from negative reactions by parents—are claimed as fact, but no substantiation is provided:

> Some of the pre-adolescent contacts had provided emotional satisfactions which had conditioned the female for the acceptance of later sexual activities. . . . [But] guilt reactions [caused by parental reprimands] had, in many instances, prevented the female from accepting sexual relations in her adult married relationships [Female Report, p. 115].

In contrast, topics on which the Kinsey team appear to have had significant data—for example, incest and statutory rape—are treated in the most trivial manner. Incest is not mentioned in the index to the Female Report, and the word is conspicuously missing in the discussion of sexual contacts between girls and their relatives! Moreover, the data which the authors provide on this subject are buried in a small table (see below) describing the sexual relationships of female children with various categories of "adult partner," including "father," "brother" and "grandfather." However, without supporting evidence of any kind, the authors take care to make the point that when repetitive sexual relations between young girls and "fathers," "grandfathers" and other family members take place it is because the children "become interested" in the activity and "actively seek" more contact.

All sexual relationships between girls and adult strangers, friends or relatives fall under the heading of "contacts" with an "adult partner." These contacts, it is reported, can be beneficial.

Although these unfounded generalizations (like those from Kinsey's male research) are not based on any demonstrable facts, they are treated as scientific truth by many in the sexology community. From the beginning, it seems, there were "experts" as eager to be true believers in child sex as Kinsey was to sell the idea. In an essay reprinted in the 1955 book *Sexual Behavior in American Society: An Appraisal of the First Two Kinsey Reports* (Himeloch and Fava [eds.],

W.W. Norton & Co.), Lawrence Kubie of Yale University's Department of Psychiatry wrote (with reference to the earlier Male Report):

> If ... Dr. Kinsey and his coworkers [do] no more than present us with incontrovertible statistics concerning the incidence of   manifest infantile sexuality and of manifest adult   polymorphous   sexual tendencies, it will be a major contribution to our understanding of human development and culture [p. 291].

As well as not being related to facts, Kinsey's sweeping conclusions on female sexual behavior in America were based on interviews with a group of women who were quite atypical.

THE FEMALE SAMPLE

The Kinsey female sample—the basis for the historic findings defining "normal" human female sexuality in the U.S. in the 1940s—was a non-random, unconventional, wholly unrepresentative sample of women for that period.

By January 1, 1950, Kinsey claimed to have secured interview data from 7,789 females, aged 2 to over 70 years, for his study of human female sexual behavior. The Kinsey team also claimed to have direct observation/experimentation data on sexual response in seven girls—apparently under the age of 4 years. Whether or not these seven girls were part of the original 7,789-member group of interviewees is nowhere explained. In fact almost no details about these seven children are provided—a characteristic of how the Kinsey team often withheld information about research methods that is both important and of interest to other scientists.

Of the non-random sample of 7,789 females, 5,940 were chosen for evaluation—1,849 (24%) were excluded because they were either non-white (934 [12%]) or prison inmates (915 [11.7%]). One hundred forty-seven (147) are described as "preadolescent," ranging in age from 2 to 15 years, and the remaining 5,793 are described as "adolescent and adult females," ranging in age from 11 to over 70 years, with the greatest number (75%) being in the 16- to 35-year age group.

Essentially, the women in Kinsey's sample volunteered   their services or were recruited. For a landmark scientific project it is amazing that Kinsey obscures the selection process and the demographics of his final subject population. But enough can be learned to know that the sample he used was significantly different than a randomly chosen sample of the population of his day would have been. In fact it was skewed in the direction of emphasizing unconventional sexual behavior. Moreover, Kinsey was warned about a "volunteering" bias in his sample well in advance of completing his research. He refused to correct for it.

Among Kinsey's females, roughly 30% were married and 75% were college educated, versus a 70% married and 13% college-educated figure for the general population of the time. Furthermore, Kinsey's definition of "married" included all females living with a man for over a year (Female Report, p. 53). Kinsey called these "common-law relationships," but he did not require that they satisfy the usual "understanding that a marital arrangement exists."[2] Needless to say, in the late 1940s and early 1950s, when the prevalence of such arrangements was considerably lower and society frowned on cohabitation, the women so involved were "extraordinary" by definition. Regarding the educational background of Kinsey's female interviewees, social scientists Herbert Hyman and Paul Sheatsley made the following comment:

> . . . seventy-five percent of the total female sample had attended college, and a surprising nineteen percent—practically one woman in five—had gone on to post-graduate work . . . a rather unique group to sample so heavily and without apparent reason [In Geddes DP: *An Analysis of the Kinsey Reports on the Human Male and Female*, Mentor Books, 1954, p. 100; emphasis added].

In his 1954 review of the Female Report, Judson Landis of the University of California at Berkeley, pointed out that

> Of all the women who had married, 32% were divorced, separated, or widowed at the time of the interview. Since the women at the time of the interview were relatively young (median age 34), we can assume that few were widowed. We queried Dr. Kinsey about the number who were widowed, but in a letter dated November, 1953, Dr. Kinsey states that "I am sorry that our tabulated statistics do not distinguish between females who were widowed, separated or divorced" ["The Women Kinsey Studied," *Social Problems*, April 1954, pp. 139-142].

Ashley Montagu, chairman of the department of anthropology at Rutgers University and author of *The Natural Superiority of Women*, noted in his 1954 review of the Female Report that devout Catholics and orthodox Jews were inadequately represented, leaving the sample, in terms of religious background, "heavily weighted with women who are likely to be sexually unconventional . . ." ("A Most Important Book, But . . . ." In Geddes, 1954, p. 125).

In a critical essay on the Female Report, published alongside that of Judson Landis, Harvey Locke of the department of sociology, University of Southern California, questioned, among other things, Kinsey's claim that 15% of his female subjects were from 100% samples ("Are Volunteer Interviewees Representative?" *Social Problems*, April 1954, pp. 143-146). Locke's skepticism about these 100% groups (a claimed substitute for randomization) may have been well founded. Kinsey co-author Paul Gebhard let it be known in 1979, for the first time, that "The term '100%' [was] actually a misnomer" as far as the male sample was concerned (Gebhard and Johnson, *The Kinsey Data*, W.B. Saunders, 1979, p. 31). This likely holds true for the female sample also. The statistical importance of this, however, is academic, given the more basic problems of the Kinsey interviewee group.

Concerning the legitimacy of extrapolating conclusions from Kinsey's female sample to the general population, George Simpson of the department of sociology at Brooklyn College made the following observation:

---

2   Rothenberg RE, *The Plain Language Law Dictionary*, Penguin, 1981.

[T]he adequacy of the sample as a basis for generalizing concerning *all* female sexual behavior in our society is almost nil ["Nonsense About Women," *The Humanist*, March-April 1954, pp. 49-56; emphasis in original].

Yet, as Ashley Montagu pointed out, the popular impression given by the media—and enduring to this day—was just the opposite:

With very few exceptions, [newspaper and magazine articles] generalize[d] Kinsey's findings for American women as a whole [Geddes, 1954, p. 128].

Compounding the unrepresentativeness of Kinsey's sample were two further problems: one of data handling, and one concerning the type of person likely to volunteer for a "sex" study. In the presentation of his female data, Kinsey continued to use the accumulative incidence technique he had used in his earlier Male Report—yet this was four years after Hobbs and Lambert in the *American Journal of Psychiatry* had clearly illustrated the inapplicability of this method to Kinsey's study of human sexual behavior (Hobbs AH, Lambert RD. "An Evaluation of 'Sexual Behavior in the Human Male.'" *American Journal of Psychiatry* 104:758-764, 1948). Using the accumulative incidence technique, behaviors that may occur only once are assumed to occur throughout the lifetime of an individual.

On the matter of error deriving from the type of person likely to volunteer for a study of sexual behavior, Kinsey pointedly chose to ignore expert advice based on information gathered from among his own subjects and published in the scientific literature in the year before his Female Report appeared.

The research of Abraham Maslow made clear there would be a "volunteer error" in Kinsey's female sample, which, unless corrected for, would significantly inflate the numbers of women reporting unconventional sexual behavior such as masturbation, oral sexuality, petting to climax and premarital and extramarital intercourse (Maslow AH, Sakoda JM. "Volunteer Error in the Kinsey Study." *Journal of Abnormal and Social Psychology* 47:259-262, 1952). Kinsey refused Maslow's advice to correct for this volunteer factor.

Maslow is mentioned in the Male Report, where Kinsey misled his readers by saying it was not known how Maslow's findings would affect that sample. The volunteer-error issue is completely ignored in the Female Report. This is indefensible in view of Maslow's 1952 publication and Lewis Terman's 1948 critique of the Male Report in the *Psychological Bulletin*, pointing out evidence of volunteer error in Kinsey's male population just from a close examination of Kinsey's own statistics (*Psychological Bulletin* 45:449, 1948). [See chapter 6 for a fuller discussion of Maslow's volunteer-error principle, and Appendix A for reproduction of a letter containing Maslow's thoughts on having his research ignored in Kinsey's books.]

Remarkably, considering the unconventional sample of women Kinsey used, his data do not demonstrate, as claimed, that premarital intercourse leads to better anything in marriage. They do show, however, a relationship between premarital and extramarital sex, which Kinsey glossed over. Kinsey was caught in another contradiction on this subject. His data do illustrate the attainment of orgasm in women is a learning process, which is incompatible with his philosophy that engaging in coitus and reaching orgasm is an activity that humans do not have to learn any more than do other mammals.

A related contradiction, noted by Judson Landis, was that "throughout the [Female] report [Kinsey] seems to assume that the frequency of orgasm is very important to and closely associated with marital success. Yet the sample would indicate almost the opposite, for the promiscuous group were highly responsive in orgasm both in and out of marriage (p. 418) but they represent marriage failure in that they had either failed to marry or failed in marriage" ("The Women Kinsey Studied," *Social Problems*, April 1954).

The Kinsey team justified the exclusion from analysis of almost one quarter of their sample (the non-white and the prison inmates) in the following statement:

> Because the sexual histories which we have of white females who had served prison sentences (915 cases) prove, upon analysis, to differ as a group from the histories of the females who have not become involved with the law, their inclusion in the present volume would have seriously distorted the calculations on the total sample. Neither has the non-white sample (934 cases) of females been included in the calculations, primarily because that sample is not large enough to warrant comparisons of the sub-groups in it [Female Report, p. 22].

The removal of non-white females was said to be because of their small number, although this same reasoning did not apply to several other significantly smaller groups within the female and male samples. The removal of prison inmates from the female sample is in stark contrast to the inclusion of male prisoners (including rapists and incest offenders) among the male sample used for Kinsey's earlier 1948 Male Report (chapter 1). Although Kinsey had been criticized for including male prisoners in his earlier work, he did so, co-author Pomeroy later explained, because he felt they were no different from the rest of the population:

> We were under attack at different times from people who insisted that we should not have included in our [Male] sample the history of anyone who had ever been in a penal institution. That, as Kinsey liked to point out, was based on the old fallacy that criminals are made of different stuff from the rest of the population [Wardell Pomeroy, *Dr. Kinsey and the Institute for Sex Research*, Harper & Row, 1972, p. 202].

However, Paul Gebhard (Female Report co-author) pointed out in his 1965 book, *Sex Offenders: An Analysis of Types* (Gebhard, Gagnon, Pomeroy and Christenson, Harper & Row, 1965, pp. 32, 33), that the prison population *was* significantly different from the non-prison population in their male and female samples. While it was wholly reasonable to exclude prison women (and men), there may have been a deeper motivation behind such exclusion so late in the research. There is the question of whether these people were removed from the female sample because they compromised Kinsey's theories of harmless adult-child sex. Certainly, there was an opportunity to analyze this group separately for the valuable information that might have been obtained on sex abuse and its consequences.[3]

As mentioned earlier, the Kinsey team also had records of sexual response in seven girls under 4 years of age, who constituted a small sample on whom direct observations had been made or upon whom experiments had been performed. Kinsey explained:

> We have similar records of observations made by some of our other subjects on a total of 7 pre-adolescent girls and 27 pre-adolescent boys under four years of age (see our 1948: 175-181) [Female Report, p. 105].

Just exactly who comprised the "7 preadolescent girls" is never explained, although Kinsey gave details of a 3-year-old girl ostensibly observed and timed during masturbation and subsequent "orgasm." In addition, in the 1948 Male Report Kinsey referred to an "orgasm—in our records for a female babe of 4 months" (p. 177). Since this "babe" is not discussed in the Female Report, it is unclear whether or not this infant is one of the "seven."

In a project of this nature it is both inexcusable and revealing that there is no more precise information on these seven children—not even their ages are given—or the circumstances in which they underwent "observation." The "some of our other subjects" who observed (performed?) orgasm experiments on female infants should have been a subject of some scientific interest/concern. Details were withheld by the authors, and, once again (as with the Male Report), reviewers seem not to have noticed.

I - ADULT SEXUAL ACTIVITY WITH CHILDREN

The Kinsey team in their Female Report addressed the issue of adult male sexual activity with female children in a section titled "Preadolescent Contacts with Adult Males." Psychiatrist Dr. Judith Herman of Harvard Medical School later pointed out in her 1981 book *Father-Daughter Incest* (see below) that the Kinsey data on this subject would have included the largest amount of information on incest ever collected from the population at large. Yet, Kinsey's analysis of these data raises more questions than answers about his findings on incest in particular and other adult-child sexual interactions in general.

Kinsey's use of definitions for certain types of sexual activity is such as to remove altogether from his results the record of some types of adult sexual contact with female children (see below).

---

3   There is an apparent contradiction in what the Kinsey authors have said about the analysis of the sex histories of their female prison sample. According to the Female Report (p. 22) and Gebhard's book *Sex Offenders: An Analysis of Types*, there was an analysis done. According to a 1981 letter from Gebhard to Reisman there was no analysis beyond pregnancy, birth and abortion data. See Appendix B.

The results—both physical and psychological—of adult sexual contact with female children would have been one of the most important data analyses the Kinsey team could have performed. However, a quote from the Kinsey researchers indicates a pre-existing bias that would color their findings:

> There is a growing concern in our culture over the sexual contacts that pre-adolescent children sometimes have with adults. Most persons feel that all such contacts are undesirable because of the immediate disturbance they may cause the child, and because of the conditioning and possibly traumatic effects which they may have on the child's socio-sexual development and subsequent sexual adjustments in marriage. *Press reports might lead one to conclude that an appreciable percentage of all children are subjected . . . to sexual approaches by adult males, and that physical injury is a frequent consequence of such contacts. But most of the published data are based on cases which come to the attention of physicians, the police, and other social agencies,* and there has hitherto been no opportunity to know what proportion of all children is ever involved [Female Report, p. 116; emphasis added].

Kinsey presented data in such a way as to confirm that the "press reports" were, in fact, misleading with regard to children being damaged by adult sexual contact.

PREVALENCE OF ADULT SEXUAL ABUSE OF CHILDREN

Of the 5,940 females who gave evaluable interview data, the Kinsey team found that 4,441 (75%) provided information allowing a determination of the frequency of preadolescent "sexual activity with adult males" — what today would be called child sexual abuse.

> We have data from 4441 of our female subjects which allow us to determine the incidence of pre-adolescent sexual contacts with adult males, and the frequency of such contacts. For the sake of the present calculations we have defined an adult male as one who has turned adolescent and who is at least fifteen years of age; and, in order to eliminate experiences that amount to nothing more than adolescent sex play, we have considered only those cases in which the male was at least five years older than the female, while the female was still pre-adolescent. On this basis, we find that some 24 per cent (1075) of the females in the sample had been approached while they were pre-adolescent by adult males who *appeared to be making sexual advances, or who had made sexual contacts with the child.* Three-fourths of the females (76 per cent) had not recognized any such approach [Female Report, p. 117; emphasis added].

The italicized portion of the above quote is an illustration of Kinsey's habit—despite all his claims to exactitude—of converting non-facts to "facts."

KINSEY'S CRITERIA FOR SEX OFFENDER

According to Kinsey's criteria, a sex offender could only be an adult. And an "adult male" offender was one who was at least 15 years old, was at least 5 years older than the victim at the time of the incident and was physiologically adolescent or adult. It would have been extremely difficult to ascertain these details about male contacts by interviewing females many years after events that mostly took place between the ages of 4 and 10. It would have been especially difficult to know if the involved male was an adolescent if Kinsey adhered to anything like the criteria for puberty given by Pomeroy *et al.* in their 1982 book *Taking a Sex History: Interviewing and Recording*:

> Note that the age of puberty is not asked of the respondent but is completed by the interviewer after all the questions are answered. The interviewer's estimate of the age of puberty is a very important peg because there are many behaviors that relate to before and after puberty. This estimation is based on the respondent's recall of his or her age at the manifestation of pubic hair, first ejaculation, menses, breast development, and/or voice change. From this information the interviewer is able to make a fairly accurate judgment of age at puberty [Pomeroy, Flax and Wheeler, The Free Press, 1982, p. 182].

According to the Kinsey team's definition, an assault on a 9-year-old girl by a 13-year-old male would not qualify as child sexual abuse, even if the male had reached puberty. The case of a 13-year-old girl raped by a 17-year-old male would not constitute sexual abuse—it would be "adolescent sex play."

Based on these stringent criteria, 1,075 (24%) of the Kinsey team's unconventional volunteer female sample (4,441) reported childhood experiences qualifying as child sexual abuse by an adult. (In the Female Report, however, these incidents are described as "contacts" with "partners" rather than sexual abuse.) Data from the remaining 3,366 female interviewees have been discarded, including an unknown amount of information on various types of sexual assault concealed within the blanket terminology "adolescent sex play." This is a considerable loss of potentially important information, given the serious phenomenon of teenage sex offenders.

AGE WHEN VICTIMIZED BY ADULT MALE

Kinsey provided a tabular breakdown of the ages at which preadolescent females were approached sexually by adult males. If this table had been based on a random sample of the population and if an unknown amount of data that might have been in this table had not been discarded (see above), it might actually have been useful. However, the table serves another purpose: it illustrates a carelessness with numbers that can be found throughout the Kinsey team's work.

Age of [Preadolescent] Females Having Adult Contacts
[Female Report, p. 118; column in italics added]

AGE	% OF ACTIVE SAMPLE	INCIDENTS (TAKING % OF 1,039)	% OF TOTAL SAMPLE
4	5	52	1
5	8	83	2
6	9	94	2
7	13	135	3
8	17	177	4
9	16	177	4
10	26	270	6
11	24	249	6
12	25	260	7(sic)
13	19	197	6(sic)
CASES	1,039	1,683	4,407

It is not clear how the total number of females with adult contacts has been reduced from 1,075 to 1,039 (-36) and how the total sample has shrunk from 4,441 to 4,407 (-34). Neither is it explained what data, if any, are from preadolescents or adolescents themselves.

RELATIONSHIP BETWEEN ADULT OFFENDER AND CHILD VICTIM

Kinsey Incest Data

(Note: For the purposes of the discussion that follows, the term *incest* is used in the sense described by Suzanne Sgroi, M.D., coordinator of the St. Joseph College Institute for the Treatment of Child Sexual Abuse. As defined by Sgroi from a psychosocial perspective, "incestuous child sexual abuse encompasses any form of sexual activity between a child and a parent, or stepparent, or extended family member [for example, grandparent, aunt or uncle], or surrogate parent figure [for example, common-law spouse or foster parent]. . . . Sexual activity between an adult and a child may range from exhibitionism to intercourse . . ." [Sgroi S, *Handbook of Clinical Intervention in Child Sexual Abuse*, Lexington Books, 1982, p. 10].)

The Kinsey team described and tabulated the nature of the sexual relationships that their female interviewees recalled having had, as children, with adult "partners." The term adult "partner" is a euphemism found frequently in both the Male and Female Reports that describes adult males involved in activities normally defined in society as sex abuse. The Kinsey authors' employment of these euphemisms enabled them to avoid the use of terminology such as sex abuse, molestation or rape, which imply crime, moral judgment or guilt.

Kinsey's table on the relationship of prepubescent girls to their male sexual "partners" is reproduced below. The column in *italics* and the dividing line between incestuous and non incestuous relationships have been added for clarity.

"Adult Partner" Table
[Female Report, p.118]

ADULT PARTNERS	INCIDENTS (TAKING % OF 609)	% OF ACTIVE SAMPLE
Strangers	317	52
Friends and acquaintances	195	32
Uncles	55	9
Fathers	24	4
Brothers	18	3
Grandfathers	12	2
Other Relatives	30	5
CASES REPORTING	(651)	609

This is the Kinsey authors' table of incest data, though it does not have this heading and is nowhere referred to as such. The column in italics indicates that some multiple contacts were taking place (discussed below).

If Kinsey's denominator for incestuous contact is taken as 4,441, then there was an occurrence rate of 3% (140 cases). Almost all other important information on this subject (especially important in the 1950s, when so little was known about incest) has been ignored or held back.

Valuable data would have been:

. The number of girls victimized by more than one relative

. The duration of incestuous relationships and the number of incidents involved per child

. The number of girls reporting incidents to parents or authorities

. The ages at which incidents occurred and at which they were reported

. Most importantly, the nature of the physical, psychological and emotional consequences assessed by follow-up

The fact that long-term data have not been made public after all these years would seem to indicate that the Kinsey team (and their successors) are withholding information, or do not have it. The responsible scientific position on a subject of this importance would be to publish data on the long-term consequences of this serious behavior and to continue to follow and monitor at least a portion of these individuals.

Dr. Judith Herman, and her co-author, Hirschman, critiqued Kinsey's superficial treatment of incest in their 1981 book *Father-Daughter Incest* (Harvard University Press):

On the subject of incest, apparently, they felt the less said the better.
This in spite of the fact that they had accumulated the largest body of
data on overt incest that had ever appeared in the scientific
literature. . . . To date this remains the largest number of incest cases
ever collected from the population at large, rather than from advertise-
ments, clinic files, or court records. The wealth of information contained in these interviews remained buried in the files of the Institute
for Sex Research. *The public, in the judgment of these men, was not
ready to hear about incest* [p. 17; emphasis added].

The question, of course, is *what* exactly was it the Kinsey team did
not want the public of their day to know about incest, or, for that matter,
about sex abuse in general. More recent comments from Kinsey-team
members (see below) may shed some light on this point. In any event,
it seems that Herman and Hirschman were not totally correct in saying
that Kinsey's incest information "remained buried in the files of the
Institute for Sex Research." In a 1981 letter to Judith Reisman, Paul
Gebhard related that the incest data had been passed on to one, Warren
Farrell, who was said to be working on a book (to be titled *The Last
Taboo*). Gebhard wrote:

We omitted incest [in the Female Report], except for one brief mention, because we felt we had too few cases: 47 white females and 96
white males, and most of the incest was with siblings. We have turned
our incest data over to Warren Farrell to supplement his larger study
which I think is still unpublished [Letter: Gebhard to Reisman, March
11, 1981; reproduced in full, Appendix B].

Reisman followed up with a request for similar access to this
information, but received no reply. At the time of this writing, Farrell's
book remains unpublished. [Note: Gebhard's comment about siblings
does not appear to fit with the Kinsey table examined earlier.]

CURRENT ATTITUDES OF KINSEY TEAM
MEMBERS TOWARD INCEST

Having achieved a measure of fame and credibility as Kinsey
co-authors, Gebhard and Pomeroy have been considered authorities
(especially by sex-industry publications) on child sexuality and incest.
Their expertise has been sought and quoted by others interested in this
subject. Thus Philip Nobile, [subsequently] editorial director of *Forum*,
writing in the December 1977 issue of *Penthouse* on the theme of
"positive incest," relied on the views and data interpretations of Paul
Gebhard:

Actually, Kinsey was the first sex researcher to uncover evidence that
violation of the [incest] taboo does not necessarily shake heaven and
earth. Unpublished data taken from his original sex histories (some
18,000 in number) imply that lying with a near relative rarely ends in
tragedy. "In our basic sample, that is, our random sample, only a tiny
percentage of our incest cases had been reported to police or
psychologists," states Kinsey collaborator Dr. Paul Gebhard, currently
director of the Institute for Sex Research in Bloomington, Ind. "In
fact, in the ones that were not reported, I'm having a hard time
recalling any traumatic effects at all. I certainly can't recall any from

among the brother-sister participants, and I can't put my finger on any among the parent-child participants." The nation was hardly prepared for such talk in the fifties, but Gebhard is releasing Kinsey's startling incest material for incorporation in Warren Farrell's work-in-progress, *The Last Taboo* [*Penthouse,* December 1977, p. 118].

Is what Nobile referred to in 1977 as "Kinsey's startling incest material" the same data Gebhard described as "too few cases [so that] we omitted incest, except for one brief mention . . ."?

Some other apparent errors and/or contradictions in this Nobile excerpt are worthy of note:

1. The number 18,000 includes female *and* male interviews. Yet, according to Gebhard and Johnson's 1979 book *The Kinsey Data: Marginal Tabulations of the 1938-1963 Interviews Conducted by the Institute for Sex Research,* no questions regarding prepubertal incest were routinely asked of males (see Gebhard and Johnson, 1979, Table 147). (In fact, it is a very curious omission in research about sexuality, by one who claimed expertise on sex offenders, that data on sexual abuse of male children by adult male family members and relatives have been ignored.)

2. The term "random sample" used by Gebhard is a misstatement. Kinsey's incest data in the Female Report is not from a scientifically drawn random sample.

3. Gebhard is quoted as saying that he is "having a hard time recalling any traumatic effects [from incest] at all." He may have forgotten that in the Female Report he and co-authors state that 80% of their female subjects found childhood sexual interaction with an adult to be traumatic (see below), although they did downplay the degree of this trauma. It seems unlikely that this "trauma" was confined to those who only had sexual contact with non-relatives.

Nobile continues the Kinsey practice of euphemizing incest. In this case it is "lying with a near relative."

Pomeroy, in another incest article ("A New Look at Incest") in a 1977 *Forum* publication, *Variations,* claimed that adult-child incest could not only be harmless, but could benefit the child emotionally:

[I]ncest between adults and younger children can also prove to be a satisfying and enriching experience . . . . When there is a mutual and unselfish concern for the other person, rather than a feeling of possessiveness and a selfish concern with one's own sexual gratification, then incestuous relationships can—and do—work out well. . . . [Incest] can be a satisfying, non-threatening, and even an enriching emotional experience, as I said earlier [*Variations,* 1977, pp. 86-88].

While these opinions may reflect "Kinsey's startling incest material," a growing body of research strongly argues against the possibility of mutually satisfactory adult-child sexual relationships—especially in the case of incest (eg, Burgess and Holmstrom, 1975; Densen-Gerber and Benward, 1976; Finkelhor, 1979; Herman and Hirschman, 1981; Sgroi, 1982; McNaron and Morgan, 1982[4]). An

4   See Books Referenced section for full references.

increased understanding of the nature of such exploitation has led to a comprehension of the child as the powerless, vulnerable and wholly dependent party in an "intergenerational" sex situation. Lanning and Burgess defined this situation as follows:

> [T]he term "victim" is used to denote all underage persons for several reasons. First, in adult/child and adult/youth relationships, *there is an imbalance of power and thus the young person is unable to make an informed consent when sex is the issue* [Lanning and Burgess, *FBI Law Enforcement Bulletin* (Vol. 53, No. 1), January 1984, p. 11; emphasis added].

It is not intended here to debate the subject of incest sequelae, except to say that the weight of evidence clearly indicates an unfavorable outcome for many girls in terms of adjustment problems, future sexual difficulties, promiscuity, frigidity, prostitution, drug addiction and even a tendency to repeat the pattern by choosing husbands who will sexually abuse their own daughters.

Kinsey co-authors Pomeroy and Gebhard clearly have established a bias on the subject of incest as a positive experience for children. This bias is evident among the full Kinsey team in their treatment of this subject in the Female Report. If, instead of making unsupported claims on the benefits of incest, the Kinsey authors had provided credible data on long-term effects, they might have been able to salvage some credibility on this subject.

In fact, almost everything the Kinsey authors have written about incest has a ring of irresponsibility and falsity about it, as, for example, this piece from Wardell Pomeroy's 1969 sex-ed book for teenage girls, *Girls and Sex*:

> There are also medical reasons for the [incest] taboo. *The children of an incestuous union will be likely to inherit the outstanding good characteristics of both.* Genetically, however, *continuing* incestuous relationships in a group *tend* to 'breed out'—that is, the bad traits *eventually* overcome the good ones in successive generations [Penguin 1978 edition, pp. 133, 134; emphasis added].

In contrast, a *British Medical Journal* editorial, looking at the combined data from two 1967 studies on this subject, reported that of 31 children born to father-daughter (12) and brother-sister matings (19) only 13 were normal. "Two died from recessive disorders (optic fibrosis and glycogen-storage disease) and one from an almost certainly recessive disorder causing progressive cerebral degeneration and loss of vision. Two of those alive probably had disorders, both with severe mental retardation with cerebral palsy, and one a possibly recessive disorder, severe non-specific mental retardation. Two others died in the neonatal period . . . . Two had congenital malformations . . . . Eight others . . . were mentally retarded, with IQs in seven ranging from 59 to 76" (*British Medical Journal* 282:250, 1981).

Pomeroy's glamorized view of incest in his *Variations* article was prefaced by a purported letter from a 20-year-old woman. Her "positive" experience was described thus:

My early memories of a typical morning when I was five or six are of getting in bed with dad when my mother left for work . . . . I can't even remember a morning when he didn't have a hard-on. He would let me play with it, and he would put it between my legs as I lay with my back to his belly. I learned that by moving back and forth, it would rub against my vulva and clitoris. It felt marvelous. Sometimes he squirted all over the bed. What a mystery that was! [*Variations*, 1977, p. 84].

Drawing this time on his experience with Kinsey's incest data, Pomeroy further testified to the *Variations* readers:

When we examine a cross-section of the population, as we did in the Kinsey Report, rather than a selection of those in prison for incest or those who seek therapy because they are disturbed by incest, we find many beautiful and mutually satisfying relationships between fathers and daughters. These may be transient or ongoing, but they have no harmful effects [*Variations*, 1977, p. 86; emphasis added].

Pomeroy's claim to have examined a "cross-section" of the female population for the Kinsey Report is, of course, totally false, as he must have known. And his retrospective reference to the "many beautiful and mutually satisfying" father-daughter incest cases in the Kinsey data stands in stark contrast to the previously quoted Gebhard letter to Reisman: "We omitted incest [in the Female Report], except for one brief mention, because we felt we had too few cases . . . ."

It seems that the Gebhard/Pomeroy—or Kinsey-school—view of incest as a positive experience, a bias that was detected in the Female Report, but a view not supportable by the Report, now is claimed to have its basis in the data of that Report.

[The trend toward legitimizing incest, which has its "research" foundation in Kinsey's work, still is very much on the agenda of some academic sexologists (see Appendix C for a brief review from *Time* magazine).]

EXCLUDED DATA

Apart from the loss (mentioned earlier) of sexual assault data under the heading of "adolescent sex play" and the withholding of data on incest, considerable information on child sex-abuse in general probably has been eliminated from Kinsey's Female Report. As Kinsey put it,

Approaches had occurred most frequently in poorer city communities where the population was densely crowded in tenement districts. . . . [W]e would have found higher incidences of pre-adolescent contacts with adults . . . if we had included the data which we have on females who had served penal sentences, and on Negro females. These latter groups, however, were excluded from the calculations in the present volume for reasons which we have already explained (p. 22) [Female Report, pp. 117, 118].

One of the reasons these people were excluded is that they provided different results (Female Report, p. 22). However, Kinsey is more likely to have found information among the excluded group on the negative consequences of adult-child sexual relationships. And in research such as Kinsey's purports to be, this group could, and should, have been studied separately for this purpose. It does appear that what the public learned about incest and sexual abuse of female children from the Kinsey Female Report was more or less what the Kinsey team wanted it to learn.

MINIMIZING CHILD SEXUAL ABUSE

Accepting the Kinsey research at face value, continuing analysis reveals an attempt to downplay the consequences of adult-child sexual activity, even as revealed in the data that *were* presented. Herman and Hirschman made this comment in *Father-Daughter Incest*:

> Kinsey . . . though he never denied the reality of child sexual abuse, did as much as he could to minimize its importance. Some 80 per cent of the women who had experienced a childhood sexual approach by an adult reported to Kinsey's investigative team that they had been frightened and upset by the incident. Kinsey cavalierly belittled these reports. He hastened to assure the public that children should not be upset by these experiences. If they were, this was the fault not of the sexual aggressor, but of prudish parents and teachers who caused the child to become "hysterical" [p. 16].

Wardell Pomeroy apparently still maintains the view that adults having sex with minors is not a problem. This information comes to light following a custody battle in California between a homosexual father and a Christian mother (Pomeroy was an expert witness on behalf of the father). Warren Farris, attorney for the mother, has described a conversation during which Pomeroy stated he "would not counsel one of his patients who was having sex with a minor to stop, but would ask why [the person] felt guilty about such activities."[5]

TYPE OF SEXUAL ABUSE

The types of sexual abuse recorded among Kinsey's whittled-down sample of 1,075 female interviewees were tabulated in the Female Report (p. 119) as follows (the column in *italics*, is added to represent the number of incidents):

---

5   Personal communication from Warren Farris to Edward Eichel, December 1989.

NATURE OF CONTACT	NUMBER OF INCIDENTS	PERCENT OF ACTIVE SAMPLE
Approach only	97	9
Exhibition, male genitalia	559	52
Exhibition, female genitalia	11	1
Fondling, no genital contact	333	31
Manipulation of female genitalia	237	22
Manipulation of male genitalia	54	5
Oral contact, female genitalia	11	1
Oral contact, male genitalia	11	1
Coitus	32	3
NUMBER OF CASES WITH EXPERIENCE	1,345	1,075

Clearly, some children experienced more than one incident. Without offering any evidence, Kinsey attributed this repetition "in many instances" to a desire on the part of the children:

> In many instances, the experiences were repeated because *the children had become interested in the sexual activity* and had more or less actively *sought* repetitions of their experience [Female Report, p. 118; emphasis added].

This is a rather important observation within the framework of Kinsey's general conclusions on childhood sexuality. A statement of this nature should have received some substantiation and elaboration. No analysis, however, is provided as to how many children "sought" repeat activity, or what kinds of "sexual activity" mainly interested them. Perhaps most importantly, how did Kinsey know the children "sought" repetitions? This is an example—one of many—where a sweeping statement needs some supporting documentation (a typical instance of Kinsey's habit of creating his own "facts").

THE CHILD AS SEXUAL OPPRESSOR

Historian Paul Robinson pointed out in his 1976 book *The Modernization of Sex* (Harper & Row) that Kinsey's view of *female* children as sexual oppressors (and thus male child molesters as, somehow, "victims") was an expression of anti-female, more than anti-child, bias:

> Kinsey complemented his defense of the old by putting in a good word for child molesters. This represented the only instance in the Reports where adults appeared in the role of victims and children in that of oppressors. *The threat posed by middle-aged and elderly men to the sexual integrity of young girls, he argued, had been greatly exaggerated. . . . Indeed, he was brazen enough to suggest that children sometimes enjoyed their sexual encounters with adults. . . .* [I]t should be noted, *Kinsey assigned the villainous role not to children as such, but specifically to female children,* just as in his examination of the

sexual hardships endured by teenagers L# #e ji #ned the role of repressors to mothers and female teachers. Inevitably, Une #I# I## that his sympathies went out not so much to the young in general as to thuse among them who happened to be male [p. 92; emphasis added].

This representation of *female* children seeking adult male prey became standard fare over the next 40 years in pornographic literature. It appears from time to time in case law.

DAMAGE TO THE CHILD

According to Kinsey's data, adult sexual "contact" with female children included coitus, which the Kinsey team defined as "genital intercourse" (footnote in Female Report, p. 101). How much physical damage was done to the children? Almost none, if this description by the Kinsey team is correct:

There are, of course, instances of adults who have done physical damage to children with whom they have attempted sexual contacts, and we have the histories of a few males who had been responsible for such damage. But these cases are in the minority, and *the public should learn to distinguish such serious contacts from other adult contacts which are not likely to do the child any appreciable harm if the child's parents do not become disturbed.* The exceedingly small number of cases in which physical harm is ever done the child is to be measured by the fact that *among the 4441 females on whom we have data, we have only one clear-cut case of serious injury done to the child, and a very few instances of vaginal bleeding which, however, did not appear to do any appreciable damage* [Female Report, pp. 121, 122; emphasis added].

The tone and the language clearly suggest that the Kinsey team would minimize the consequences of even vaginal intercourse between adults and prepubescent girls (rape). It was not made clear by what educational process the public was supposed to "learn to distinguish" serious from non-serious injury in female children with whom adult males have attempted or completed intercourse. The Kinsey discussion stands in clear contrast to other accounts of the consequences, immediate and long term, that often result from such activity. The following description of injury to female children from adult molestation is from Clifford Linedecker's 1981 book *Children in Chains* (Everest House):

Severe injury can occur to small children who cannot physically accommodate an adult sex partner, and some have died from internal bleeding or asphyxiation . . . . Little girls suffer lacerations of the genitals, and both boys and girls have incurred severe damage to their rectums after anal intercourse with adults . . . . [Coppleson's study and others] establish the link between early sexual intercourse and the premature incidence of cervical cancer among females in their twenties and thirties. Hysterectomies, or death, are almost always the ultimate result. Also prepubescent girls do not have the vaginal pH that older women have to protect against infection and they commonly contract vaginitis and other local genital infections [pp. 120, 121].

Some of the infectious complications of child sex abuse are gonorrhea, syphilis, herpes, chlamydia, chancroid, lymphopathia venereum, lymphogranuloma inguinale, group B beta-streptococcal infections, Trichomonas infection, inclusion blenorrhea and pubic lice. It appears that Kinsey's research took absolutely no account of the possibility of these consequences, even allowing that some of these infections were not known in his day.

Regarding the possibility of emotional or psychological problems resulting from adults making sexual "contacts" with girls, Kinsey had this to say:

On the other hand, *some 80 per cent of the children had been emotionally upset or frightened by their contacts with adults.* A small portion had been seriously disturbed; but in most instances *the reported fright was nearer the level that children will show when they see insects, spiders, or other objects against which they have been adversely conditioned.* If a child were not culturally conditioned, it is doubtful if it would be disturbed by sexual approaches . . . . *It is difficult to understand why a child, except for its cultural conditioning, should be disturbed at having its genitalia touched, or disturbed at seeing the genitalia of other persons, or disturbed at even more specific sexual contacts [eg, attempted intercourse].* When children are constantly warned by parents and teachers against contacts with adults, and when they receive no explanation of the exact nature of the forbidden contacts, they are ready to become hysterical as soon as any older person approaches, or stops and speaks to them in the street, *or fondles them* . . . even though the adult may have had no sexual objective in mind. *Some of the more experienced students of juvenile problems have come to believe that the emotional reactions of the parents, police officers, and other adults who discover that the child has had such a contact, may disturb the child more seriously than the sexual contacts themselves.* The current hysteria over sex offenders may very well have serious effects on the ability of many of these children to work out sexual adjustments some years later . . . [Female Report, p. 121; emphasis added].

Here is one illustration of Herman and Hirschman's charge that Kinsey tried to minimize child sexual abuse. It would appear that a measure of blame is apportioned to everyone—parents, teachers, police, society—except the sex offender or "adult contact." No evidence is provided anywhere in Kinsey's research to support these opinions, yet some authorities of the period (as is the case today) apparently agreed with them. In a 1954 analysis of the Kinsey Reports, titled "Sexual Behavior in the Young Human Female and Male," psychiatry professor Frank Curran observed:

The authors point out, however, that there are *emotional* disturbances as a result of such contact in about eighty per cent of the children having such experiences. However, they, as well as many other observers, have concluded (and accurately, I believe) that these psychological effects are primarily the result of the emotional disturbances of parents, police officers, or other adults who discover that the child has had such a sexual contact [In Geddes, 1954, p. 169; author's emphasis].

Since physical trauma, according to Kinsey, is rare and emotional trauma the result only of "adverse conditioning," it might be expected that Kinsey's research discovered benefits to at least some children from sexual activity with adults. And this indeed is claimed:

> The adult contacts are a source of pleasure to some children, and sometimes may arouse the child erotically (5 per cent) and bring it to orgasm (1 per cent). The contacts had often involved considerable affection, and some of the older females in the sample felt that their pre-adolescent experience had contributed favorably to their later socio-sexual development [Female Report, pp. 120, 121; emphasis added].

RAPE

Since the handling of sexuality data in Kinsey's books, and the generalizing from that data, is clearly somewhat bizarre at times, Kinsey's treatment of the subject of rape might be expected to be unusual. It is. The topic is dealt with as if it does not exist. Yet it is clear from Kinsey's "adult partner" table, and from other material discussed earlier, that Kinsey had considerable data on rape.

In this major work on female sexuality, rape is mentioned in two footnotes (one about penalties, the other a definition in canon law) and in a table about dreams that went beyond actual experience. In the "dream" table, perhaps the most notable point is that rape dreams led to orgasm more often than dreams about petting!

Rape receives no better coverage in Kinsey's prior Male Report. Here it is mentioned once, as a problem for some older men whose "affectionate fondling" of children is sometimes misinterpreted as attempted rape. As Kinsey put it:

> Many small girls reflect the public hysteria over the prospect of "being touched" by a strange person; and many a child, who has no idea at all of the mechanics of intercourse, interprets affection and simple caressing, from anyone except her own parents, as attempts at rape. In consequence, not a few older men serve time in penal institutions for attempting to engage in a sexual act which at their age would not interest most of them ..." (Male Report, p. 238).

This treatment of rape is one of many remarkable features in Kinsey's remarkable research. Perhaps there was no rape in the 1940s.

II - PREADOLESCENT SEXUAL AROUSAL AND ORGASM

The Kinsey authors have argued that sexual contacts with adults are a source of pleasure to some children. They have implied—and in later years overtly claimed—the same for incest. In order to provide a theoretical basis for this position, it would be necessary to show that children are sexual beings. Kinsey and colleagues claim to have demonstrated this through 1) data gathered by the interview technique, and 2) by documenting "what seem to be sexual responses . . . observed in . . . both female and male infants as young as four months of age, and in infants and adolescent children of every older age" (Female Report, p. 103). Making use again of the non-fact as "fact," the Kinsey team preface their data by stating,

> It is *certain*, however, that there are children, both female and male, who are quite capable of *true* sexual response [Female Report, p. 103; emphasis added].

A scientist does not claim that something "is certain" when there is no evidence for it. Moreover, what is "true sexual response" in a child? It is in the attempt to demonstrate and document this "true" response for male children that the Kinsey research is most compromised (see chapter 1). However, the data on female child sexuality have some problems of their own, though minor by comparison.

The Kinsey data on female child sexual response are summed up in the following statement.

> About one per cent of the older females who have contributed histories to the present study recalled that they were making specifically sexual responses to physical stimuli, and in some cases to psychologic stimuli, when they were as young as three years of age (Table 146, Figure 98). This, however, *must* represent only a portion of the children who were responding at that age, for many children would not recognize the sexual nature of their early responses. About 4 per cent of the females in our sample thought they were responding sexually by five years of age. Nearly 16 per cent recalled such responses by ten years of age. All told, some 27 per cent recalled that they had been aroused erotically—sexually—at some time before the age of adolescence which, for the average female, occurs sometime between her twelfth and thirteenth birthdays (see pp. 122-7). However, *the number of pre-adolescent girls who are ever aroused sexually must be much higher than this record indicates* [Female Report, pp. 103, 104; emphasis added].

Again, the Kinsey team speak for the children as though they understood normal patterns of child development. They assert the low (1%) sexual response rate by age 3 is due to the inability of many children to recognize their sexual response. The overall figure for preadolescent girls experiencing what Kinsey called "orgasm" was "about fourteen percent." The low figure here is justified by saying "it is not at all impossible that a still higher percentage had actually had such experience without recognizing its nature" (Female Report, p. 105). But such commentary by Kinsey is mere opinion, based on personal views, and has no scientific basis. (In the above quotes the non-fact to fact conversion is quite evident, including the use of the double negative technique: "it is *not* at all *im*possible . . . .")

Readers might find it difficult to accept that "older" interviewees were able to recall at all that they were experiencing "specifically sexual responses to physical stimuli" at the age of 3 years, or that it was remotely possible for adults to recall what struck them at age 3 as a "psychologic" sexual stimulus. This would require prodigious feats of memory. In weighing the validity of such answers to interview questions, it is necessary to bear in mind three facts about the Kinsey team's research that have been discussed previously: 1) the "burden of denial" strategy of interviewing—"We always assume that everyone has engaged in every type of activity. . . . This places a heavier burden on the individual who is inclined to deny his experience" (Male Report, p. 53); 2) the bias in the sample and the bias implicit in volunteering; 3) Kinsey and team's personal bias.

[Elsewhere, Kinsey's technique of "forcing" the answers he wants is discussed (chapter 4).]

ORGASM NUMBERS

According to the Kinsey data (Female Report, p. 105), 16 girls "recall orgasm" by age 3 and another seven were directly observed in orgasm by that age. Four of these girls (it is not stated whether observed or not) experienced "orgasm" at less than 1 year. (Presumably these *were* observations. It is difficult to imagine recall to this age, even with the most aggressive interviewing techniques.) It is strange that the seven girls under 4 years, who were directly observed in "orgasm," are not handled as a separate group. In a scientific work of this nature, some description of the girls, the observers and their qualifications, and the circumstances of these observations is called for. But no information was given in the Female Report, and none has been offered since.

Combining Kinsey's Table 10 (Female Report, p. 127) and Table 147 (p. 544), the following numbers are given on "pre-adolescent orgasm from any source."

Incidence Of Preadolescent Orgasm From Any Source
[Female Report, Tables 10 and 147]

BY AGE	ACCUMULATIVE % OF TOTAL SAMPLE	TOTAL SAMPLE SIZE
3	-	5,908
5	2	5,862
7	4	5,835
9	6	5,772
* 10	8	5,762
11	9	4,577
* 12	13	5,738
13	14	1,144

* From Table 147

From a technical point of view, it is unsatisfactory that the fluctuating sample sizes are not explained.

Combining two other Kinsey tables (Table 21, p. 177 and Table 25, p. 180) provides the following information on those girls Kinsey described as masturbating and those masturbating to "orgasm":

BY AGE	EXPERIENCE IN MASTURBATION (Table 21)	MASTURBATION TO ORGASM (Table 25)
3	1% (of 5,913)	-% (of 5,913)
5	4% (of 5,866)	2% (of 5,866)
7	7% (of 5,841)	4% (of 5,838)
10	13% (of 5,808)	8% (of 5,802)
12	19% (of 5,784)	12% (of 5,778)

Fluctuating sample totals are, again, not explained and there is the contradiction that the sample size for orgasm from one source—masturbation (Table 25)—is larger than the sample size for orgasm from all sources (Tables 10 and 147) for ages 3, 5, 7, 10 and 12.

EARLY CHILDHOOD "ORGASM"

Kinsey spoke of "the typical reactions of small girls in orgasm" and claimed he had observed—or had observational data—on "orgasm" in seven girls under 4 years of age.

The following description, according to Kinsey, is provided by an "intelligent mother" who allegedly had frequently observed her 3-year-old in masturbation:

Lying face down on the bed, with her knees drawn up, she started rhythmic pelvic thrusts, about one second or less apart. The thrusts were primarily pelvic, with the legs tensed in a fixed position. The forward components of the thrusts were in a smooth and perfect rhythm which was unbroken except for momentary pauses during which the genitalia were readjusted against the doll on which they were pressed; the return from each thrust was convulsive, jerky. There were 44 thrusts in unbroken rhythm, a slight momentary pause, 87 thrusts followed by a slight momentary pause, then 10 thrusts, and then a cessation of all movement. There was marked concentration and intense breathing with abrupt jerks as orgasm approached. She was completely oblivious to everything during these later stages of the activity. Her eyes were glassy and fixed in a vacant stare. There was noticeable relief and relaxation after orgasm. A second series of reactions began two minutes later with series of 48, 18, and 57 thrusts, with slight momentary pauses between each series. With the mounting tensions, there were audible gasps, but immediately following the cessation of pelvic thrusts there was complete relaxation and only desultory movements thereafter [Female Report, pp. 104, 105].

The above description still is used by sexologists (eg, Crooks and Baur's Our Sexuality, 1983) as evidence that very young children are potentially capable of sexual arousal and pleasure.

However, this account leaves some key questions unanswered. For example, it is known today that masturbation in a young child may follow from prior sexual molestation. What was this child's history? And, given the type of *repeat* sexual experimentation on male children documented in Kinsey's earlier Male Report, was there a "training" effect here? Was this child, or others of the seven girls under 4 years of age allegedly observed in orgasm, the subject of *earlier* hands-on masturbation experiments?

Kinsey claimed to have "similar records" of orgasm for his seven girls as for 27 boys under 4 years (Female Report, p. 105). And from the Male Report it appears that these 27 boys are among those whose "original data [were] gathered by certain of our subjects . . . for use in the present [Male] volume" and who were included in the sex stimulation experiments described in the previous chapter. In Table 30 (p. 175) of the Male Report there are exactly 27 boys under 4 years of age listed as observed in orgasm by the "other subjects," who, as was made clear in the previous chapter, may well have been Kinsey team members themselves. At least some of these 27 boys—and possibly, therefore, some of the 7 girls—were involved in *repeat* experiments (Male Report, p. 175, footnote to Table 30). Thus the questions remaining to be answered concerning Kinsey's male child sexuality research apply on a lesser scale to his female child studies.

SEXUAL CAPACITY VS. REPRODUCTIVE CAPACITY

The above sexual response and orgasm data for female infants and children, together with the earlier experimental data from males as young as 2 months, were the support material for Kinsey's conclusion on childhood sexuality. In his own words this was summed up as follows:

> [T]he record supplied by the recall of the adult females and males who have contributed to the present study [Male and Female Reports], and direct observations made by a number of qualified observers, indicate that some children are quite capable of responding in a way which may show all of the essential physiologic changes which characterize the sexual responses of an adult [Female Report, p. 102].

This, if true, introduces a dichotomy into sexual development in the child. The capacity for sexual reproduction, which is not present until puberty, is thus preceded by the capacity for sexual response (and pleasure), which is present from birth. As Kinsey put it, "the capacity to reproduce is not synonymous with the capacity to be aroused erotically" (Female Report, p. 125). The acquisition of the full ability to respond erotically in preadolescence is, according to Kinsey, a function of experience and conditioning (Female Report, p. 126) and thus has little to do with later hormonal effects. Kinsey made it very clear, particularly in his Male Report—as noted in chapter 1—that the full development of these capacities in preadolescence is held back by the negative influence of "societal restraints" and "cultural inhibitions."

Kinsey's ideology of the separation of sexual developments is accepted "fact" in academic sexology, where "experts" now even refer to the "sexuality of the fetus" and talk of the "need for a massive paradigm shift on the parts of professionals, parents, and society in viewing, nurturing, and protecting the sexuality of infancy and early childhood . . . " (see Mary Calderone's article, "Adolescent Sexuality: Elements and Genesis," *Pediatrics* 76 [suppl. 4, part 2]:699, 1985). This ideology also is the "scientific" justification used by proponents of pedophilia and the supporters of "children's rights" to promote the legality of sexual access to children.

KINSEY AND THE FBI

Although some early reviewers of Kinsey's work expressed concern for the effect of his results on society's attitudes to human sexuality, no one seemed to want to make a specific major issue of Kinsey's most stunning finding: the beneficence of adult sexual relations with children. The FBI, however, appears to have been concerned.

Intimation of the FBI's interest comes from an unlikely source, namely, pedophile David Sonenschein of the Austin Pedophile Study Group II and author of the booklet *How to Have Sex With Kids*. In a 1987 article in the *Journal of Sex Research*, titled "Having One's Research Seized," Sonenschein, who claims to be a former employee of the Kinsey Institute, provided the following interesting account of a Kinsey-FBI connection:

> . . . in the mid-1950s the FBI approached Kinsey wanting him to reveal to them his sources of sexually explicit materials. Kinsey and Wardell Pomeroy resisted, and, in turn, pressed the agency to share its holdings with the Institute for research, causing great indignation at the Bureau. Internal memos indicate that the FBI continued to monitor Kinsey's "intrepid band" (as the agency referred to them), particularly because they were afraid the research would lead to an increase in "permissiveness" and "sexual deviancy." Further, the FBI condemned the Rockefeller Foundation's funding of the Institute, feeling that continued research in Kinsey's direction would corrupt and endanger the nation's children. A May 19, 1959, memo says that the foundations have "a stranglehold on the training ground of youth," but goes on to say that "no better instance of a reputable name being lent to enhance an unsavory cause can be found than that offered by the Rockefeller Foundation's support of the Kinsey sex studies." *The Agency was very upset by Kinsey's "revelation" that sex between adults and children can "contribute favorably to their later sociosexual development"* [*Journal of Sex Research* 23:408-414, 1987; emphasis added].

In pondering the future effect of Kinsey's research on the nation's children, the FBI showed commendable concern, but was not addressing the most serious question. If the agency had decided to find out how Kinsey's child sex experiments were carried out, a fruitful investigation would have been likely.

CHAPTER THREE

FROM PRUDERY TO "FREEDOM": A BRIEF REVIEW OF THE SEXUAL REVOLUTION

Dr. J. Gordon Muir

Chapter Overview

From the preceding chapters, it follows that if Alfred Kinsey and his team had a major effect on social mores it was from a basis of fake science. The sexual revolution that followed in the wake of Kinsey's two landmark books does seem to owe some of its character to Kinsey's research—certainly it bears the stamp of key tenets of Kinsey's philosophy: in particular the notion that all sex is good, including "outlawed practices," and that it is good for people to engage in sexual activity from as young an age as possible.

Several contemporary reviewers of Kinsey's work felt at the time that it would influence sexual mores in the United States. Sociologist Bernard Barber, author of Science and the Social Order, *was in no doubt about the impact of Kinsey's research. He wrote in Geddes' 1954 book* An Analysis of the Kinsey Reports on the Sexual Behavior of the Human Male and Female *(Mentor Books) that*

> *There can be no question that the Kinsey reports will change the pattern of sexual behavior in American society [p. 61].*

Just how far things have changed is described below. In terms of social upheaval and infectious disease, the application of Kinsey's new morality has been disastrous. And this "revolution" is not yet over. If it proceeds according to Kinsey's original vision, then there still is some way to go.

Revolutions often produce chaos without delivering the freedoms the participants were led to expect. The sexual revolution (which some say began with Alfred Kinsey) has been a case in point. The social consequences are everyday news: teenage pregnancy, teenage abortion, child parents (often single and in poverty), unwanted children, child abuse, and the list goes on. The medical consequences are equally devastating: several venereal disease epidemics (some unrecognized by those unaffected) with untold suffering and a cost to the U.S. economy of several billion dollars each year. There are additional effects in terms of divorce, abandoned families, disturbed children, and all the host of social and psychological consequences that follows these traumas.

What happened in the rush to sexual freedom was not the discovery of a new, free and imaginative society but the throwing out of the baby (necessary codes of conduct for a healthy society) with the bath water (Victorian prudery, repression and hypocrisy). Of course it was impossible for this morality pendulum to have stopped in some sane middle ground because, in addition to its own momentum, it was commercially driven by the vast profits to be reaped by catering to a society in which there were sufficiently large numbers of people who wanted to see and hear everything. And a whole generation was told by many of the people it placed credence in that it was good to see and hear *and do* everything.

The result now is a society in the United States (and most "Western" countries) that is behaviorally off the ecological tracks—even more than its environmental ecology is derailed. The specifically human ecology is the biological and mental (some would add spiritual) state of society and its members and the interplay of factors (conduct, attitudes) that affect its well-being. Biologically the sexual revolution has been devastating—as we shall see. It follows that the psychological impact has been equally serious, if less easy to measure.

DEATH OF THE "OLD TABOOS"

By the late 1960s society's moral ozone—the "old taboos"—was fast disappearing. A 1967 *Newsweek* special report chronicling the progress of the sexual revolution to that high point of the tumultuous '60s makes fascinating reading in retrospect:

> The old taboos are dead or dying. A new, more permissive society is taking shape. Its outlines are etched most prominently in the arts—in the increasing nudity and frankness of today's films, in the blunt, often obscene language seemingly endemic in American novels and plays, in the candid lyrics of pop songs and the undress of the avant-garde ballet, in erotic art and television talk shows, in freer fashions and franker advertising. And, behind this expanding permissiveness in the arts stands a society in transition, a society that has lost its consensus on such crucial issues as premarital sex and clerical celibacy, marriage, birth control and sex education; a society that cannot agree on standards of conduct, language and manners, on what can be seen and heard.

These new postures alarm many citizens, psychologists and social thinkers who see in this rapid destruction of taboos a dangerous swing toward irresponsible hedonism and, ultimately, social decay [*Newsweek*, November 13, 1967, p. 74].

Many celebrities of the period were leading the drive to what they thought was a saner, more adult civilization. The rationale was, as *Newsweek* described it, that people were "breaking the bonds of puritan society and helping America to grow up. . . . Agencies of moral order like the church, the government, the family and the community . . . [were] overrun . . . ." Parents were more "bewildered" than "horrified" by the new candor which "[forced] them to reassess their role as moral arbiter for their family."

Geoffrey Shurlock, who was chief executor of the old (1930s) Hollywood Production Code, told *Newsweek*: "America has in time grown up to accept sex. All the taboos are beginning to break down, which is probably the most healthy thing that could happen." Keith Richards, Rolling Stones' guitarist, proclaimed: "We are not old men. We are not worried about petty morals." Television impresario David Susskind said "[The new generation] wants to strip away all the sham and all the cant of their elders and to strive instead for truth and honesty. This revolution has been made by young people and nothing will thwart it for the simple reason that truth will out. 'Tell it to me, baby. Tell it the way it really is.' These are the battle cries of the young."

Words like "truth" and "honesty" became the property of those who wanted to break down the moral conventions. An intimidating feature of the times was that those not for this revolution were considered against it and on the side of cant, bigotry and hypocrisy. Of course fueling the sexual revolution, and comprising part of it, were the revolutions in fashion, books, theater, music, advertising, art and movies. Another contributing and intimidating factor was that those responsible for the Vietnam War were symbolic of the "old morality," a morality which was also hopelessly out of touch by being against, among other things, the growing fashion in the use of life-enhancing drugs like marijuana and LSD.

THE NEW BABYLON

Some saw a Babylonian parallel. Historian and columnist Max Lerner observed:

We're living in a Babylonian society perhaps more Babylonian than Babylon itself. It's what's called a late senate period. The emphasis in our society today is on the senses and the release of the sensual. All the old codes have been broken down [*Newsweek*, November 13, 1967].

That was more than 20 years ago. The "golden years" of the sexual revolution were still ahead when Lerner made these comments in 1967. The fruits of the drug culture have been fully witnessed and understood since then, but the mayhem from the sexual revolution has not yet got its message through. Movies, television and rock music, for example, became more sexually explicit than they ever were.

Free-lance journalist Kandy Stroud, writing in *Newsweek* in 1985, noted that what used to be innuendo in rock was now explicit. The English group Frankie Goes to Hollywood sang "Relax when you want to come"; Sheena Easton's "Sugar Walls" signified genital arousal; Judas Priest intoned "Eat Me Alive," about a girl being forced to commit oral sex at gunpoint; Motley Crue crooned about intercourse on an elevator. Stroud noted that "Unabashedly sexual lyrics like these, augmented by orgasmic moans and howls, compose the musical diet millions of children are now being fed at concerts, on albums, on radio and MTV."

Since 1985, a new "cultural development" in "music" has arrived— rap music, expressing the "culture of *attitude*." Pulsing with anger, hatred and sexual violence, this new art form, pioneered by groups with names like Public Enemy, N.W.A. (Niggas With Attitude) and Guns N' Roses, comes to us courtesy of major companies like CBS/Columbia Records, according to *Newsweek* (March 19, 1990). Lyrics can "glorify 'taking out a cop or two'" or glamorize abusing a woman with a flashlight or even raking her with an Uzi. According to the *Newsweek* writers, with this cultural advance

> It is not just that romance has gone out of music—attitude has done the seemingly impossible and taken sex out of teenage culture, substituting brutal fantasies of penetration and destruction.

(Commenting on this new "X-rated," "toxic pop" culture, two *Time* writers asked in a cover story, "what impact will this culture have on the first generation to grow up within it?" Not much, they figured— without any evidence—which was strange in a magazine that takes an activist—cigarette ads excepted—position on the environment. In any case, they argued, the government has no place monitoring cultural pollution. Clearly, environmental damage to the human psyche is not something that society is going to be able easily to take pre-emptive action on—like, say, global warming.)

With the development of the communications and entertainment revolutions of the past 40 years, adolescents and preteens have been exposed to an increasingly blaring sexual marketplace without any instruction in the role of sex in a responsible society. In addition, the liberal-intellectual message of the day has been that attaching rules to sexual behavior is the province of narrow-minded "moralists" trying to "impose" values. Not unsurprisingly, many young people developed lifestyles in tune with the commercial sexual onslaught. In fact the values adopted by the young, popularized by their role models and justified by a minority intellectual elite, have become the new standards. Looking back at the New Morality from a 1982 perspective, Paul Ramsey, professor of religion at Princeton University, noted a remarkable fact about Western culture:

> ... ours is the only era in the history of human life on this planet in which the "elders" of the tribe ask the young what the tribal rules and standards of expected behavior should be. We aspire to be rationalists, liberals, egalitarians. No heritage can be transmitted for that would be imposition. Thus we are a civilization without puberty rites, without

rites of passage, without rituals, ordeals or vigils that the young must pass through to be accepted as men and women among the elders. The nearest approximation we have to a rite of passage to adulthood is getting a driver's licence [*Postgraduate Medicine* 72:233, 1982].

At the beginning of the 1980s some writers were calling for, and forecasting, a turn away from the self-indulgence (euphemistically called "self actualization") of Tom Wolfe's "me" decade. Lance Morrow in *Time* was expressing the hope for a revival of responsibility and a return to excellence and seemed to think it might be possible because "large numbers of Americans [were] sick of a society in which so many standards of conduct have collapsed" (*Time*, February 22, 1981, March 22, 1982). Pollster and social critic Daniel Yankelovich in his book *New Rules: Searching for Self-Fulfillment in a World Turned Upside Down* (Random House, 1981) thought that a new "ethic of commitment" was at hand in reaction to the ideas of reward without effort and sexual freedom without consequences. But it was not to be.

Strangely, even today, education for the young does not include the vital, clear lessons of the 20th century's sexual revolution—one of the most significant events of human history. (It does, however, belatedly recognize the lessons of the drug revolution, so there is hope.) What sort of education can this be that can only (and barely) teach students how to get passing grades but cannot teach the obvious conclusions of recent history because such lessons would make a point about moral values—something that is not supposed to happen in schools? The clearest lesson of the sexual revolution is the human ecological effect— the damage done to human social and physical health. This is the most precise yardstick by which to chart the progress of this turnover in moral values and by which to judge its results, good or bad.

SOCIAL DISORIENTATION

Socially, the sexual revolution has wrought upheaval. There are about 11 to 12 million sexually active adolescents in the U.S.: 10 million (of the 19 million) in the 15- to 19-year age group and about 1.4 million (of the 16.5 million) in the 10- to 14-year age group. About 860,000 teenagers will become pregnant this year—23,000 aged 14 or younger. More than 40% of pregnancies in the 15- to 19-year-olds will be aborted and 60% of those in girls under 15 (*Family Planning Perspectives* 20:263, 1988). About 75% of pregnancies in 15- to 19-year-olds are premarital and unplanned, as are presumably virtually all pregnancies under 15.

Between 1950 and 1968 the number of out-of-wedlock births to teenagers almost tripled to about 165,000 per year (*Clinical Obstetrics and Gynecology* 14(2):442, 1971). Legalization of abortion in 1973 has ended this trend. Nevertheless, today there will be about 230,000 births per year to women under 20 who are both poor and unmarried, a testimony to significantly increased rates of sexual activity among teenage females. According to two researchers at the Johns Hopkins School of Hygiene and Public Health, a large survey of metropolitan-area teenagers nationwide revealed a steady growth in the numbers of girls having premarital sexual intercourse: 30% of female teenagers surveyed in 1971, 43% in 1976, and 50% in 1979 (*Family Planning Perspectives* 12:230, 1980).

In the absence of special programs, a high percentage of pregnant teenagers will drop out of school and about 40% will become pregnant again within two years (*Clinical Obstetrics and Gynecology* 21(4):1215, 1978). Dr. Janet Hardy, professor of pediatrics at The Johns Hopkins University Hospital, Baltimore, gives an example of an inner-city junior high school where more than 50% of seventh graders are sexually active and 18% of the girls in the seventh, eighth and ninth grades have been pregnant once or more.[1]

One study, now more than 12 years old, found that 45% of white boys 14 years or younger had experienced intercourse. The percentages for Hispanics and blacks were, respectively, 66% and 88% (*Family Planning Perspectives* 7:256, 1975). These figures help to explain the high sexual experience rate among teenage females. As Dr. Luella Klein of Emory University School of Medicine, Atlanta, has pointed out, "many [teenage females] see sex as necessary for the social rewards of dating. Sex is often seen as necessary payment to a male if a female is to be popular, go places and do things" (*Clinical Obstetrics and Gynecology* 21(4):1151, 1978).

In big-city ghetto areas it may almost have become a rite of passage for girls to get pregnant by the mid-teens. According to the director of a Chicago Board of Health teenage clinic serving the South Side ghetto, "If a girl gets to be 15 or 16 years old and she hasn't had a baby yet, her friends think there must be something wrong with her" (*Newsweek*, February 16, 1987).

Although premarital sexual activity among girls increased by two thirds during the 1970s, the teenage birthrate declined because of the great increase in abortion. Still, by 1978 there were about 1.3 million children living with 1.1 million adolescent mothers, half of whom were unwed.

Today, commonly quoted figures state that about one out of four children is being raised by a single parent, about 22% were born out of wedlock (a third of these to teenage mothers) and one out of five lives in poverty—the poverty rate being twice as high among blacks and Hispanics.

Here is one major cause of welfare dependency. James Marks and Marshall Kreuter of the CDC pointed out in an editorial in the *Journal of the American Medical Association* that "In 1985, $16.65 billion was spent on families begun when the mother was a teen; virtually all of those costs are associated with public assistance including Aid to Families With Dependent Children, Medicaid, and Food Stamps" (*Journal of the American Medical Association*, 257:3410, 1987).

---

[1]   In McAnarney ER (ed.): *The Adolescent Family,* Report of the Fifteenth Ross Roundtable on Critical Approaches to Common Pediatric Problems, Ross Laboratories, Columbus, OH, 1984.

Behind the cold statistics, in addition to the massive welfare problem, are damaged lives, unwanted children, lost educations and a raging "hyper-epidemic" of venereal diseases. A further problem is a predisposition to drug abuse. According to psychiatrist Armand Nicholi, Jr., of Massachusetts General Hospital and Harvard Medical School, there is a connection between the child drug epidemic and today's family environment. For example, the characteristics of children from single-parent homes are the same as those who are prone to drug abuse—ie, lack of a close relationship with parents, a large amount of time spent away from home and increased reliance on peers as opposed to parents (*New England Journal of Medicine* 308:925, 1983).

Sex education does not seem to be helping. In the journal *Pediatrics*, Dr. James Stout and Dr. Frederick Rivera of the University of Washington and Children's Hospital and Medical Center, Seattle, reviewed studies of the effects of sex education on teenage sexual behavior (*Pediatrics* 83:375, 1989). They concluded that "sex education programs in junior and senior high schools have little or no effect either positively or negatively on altering the age of onset or frequency of adolescent sexual activity, on increasing contraceptive use, or on preventing unplanned teenage pregnancy." They noted that "a classroom course alone cannot be expected to change sexual behavior in a direction that is in opposition to the adolescent's sexual world as molded by the television, motion picture, music and advertising industries, as well as peer group and adult role models." Besides, as will be seen in the following two chapters, some classroom courses seem designed to increase teenage sexual activity.

The rising divorce rate in America may or may not be related to the sexual revolution. Logic would suggest a connection. Certainly, Kinsey's research indicates that marital infidelity is higher among women with premarital sexual experience. (There were just over 400,000 divorces in 1962, 845,000 in 1972, and 1.2 million in 1981.)

In a new book, *Second Chances: Men, Women and Children a Decade After Divorce* (Ticknor & Fields, 1989), Dr. Judith Wallerstein presents results of the first long-term study of the effects of divorce on children. After following 60 families over a period of 10 to 15 years, Wallerstein found that ten years after the event "almost half of the children entered adulthood as worried, under-achieving, self-deprecating, and sometimes angry young men and women." Daughters had difficulty with intimacy and relationships. In other words, as with child abuse, the cycle probably has a tendency to repeat itself.

ADOLESCENT SUICIDE

Adolescent suicide (up 300% in the last 20 years, according to a 1982 *Medical Tribune* report) may be another tragic end point for at least some children under the sexual pressures of modern-day America. Harvard psychiatry professor John D. Mack provides an illustration in his book *Vivienne: The Life and Suicide of an Adolescent Girl* (Little, Brown, 1981).

A special report on the subject of teenage suicide in *Sexual Medicine Today*, a supplement to the May 12, 1982 *Medical Tribune*, noted that "sexual matters often predominate among the risk factors for adolescent depression and suicide." Supporting this conclusion were data provided by Dr. Marlene Payne, a psychiatrist at Georgetown University School of Medicine: 22% of all female adolescents who tried to kill themselves were either pregnant or believed they were pregnant at the time; in 36% of suicide attempts, the teenager was breaking up from a serious romantic involvement. Payne also noted that 72% were living in a household from which one or both biological parents were absent.

Some current figures on adolescent suicide are alarming. The National Adolescent Student Health Survey, conducted in 1987 among 11,419 eighth and tenth grade students from 217 schools in 20 states, showed that 25% of the boys and 42% of the girls had at some point in their lives seriously considered committing suicide. Self-inflicted injury that could have resulted in death was reported by 11% of the boys and 18% of the girls. In 1987, approximately 10% of deaths among persons aged 1-24 years were suicides (*Morbidity and Mortality Weekly Report* 38:147, 1989; CDC, Atlanta). (It also was noted in this survey that 6% of the girls reported someone had tried to force them to have sex at school during the past year; 19% reported the same for outside of school.)

Adolescent suicide statistics may be less of a shock when viewed in the framework of current information on the mental health of American youth. Child psychiatrist James F. Leckman of the Yale University Child Study Center, chairman of the Institute of Medicine Committee (of the National Academy of Sciences) that compiled the report "Research on Children and Adolescents with Mental, Behavioral and Developmental Disorders," recently pointed out that about 12% of the U.S. population under the age of 18—ie, 7.5 million children and teenagers—"have a diagnosable mental disorder." Other estimates put the number as high as 11 to 14 million children, according to Sandy Rovner of the *Washington Post* (*Washington Post*, June 13, 1989, Health section, p. 11).

SEXUAL VIOLENCE

As Brooklyn District Attorney Elizabeth Holtzman pointed out in *The New York Times* (May 5, 1989), "Sexual violence against women is rampant. More than 3,400 women will report being raped [in 1989] in New York City, and thousands more will be raped and never report it. The FBI says a woman is raped in the U.S. every six minutes; one out of ten women will be raped in her lifetime."

Holtzman blames dehumanizing attitudes about women, citing "a recent study of junior high school students in Rhode Island [in which] 50% of the boys said it was acceptable to rape a woman if a man spent at least $15 on her." She noted another "survey of college students [in which] one man in 12 admitted to a rape—but not one considered himself a rapist." According to Holtzman, in New York City there has been a 27% increase in rape arrests of boys under 18 and a 200% increase among boys under 13.

An overview of trends in sexual violence in the United States over the last several decades has been summarized in the following terms by Dr. John Court:

Historically, civilized societies have respected two major taboos—that of violating another physically and that of sexual violation. And whereas these restraints applied to the adult world at risk of social punishment, they were even more fully acknowledged in relation to the protection of children. Where the taboos were broken, a high level of shame existed.

Since the sixties there has been an escalating pattern of reported activities in such areas as rape, sexual assault and the sexual abuse of children. Although there was initially public denial of the significance of startling increases in such criminal statistics, with efforts to explain them away as merely changes in reporting rates, the stark reality that a real increase has occurred is now undeniable.

From 1933 to 1963 the reported rape rate in the U.S. increased from 3.7 to 9.2 per 100,000 persons. Over the next decade this jumped to 24.3 and by 1983 to 33.7. Or, to put it another way, the number of rapes increased by 526% between 1960 and 1986. Serious writers such as Hindelang and Davis (1977)[2] refer to the trend as "phenomenal" and "dramatic," even when writing in the context of other serious crimes which were also increasing. The Uniform Crime Report was still saying in 1984 that "forcible rape . . . is still recognized as one of the most underreported of all Index crimes."

That such increases are linked in complex and powerful ways to the messages of pornography has been convincingly argued by feminists among others who, without adopting simplistic causal explanations, have nonetheless indicted the use of women in humiliating ways for the entertainment of men as a major contributor in shifting attitudes toward acceptance of sexual violence, and desensitization to the negative consequences of such behavior. Such relations have been argued theoretically, shown in laboratory experiments and correlated in social-psychological studies (eg, Baron and Strauss, 1984).[3] The Surgeon General summarized the research by saying that "I am certain that pornography that portrays sexual aggression as pleasurable for the victim is at the root of much of the rape that occurs today."

The pervasive availability of sexually aggressive materials (and probably non-violent materials also) in magazines, books, films and videos has sexualized the home environment in an unprecedented manner, such that home is no longer a place of safety from sexual harassment. There are many to tell us it never was totally safe, but the steep increase of child sexual abuse being reported strongly

2   Hindelang MJ, Davis BJ: Forcible rape: A statistical profile. In Chappell D, Geis R, Geis G (eds.): *The Crime, The Victim and the Offender*, Columbia University Press, 1977.

3   Baron LA, Strauss MA: Sexual stratification, pornography, and rape in the United States. In Malamuth NM, Donnerstein E (eds.): *Pornography and Sexual Agression*, Academic Press, 1984.

suggests that even the appearance of civilized taboos is under threat from the advocates of the sexual revolution.

Child sexual abuse reporting is still new enough to provide only a partial indicator of the extent of such abuse, and estimates vary widely. A responsible representative estimate based on the reporting of cases to state reporting agencies in the U.S. moves from 7,559 in 1976 to 37,366 in 1980 and 71,961 in 1983 (Finkelhor, 1986).[4] Clearly this is an alarming upward trend.[5]

Many sociological and psychological forces are converging to elevate child sexual abuse from a whispered rarity to a rampant tragedy of enormous proportions.

As a further footnote , it should be noted that Dr. David Finkelhor of the Family Violence Research Program at the University of New Hampshire has done research showing that 19% of American women and 9% of all men may have been sexually victimized as children. He has "speculated" that between 2 million and 5 million American women have had incestuous relationships (Newsweek, May 14, 1984, p. 31).

VD EPIDEMICS

Medically the sexual revolution has been an unmitigated disaster. According to the Centers for Disease Control's 1988 report on sexually transmitted diseases (STDs), 2.5 million teenagers had an STD (excluding HIV infection) in 1987. Today gonorrhea is the most common reportable disease in school age children—surpassing chickenpox, measles, mumps and rubella combined.

In 1960 in the U.S., approximately 57,000 cases of gonorrhea were reported in the 10- to 19-year age group. There were 256,000 cases in 1980. "Reported" diseases are, of course, only a fraction of the true incidence. There are well over 10 million new cases of various types of sexually transmitted diseases in the U.S. each year, most unreported. And for every case diagnosed, several more may be unrecognized.

The most recent upsurge in these diseases is thought to be related to increasing sex-for-drugs activity, which is also blamed for the spread of AIDS. Also, those diseases which cause ulcers or blisters may themselves assist the spread of AIDS. According to Wendy J. Wertheimer, director of public and government affairs for the American Social Health Association, based in Palo Alto, California, these diseases cost U.S. society $4 billion per year (New York Times, July 16, 1988). This likely is a considerable underestimate.

As the sexual revolution gathered steam, a few people who could see where it was headed did warn of the consequences. British venereal disease specialist Dr. Arthur Wigfield, in a 1971 article in the British Medical Journal, pointed out where this revolution was going and who was taking it there. He wrote:

4   Finkelhor D: Sourcebook on Child Sexual Abuse, Sage Publications, 1986.
5   It is currently estimated that there are about 200,000 new cases of child abuse each year in the U.S. (Raskin DC, Yuille JC: Problems in evaluating interviews of children in sexual abuse cases. In Ceci SJ, Ross DF, Toglia MP: Perspectives on Children's Testimony, Springer-Verlag, 1989).

The sexually permissive section of society shows little but ignorance, indifference or contempt for the venereal diseases. We venereologists wonder what can be done to contain them as they threaten to get out of hand. We wonder how high our graphs will climb [*British Medical Journal* 4:342, 1971].

Wigfield described how youth were being led in their revolution by people who were "utterly naive in their conception of the spread of disease." Semi-prophetically he cited the role of

the controllers of the mass media and the cult of the sensuous, salacious and sensational. These are the people in whose power lies the future sanity and sanctity of mankind. Either a malevolent materialism, with its seeking after sales and profit, or a benevolent solicitude for human happiness must ultimately prevail. It will no longer be to "great kings that nice customs curtsey," but to publishing princes and aces of advertising, to the [press] barons, and to the lords of television.

What happened, of course, is history.

Some of the STD consequences of the sexual revolution are summarized below.

HERPES (Herpes genitalis)

Before AIDS-virus infection, this was regarded as the most important sexually transmitted disease, dubbed the "new scarlet letter" by *Time* magazine in 1982. It now affects up to 25 million Americans, and new cases may be occurring at the rate of half to 1 million every year.

The disease is not only painful, it is incurable, it tends to recur and it is life threatening to the newborn of infected mothers. Herpes encephalitis in the first weeks of life is now the commonest cause of fatal encephalitis in the United States (*Western Journal of Medicine* 136:419, 1982). At least half of the babies born to mothers with the active disease will become infected with some form of herpes; half of these will die or suffer permanent neurological damage (*American Journal of Diseases in Childhood* 126:546, 1973; *Journal of the American Medical Association* 243:157, 1980; *Pediatrics* 66:147, 1980).

Briefly, the venereal condition usually starts as a tingling or burning sensation on the skin. In hours or days the skin of the sensitive area will break into a measles-like rash, followed by blister-like sores which are excruciatingly painful. In addition there may be swollen glands, fever, muscle aches and other symptoms. Psychological problems in sufferers are common—especially depression (often deep) and a sense of isolation.

Whether or not the herpes virus is a cause, it certainly appears to be a factor in cancer of the cervix and vulva. In some cases herpes causes few symptoms and diagnosis is difficult. About 80% of women who have had sexual contact with men with symptoms of herpes will become infected. The condition is rampant in college campuses throughout the U.S.

GONORRHEA

Somewhat overshadowed now by some of the "new" STDs, gonorrhea is still increasing dramatically and is now the most common reportable infectious disease of school age children. Approximately 2 million new cases will occur in the U.S. this year. It is the most prevalent notifiable disease in the world. One of the problems with this disease is that about 10% of males and more than 70% of females infected are unlikely to be aware of it.

Another problem is the increasing resistance of the gonococcus bacterium to drug treatment. Today blood levels of penicillin of up to 100 times that of 20 years ago may be required for a cure—and even that may fail. There are of course standby drug treatments, but the medical profession is barely keeping ahead of this bug. In addition, even if the gonorrhea is cured, there is often a lingering second infection with another type of organism (such as chlamydia) which remains unscathed.

Orogenital sex practices are leading to cases of gonorrhea in the mouth and tonsils—and most of these are without symptoms. The rectum is another problem area. As well as possibly being unrecognized, these extra-genital sites of infection may remain infected after successful treatment of the genital condition. Up to 10% of persons diagnosed as having genital gonorrhea may also have mouth and tonsilar infections. In the past, it was surmised that up to a quarter of the homosexual community could have gonorrhea of the tonsils (*British Medical Journal* 4:660, 1971).

The most serious and tragic consequence of this disease is its toll of chronic pelvic problems and infertility in a high percentage of women victims (see below).

CHLAMYDIA

Most people have never heard of chlamydia, but it may be more common in industrialized countries than any other principal venereal disease. Health care costs related to chlamydia may be more than $1.3 billion annually in the U.S. (*Newsweek*, April 21, 1986, p. 81). The organism responsible is a small bacterium, better known for causing blindness (trachoma) in many underdeveloped nations. In Western nations it has become a major cause of serious sexually transmitted disease. Chlamydial venereal infections are not reportable, but these are believed to be twice as common as infections with gonorrhea (ie, 4 to 5 million new cases a year—and this is likely to be an underestimate).

The reason for the uncertainty about just how commonly chlamydial organisms cause venereal infection is that until recently only specialized research laboratories have had the facilities to make a diagnosis. This bug is difficult to identify, not easy to combat, and produces serious consequences—especially chronic pelvic inflammation and sterility (see below).

According to Dr. Richard Sweet, professor of obstetrics and gynecology at the University of California-San Francisco School of Medicine, infants born to infected mothers will develop eye infections in 30-50% of cases, and worse, chlamydial pneumonia in 10-20% of cases by the third month (*Ob.Gyn.News* 17(10):15, 1982). Chlamydia is most common in the young and sexually promiscuous. A study of sexually active adolescents in Baltimore found an infection rate of 35% in boys, 27% in pregnant girls and 23% in non-pregnant girls (*Pediatrics* 73:836, 1984).

Chlamydial organisms usually cause urethritis in men and women and are probably the cause of about 50% of cases of nongonococcal urethritis (NGU)—a very common venereal condition that often coexists with gonorrhea and often persists after the gonorrhea has been treated. About 20-30% of men with gonorrhea automatically have this organism. As diagnostic services improve, chlamydial infection alone will undoubtedly be seen to be a major public health problem. In addition to causing sterility, it may be involved in a whole host of pelvic disorders, including chronic prostatitis and cancer of the cervix. It may even be a cause of premature birth and of childhood myocarditis.

As with gonorrhea, a high percentage of people infected with chlamydia are probably unaware of it.

PELVIC INFLAMMATORY DISEASE (PID)

According to some experts, this is "the most significant of all the sexually transmitted diseases in American medicine" (*American Journal of Obstetrics and Gynecology* 138:880, 1980). That, of course, was before AIDS. This disease—which in three words is the reason traditional STDs are sexist—accounts for 5-20% of hospital admissions for gynecologic problems in the U.S. and is associated with health care costs of more than $1 billion annually (*Reviews of Infectious Disease* 8:86, 1986).

In a 1980 review of the problem in the *American Journal of Obstetrics and Gynecology*, Dr. L. Westrom of the University of Lund, Sweden, noted that there were about 500,000 new cases each year in the United States. Because of associated damage to the fallopian tubes this means that "more than 60,000 women are rendered infertile because of PID annually . . . ."

The epidemic of PID today presages one of infertility tomorrow (already here, to some extent). Subsequent to gonorrhea or infection with chlamydia and a variety of other organisms, including herpes, the fallopian tubes are liable to become blocked, leaving a woman infertile for the rest of her reproductive life. About 20% of women with gonorrhea will develop PID, and each episode carries a risk of infertility estimated at about 15%. It appears that almost a third of women who get PID do so before the age of 20, ie, before starting their reproductive period in many cases.

Westrom believes PID is having a great impact on modern industrial societies, and not just because of infertility. There is a seven-to-tenfold increase of conceptions occurring outside the uterus in post-PID women. And it is estimated that 90,000 post-PID women each year in the U.S. are added to the pool of women with chronic abdominal pain. Menstrual problems and pain on intercourse are other frequently occurring consequences.

BACTERIAL VAGINOSIS

This is one of the commoner female genital tract infections, and it is believed to be a sexually transmitted disease. Until recently it was regarded as mostly a nuisance—a condition that was without symptoms in half those affected and that caused a fishy-smelling discharge in the other half.

It appears to be caused by an increased concentration of several vaginal bacteria (principally *Gardnerella vaginalis*) and a simultaneous reduction of the protective, lactic-acid-producing lactobacilli. In an up-to-date review of this condition, Dr. Jack Sobel of Wayne State University School of Medicine noted that it has been diagnosed in 15% of women at a university gynecology clinic and in 10% to 25% of pregnant women. An added nuisance has been the 20% to 30% recurrence rate after antibiotic treatment (*Annals of Internal Medicine* 111:551, 1989).

Of more serious import, however, is the recently discovered association between bacterial vaginosis, salpingitis, amniotic fluid infection, preterm rupture of the membranes and consequent prematurity. In Sobel's words, "If this association is confirmed, bacterial vaginosis will have been transformed from a common, frequently unrecognized vaginal infection that is mainly of nuisance value to one of considerable morbidity with serious potential implications in the non-pregnant woman, the postoperative patient, and especially the pregnant woman."

TRICHOMONIASIS

This (together with the ubiquitous vaginal yeast infections) is probably the commonest venereal disease of them all. It is caused by a large one-celled organism called *Trichomonas vaginalis*. This is one of a type of organisms found in the digestive tracts of many animals.

In humans it causes urogenital infections. In women it usually causes vaginitis, in men it is mostly symptomless. Thus it is spread among women by men who are unaware of their infection. The prevalence of this condition in the U.S. today is colossal. It is estimated to occur in over 50% of women with abnormal vaginal discharges, or about 20% of the female population (*Current Contents*, May 17, 1982, p. 5). The disease is more of a chronic nuisance than anything else, although it has been suggested that this, too, may be a factor in cervical cancer.

CANCER OF THE CERVIX

This disease, which is one of the commonest causes of cancer deaths in women, is now recognized to have definite association with sexual promiscuity and teenage sexual activity. The condition is relatively rare in women who do not engage in premarital or extramarital intercourse and who do not start sexual activity in their teens (see *Cancer Research* 27:603, 1967; *American Journal of Public Health* 57:815, 1967; *American Journal of Epidemiology* 98:10, 1973). However, extra-marital sexual activity by a husband increases the risk to his wife (*Lancet* 2:1010, 1981).

This disease can be largely prevented by avoiding adolescent sexual activity and extra-marital sexual activity. The human papillomavirus (cause of genital warts) is widely believed to be linked to cancer of the cervix. There is currently an "epidemic" of wart virus infections— about 12 million cases nationally, and 750,000 new ones per year— coinciding with reports of "dramatic increases" in the prevalence of precancerous changes in the cervices of young women. Some experts are fearful of a future "epidemic of cervical precancer" (*British Medical Journal* 288:735, 1984).

The genital wart virus is also linked to cancer of the vulva, vagina and rectum. It has been shown that receptive anal intercourse and the presence of genital warts closely correlate with the development of anal cancer in men. Evidence is mounting that the same wart virus that is implicated in cervical cancer in women is also associated with anal cancer in men—and women (*New England Journal of Medicine* 317:973, 1987; *Lancet* 2:765, 1989).

HEPATITIS B

Hepatitis B, a blood-borne virus infection which has become epidemic in this country in the homosexual population, still is not generally recognized as a sexually transmitted disease. The virus agent is carried principally in blood, semen and saliva. Transmission through infected semen, particularly during anal intercourse, explains the prevalence of this infection in the homosexual community. One study found that nearly 50% of homosexuals with a history of more than 40 sexual partners had evidence of previous infection (*British Journal of Venereal Diseases* 53:190, 1977). The Centers for Disease Control estimate is that there are about 200,000 new infections annually in the U.S.

The prevalence of this disease increased about 35% per year over the past ten years. The risk of becoming a carrier after acute infection is about 1% to 5%. The long-term risk is that of developing cirrhosis or liver cancer.

HEPATITIS C

The discovery of the hepatitis C virus—which has probably been responsible for many cases of post-transfusion hepatitis and perhaps sexually transmitted hepatitis—was announced by the Chiron Corporation of California in May 1988. Apart from anything else, this will be a step forward in the prevention of post-transfusion hepatitis.

It appears likely that the majority of cases of what has been called non-A, non-B hepatitis are caused by hepatitis C, and there have been about 150,000 such infections per year in the U.S. Since blood transfusion probably accounts for less than 10% of these, IV drug use and promiscuous sexual activity may account for much of the rest.

This virus may be responsible for "a substantial proportion of the acute and chronic liver disease in the United States" (*New England Journal of Medicine* 321:1539, 1989).

SYPHILIS

Syphilis, an "old" STD that was in decline, has made a major comeback in the homosexual community in the past two decades, and particularly the past five years. There was a 30% increase in reported cases nationally from 1985 to 1987, the bulk of the increase being in California, New York and South Florida. Many promiscuous gays probably have been infected unknowingly. In one study among gays attending saunas in Amsterdam, there was evidence of recent or previous infection in 34% (*British Journal of Venereal Diseases* 57:196, 1981).

AIDS

AIDS (the acquired immunodeficiency syndrome), the most written-about and emotionally charged medical condition in human history, is not a single disease but a disease syndrome that follows infection with the human immunodeficiency virus (HIV).[6] Actually, there are now two known HIV viruses, HIV-1 and HIV-2, but the latter is almost entirely confined to West Africa.

Blood and genital secretions are the main source of HIV virus transmission, which makes this a disease principally of intimate sexual contact and of passage from mother to child in the perinatal period. Transmission by blood-contaminated needles among IV drug users has increased dramatically, however.

The AIDS virus targets cells in the blood and the brain. New evidence also indicates a selectivity for bowel epithelial cells.[7] What this means is that, mechanical interventions and childbirth aside, the

---

6   HIV is a "slow" virus (ie, it has a prolonged asymptomatic incubation period). In that sense it is like the virus that causes kuru: both were not known to infect humans before epidemics gradually unfolded. According to British venereologist Dr. John Seale, HIV poses "a unique threat to humanity." For an anthropological perspective on these two infections, see chapter 7.

7   See Nelson JA *et al*.: Human immunodeficiency virus detected in bowel epithelium of patients with gastrointestinal sysmptoms. *Lancet* 1:259, 1988.

likely predominant means of spread of the AIDS virus has been anal intercourse.

This leaves unexplained the situation in Africa, where heterosexual spread is believed commonest. However, heterosexual spread there is seen as greatly facilitated by concomitant STDs which create open sores. It also has been suggested that unprotected heterosexual anal intercourse is commoner in Africa than may have been thought. Moreover, the prevalence of parasitic bowel diseases in African communities may resemble that of Western homosexual communities, where infections like amebiasis, shigellosis, salmonellosis and giardiasis (the "gay bowel syndrome") are endemic. These diseases may be a cofactor in the spread of AIDS.

The notion that there may be a cure for AIDS anytime in the near future is pure fantasy. The human immunodeficiency virus incorporates its own genetic material into the genetic material of cells in an infected patient. These cells then become potential human HIV factories. The ability to "cut and paste" within the human chromosome or to block viral reproduction in infected cells is not likely anytime soon.

February 1990 CDC data indicate that homosexuals, bisexuals and IV drug users account for about 90% of AIDS cases. Non-drug-abusing heterosexuals account for about 5% of cases, but more than half of these appear to be the result of sexual contact with IV drug users or bisexuals. Hemophiliacs and blood transfusion recipients, who became secondarily infected during treatment with blood or blood products, account for about 3% of cases.

The AIDS demographic percentages are not usually reported in this particular manner because this illustrates a major truth about AIDS: The virus gained its foothold in Western society or, at least, achieved rapid initial spread as a result of promiscuous homosexual sex practices, particularly anal intercourse.

Gay activist groups are currently intent on creating the impression that promiscuous homosexuals have just been unlucky in getting infected before heterosexuals. Major segments of the national press have unfortunately cooperated in the fostering of this myth, just one of many wrong impressions the public has been given about the AIDS epidemic.

AIDS-virus infection is, of course, a sexually transmitted disease, but most states (at the time of writing) do not categorize it as such. Moves to reclassify HIV infection as an STD are taking place in some states but will be defeated in others (eg, New York) because this could mean adopting the standard STD practice of *requiring* notification of sexual partners (including spouses) of the possibility of infection. Powerful gay rights groups are fighting partner notification schemes in the higher interest of anonymity for homosexual men.

In 1989, the U.S. passed its first 100,000 AIDS cases, and estimates are that 1.5 million (some say 3 million) people carry the virus, most without knowing it. However, with AIDS almost everything has been distorted by politics (and by Alfred Kinsey's phony statistics; see chapter 6), and a figure closer to 1 million may be more correct. Twenty percent to 70% of the U.S. homosexual population are thought to be infected. Among IV drug users, HIV infection rates are high: about 50% in New York, Newark and Puerto Rico; but rates in the West, Midwest and South are lower.

Perhaps most virus carriers will go on to develop AIDS, but the latent period may be seven years or more. If no new transmission routes emerge, current projections are that by the end of 1992 there will be a cumulative total of more than 360,000 cases of AIDS, with more than 60,000 deaths in that year alone.

A worrisome recent discovery is that a significant number of persons in high-risk groups may actually have the virus for up to three years without showing positive in standard tests. Another numbing statistic is the infection rate among newborns in some areas: standard tests indicated that one in 80 babies born in New York City in 1987 had HIV antibodies. (These antibodies actually indicate infection in the mother, but about 40% of these babies will go on to develop AIDS.)

With most sexually transmitted diseases, there are those who can become infected by causes totally beyond their control (ie, by non-behavioral means). Tragically, this is true of AIDS. Particularly devastating may be the toll among children. According to Drs. Larry Bernstein, Richard Mackenzie and James Oleske, writing in the November 15, 1989, issue of *Patient Care*, by 1991 the number of HIV-infected infants is expected to approach or exceed 20,000. Most of these children will have been infected by their mothers, who, in turn, will have been infected principally by IV drug abuse or by sex with an infected partner.

As AIDS spreads into the heterosexual community, more and more children will be born infected. There has been talk lately of the "myth of heterosexual AIDS." In some cities it already is not a myth. Whether it remains a myth nationally will depend on levels of drug abuse and promiscuity.

The recently discovered fact that HIV-infected persons may suffer a loss of mental function long before any other symptoms of AIDS has alarmed some public health officials.[8] This disclosure led the Defense Department in late 1987 to remove HIV-positive individuals from stressful high performance jobs such as flying aircraft, handling nuclear weapons or working on sophisticated machinery (*Washington Post*, December 12, 1987). The possibility of impaired judgment in otherwise apparently healthy individuals has public health implications that are liable to be too much of a hot potato for most public health officials to want to deal with, given the politics of this condition (see below).

There has not been much discussion about the brain effects of AIDS—which fits a pattern concerning other important facts about this disease—but at least 80% of adults with AIDS have brain damage, and

8   See Grant I *et al.*: Evidence for early central nervous system involvement in the acquired immunodeficiency syndrome (AIDS) and other human immunodeficiency virus (HIV) infections. *Annals of Internal Medicine* 107:828, 1987.

at least half will have clinically apparent symptoms or signs of this effect.[9] These may show as neuromuscular defects or behavioral changes, including personality change, depression and paranoia. At the end stage, the patient is usually bed-bound, "stares vacantly and is capable of only a few simple social or intellectual interactions."

Called HIV encephalopathy or "AIDS dementia complex," the neurological effects of HIV infection are estimated to be present in 2% to 3% of *asymptomatic* AIDS-virus carriers and possibly 50% of those at the swollen-lymph-node stage of pre-AIDS. A progressive HIV encephalopathy will occur in up to 50% of HIV-infected children 2 months to 5 years after exposure.

Due to estimated per-patient costs of $40,000 to $140,000 and the thousands of dollars required for intensive care of infected newborns, the AIDS epidemic may bankrupt the U.S. healthcare system. A June 1989 *New England Journal of Medicine* article points out that federal spending on HIV-related illness amounts to $5.5 billion for the years 1982 to 1989, will be $2.2 billion for 1989 alone, and will reach $4.3 billion in 1992.

One estimate is that total health care costs for persons infected with HIV could rise to as much as $13 billion by 1992. In 1989, AIDS-related expenditures will consume about 10% of the Public Health Service budget, including about 10% of the FDA budget and 40% of the Centers for Disease Control's budget. Although the possibility of effective vaccines or cures is not in sight in this century, it remains true that this is a behavioral disease and the epidemic could have a behavioral solution.[10]

AIDS ATTITUDES AND HOMOSEXUALITY

AIDS is the culmination of the sexual revolution. It is forcing mainstream Western society to confront issues of human sexuality that otherwise may never have been addressed.

It has been pointed out that AIDS is predominantly a behavioral condition. Ironically, it is caused principally by behaviors traditionally considered unhealthy (and immoral), and it is difficult to pass on from person to person (infection from blood products and childbirth aside) except by these behaviors. A major difference between AIDS and other sexually transmitted diseases that have arisen in society is that AIDS is seemingly always fatal and will not be curable for a very long time, if ever.

There is little dispute among medical experts that the launching pad for AIDS in Western (American) society was the homosexual community, where HIV suddenly found itself in the amplification system of homosexual promiscuity. What this meant was that a virus which would have had difficulty in being perpetuated in a Western

9   See Dalakas M *et al.*: AIDS and the nervous system. *Journal of the American Medical Association* 261:2396, 1989.

10   Research results in chimpanzees, reported by Genentech in 1990, indicate that a vaccine *may* one day be possible.

heterosexual population, because it was not easily passed on by conventional behaviors, was spread rapidly by multiple-partner, anal-based sex practices. (The AIDS epidemic has, of course, been fertile ground for some creative conspiracy theories. Perhaps the most bizarre was the suggestion by Harry Hay, "father" of the modern gay and lesbian movement, that cronies of Ronald Reagan may have been involved.[11])

The toehold in the homosexual corner of society was likely assisted by the presence of co-factors in the form of epidemics of bowel diseases (the "gay bowel syndrome"), which had begun to be recognized in the late 1970s, in the growing urban concentrations of homosexual men whose modal form of sexual behavior was impersonal, repeated, random and anonymous sex.

Going back a bit in history, the gay drive for public approval of "an alternative lifestyle" began in earnest in the early 1970s with efforts to portray homosexuality and its sexual practices as a valid, healthy, equally acceptable way of life. Gay activists were demanding, even then, that public school sex education courses taught by gays should present homosexuality as a healthy alternative, with, for example, gay love stories available in the school libraries (*Time*, September 8, 1975).

In the March 1975 issue of *Psychology Today*, Mark Freedman, a founding member of the Association of Gay Psychologists, urged readers to believe that homosexuality "can lead to better than average functioning and to a fuller realization of certain fundamental values." He noted the advantage for gay men of the ability to have sex without having "to feign love or any other emotion" and the benefits of "group sex [which], in my opinion, offers pleasures that are impossible for couples."

When George Will suggested in his May 30, 1977, *Newsweek* column that homosexuality was "an injury to healthy functioning," gay leaders Jean O'Leary and Bruce Voeller (in a letter of response, June 6, 1977) screamed "outrage" at this "unsupported and totally false statement."

By the end of the 1970s, the myth, at least among many homosexuals, that a promiscuous lifestyle was valid and healthy had been established. And, according to Bell and Weinberg's classic 1978 study (*Homosexuality: A Study of Diversity Among Men and Women*, Simon & Schuster), most homosexuals were reporting having more than 250 lifetime sexual partners; almost 30% were reporting 1,000 or more. A few years later, Dr. William Foege, director of the CDC, told *Time*, "The average AIDS victim has had 60 different sexual partners in the past 12 months" (*Time*, July 4, 1983).

---

11   The sudden appearance of the AIDS virus has given rise to several conspiracy theories. Most recently, Harry Hay, founder in 1950 of the Mattachine Society (forerunner of the modern gay and lesbian movement), has said: "I share with many people the secret, sneaking sensation that, on one level or another, it may have been introduced by reckless Republican reactionaries of the stripe of Ronald Reagan. Not Reagan himself—he's too stupid. . . ." He added, "The same mentality that created the Tuskegee experiments. . .still is part of the mentality of the Centers for Disease Control in Atlanta" (*OutWeek*, June 27, 1990, p. 95). However, the AIDS virus has been identified in human tissue from as far back as 1959. At that time scientists were not able to genetically engineer new viruses.

The recognition of the AIDS epidemic and its principal mode of spread should have been enough to cause a serious rethinking of the "valid," "alternative lifestyle" view of homosexuality being promoted by activists. In fact, activist homosexuals became even more militant, and, paradoxically, they were able—after a shaky start—to turn the AIDS situation to their advantage in the all-important pursuit of acceptance by the heterosexual community. AIDS was successfully transformed from a medical to a political condition (see below) and, as the slogan put it, "AIDS is not our weakness, AIDS is our strength."

In effect, there is a second pathology involved here in this process of psychological manipulation. As radio personality and stress expert Roy Masters has pointed out, militant gays have responded to the "horrible tragedy" of AIDS "by going into a state of total denial as a way of coping with the intense pain" (*New Dimensions*, March 1990). This denial includes the role of homosexual promiscuity in the epidemic; few aficionados of current affairs programs in the past several years will have missed the oft-repeated cliche that "homosexuality doesn't cause AIDS, a virus does."

Partly as a result of this "horrible tragedy," mainstream Americans—a group with a fairly strong instinct of caring and compassion—have been susceptible to having their understanding of the AIDS epidemic manipulated and distorted by powerful propaganda. One of the most persistent messages has been that "anyone can get AIDS," implying that no one particular behavior is at fault. This, of course, is a clever half-truth in the sense that anyone can also get syphilis. It seems that there is a concerted effort from many sources to dissociate what has been a prominent feature of the homosexual lifestyle, namely, homosexual promiscuity, from its genuine connection to the origins of the AIDS epidemic in the U.S.

There has been emotional manipulation of the American public. Firstly, ordinary citizens have been made to feel *guilty*, by a constant barrage of accusations, that *they* are somehow bigoted and "homophobic" for having seen the homosexual lifestyle as antagonistic to their own basically Judeo-Christian value system. Secondly, they have been disoriented by the violence of militant gays' attacks on them. Masters likens the St. Patrick's Cathedral atrocity, for example, to terrorist conduct that ultimately can produce sympathy in its victims (the "Stockholm syndrome"). This is a tactic of the homosexual militant group ACT UP, and it appears to be achieving a measure of success—even with government officials (see below). Masters has made the astute observation that

> The cruelest form of injustice employed by the gay lobby is to accuse sensitive, decent people of bigotry, hatred, and "homophobia" for simply following their own moral consciences and seeing abnormal as abnormal [*New Dimensions*, March 1990].

In this vein, University of Minnesota pediatrics professor Gary Remafedi says, "AIDS is a disease that is about racism, homophobia and discrimination. . . [t]hose underlying factors perpetuate the epidemic," according to a *Wall Street Journal* report on sex education

("Uncharted Course: Effort to Teach Teens about Homosexuality Advances in Schools," *Wall Street Journal*, June 12, 1990).

In fact, an atmosphere has been created in which "informed" and "intelligent" comment on the AIDS situation can only employ the word *moral* in limited acceptable ways, such as "mandatory screening programs [for AIDS virus carriers] . . . are not *morally* justifiable at this time" (1988 article on AIDS by a bioethicist in the journal *Science*; emphasis added).

There have, of course, been examples of horrible intolerance, bigotry and hostility directed at AIDS victims, which is indefensible regardless of the cause of infection. However, fear of the "bigot" label has also rendered some subjects virtually undiscussable. This applies to the "innocent victim" description, once used of HIV carriers like hemophiliacs and newborns, who got infected by means other than their own promiscuity or drug abuse. This has become a taboo concept because it does not fit the approved point of view being pushed by gay activists and some leading editorial writers.

With AIDS, the "approved" position is that there's no such thing as an "innocent" victim. This comes out in mocking, but factually silly, lines like, "Funny, one never hears about innocent victims of cancer." However, most people who adhere to a semblance of traditional morality, and who stop to think about it, are unlikely to be fooled into thinking there is no difference between how Ryan White and Rock Hudson got AIDS.

THE POLITICIZATION OF AIDS

What separates AIDS from the other STDs is its politicization. Never before has a political constituency arisen whose principal unifying feature was the championing of a lifestyle inimical to healthy functioning and to the public health in general. As George Annas, director of the Law, Medicine and Ethics program at the Boston University School of Public Health reportedly said, "There never was a politically savvy group of sick people before," a group that, according to *New York Times* writer Gina Kolata, "has a cohesiveness and a body of experts in politics, press relations, advertising and law that it deploys to fight for its agenda" (*New York Times*, March 11, 1990). The political muscle they have flexed has at times made a farce of what should have been serious efforts to contain the AIDS virus.

Writing in the January 1989 issue of *Private Practice*, Dr. Edward Annis, chairman of the Florida Medical Association's Speakers' Bureau and former president of the American Medical Association, noted that "gay-rights organizations have pressured legislators to place innumerable obstacles in the path of public health officials and private practitioners." He added:

Rules and regulations have been designed to *control the vast number of people who are not infected with AIDS* [virus], rather than to inhibit the actions of those who have the potential to spread the disease [emphasis added].

According to *Newsweek* (March 12, 1990), a gay lobbying group—The Human Rights Campaign Fund—was the ninth largest independent PAC during the last presidential election, and 25th on the Federal Election Commission's list of fund raisers. However, although well funded, gay organizations do not represent the large minority of the population politicians think they do. This misconception of course arises from the false belief that Kinsey's homosexuality statistics are more accurate than they really are (10% is the commonly quoted, and erroneous, figure for the prevalence of homosexuality in society; see chapters 1 and 6). And gay lobbyists have used figures such as 15 million for the size of the homosexual community.[12] Thus, the face of society is being changed by political money and politicians in thrall to a perceived powerful pressure group.

And so, remarkably, history repeats itself. Mattachine Society founder Harry Hay told his biographer Stuart Timmons in an interview for *OutWeek* that Kinsey's 1948 data on homosexuality really got his attention:

> In 1948, Alfred Kinsey said that the hard-core homosexuals would number about 6 percent [of the U.S. population] and there was a possibility that, including the people who had some amount of homosexual experience, the number might be as high as 10 percent. We'd thought the people we knew in various cliques in L.A. might number as high as 25,000. But using the Kinsey figures—that we must be 250,000—was just mind-boggling [*OutWeek*, June 27, 1990, p. 95].

With sufficient state and federal support, what *Time* magazine has called the "AIDS political machine" has been able to use the thing that gay rights activists originally feared would most hinder their progress—the AIDS virus—to achieve the most startling advances. AIDS sufferers are a specially protected class in many areas. For example, AIDS is now a handicap from an anti-discrimination point of view, and even persons regarded as at risk for HIV infection (which could include sexual contacts of AIDS patients) will be protected from discrimination under new legislation.

In this political climate it is very difficult to tell the truth about AIDS, homosexual sex practices, and how best to contain the grave AIDS virus epidemic. For gay activism this is a purposeful outcome. The political and social changes are bringing about a shift in the public's view of the legitimacy of homosexual relationships. And that appears to be, above all, gay activism's goal: the acceptance of the homosexual lifestyle and the recognition of anal intercourse as the moral equivalent of heterosexual relating. Merely stating facts about AIDS, homosexuality, and even public health, can easily be dismissed as "homophobia" and be equated with racism. This is highly intimidating to many ordinary citizens.

---

12   A December 1979 issue of *Campaigning Reports* states that there are an estimated 15 million American gays of voting age and that "the assumption can be made that as many as 10-12 million can be activated on specific issues or to support specific candidates. . . ." Cited in Rueda E, *The Homosexual Network*, Devin Adair, 1982.

Intimidation has, in fact, been a major factor in the official response to the AIDS epidemic, and it is astonishing how fearful officialdom has been of this tactic and how gentle the media have been in describing its more obscene excesses. The most visible intimidation apparatus of gay activism has been the AIDS Coalition to Unleash Power, known as ACT UP. This is an organization so feared that it may desecrate a cathedral one week and be respectfully received to advise the Food and Drug Administration and the National Institutes of Health the next.

ACT UP, whose members are overwhelmingly white, male, and homosexual, has been described in *The Wall Street Journal* as "bristling with conspiracy theories and paranoia," a group that believes in "sticking it in the face of every individual you can stick it in," and whose hallmarks have been described as "rage, anger and revenge." However, according to segments of the media, the type of excess ACT UP specializes in (eg, trashing St. Patrick's cathedral) is merely "*testing* the limits of this country's tolerance," while "homophobia remains [the] serious problem." Mr. Larry Kramer, a New York playwright and a founder of ACT UP, has been quoted in *The Wall Street Journal* as saying, "I think the time for violence has now arrived. . . . I'd like to see an AIDS terrorist army like the Irgun which led to the state of Israel."

Irrational fear of AIDS activists has now become endemic at the highest levels in Washington—perhaps a higher form of homophobia! This is one reason why the government now spends more on this disease than on any other, including more than for heart disease, stroke, hypertension and diabetes combined. This situation is most remarkable considering that the predominant mode of spread of AIDS is behavioral—involving types of behavior not practised by most of the population—and considering that those who are at risk could avoid the risk by behavior modification. AIDS is more easily avoided than numerous other diseases on which the government is now spending less effort and money. This is politics driven by fear.

The politics of AIDS, and efforts to control, intimidate and instil guilt into the non-infected and unlikely-to-be-infected, have been evident at scientific conferences, in public "health" regulations and hospital procedures, and, in the early days of the epidemic, by efforts to prevent homosexuals from being "stigmatized" by blood-donation screening measures. And in terms of what constitutes "safe sex," to be blunt, the public has been lied to.

Usurping Medical Conferences

"Activists" took over the rostrum at the 1989 international AIDS meeting in Montreal and conducted their own opening ceremony. They wanted more emphasis on cure and an end to the term "AIDS victim." These "AIDS ideologues," benefitting from an unusually gracious free-speech opportunity, later tried to drown out a talk by Dr. Stephen Joseph, [then] New York City's Public Health Commissioner (partly because they didn't like his downward revision of AIDS and homosexuality statistics in New York [see chapter 6] and his call for partner notification). Joseph was denounced as a "liar" and a "murderer." Dr. Elizabeth Whelan, president of the American Council on

Science and Health, recounted in *The New York Times* some other peculiarities of this conference that would have been unheard of at a scientific meeting only a few years ago:

> One plenary session speaker talked of the necessity of making condoms common items. He encouraged us to have our children play with condoms instead of balloons, stage condom blowing contests at birthday parties and work at ways of getting songs about condoms in the media.
>
> He also explored the idea of having the Goodyear blimp replaced with a condom. While he was speaking, AIDS activists outside the conference hall inflated a seven-story yellow condom.
>
> Another plenary speaker talked of the importance of teaching children about safer anal sex "without penetration" and later added that AIDS was good because it made the world "kinder."
>
> Yet another speaker summed up what I felt was the consensus of the AIDS establishment at this conference. He told us that, as a society, Americans had to choose between good health and "retrograde moralism"—whatever that is [*New York Times*, August 8, 1989].

As pointed out in the *British Medical Journal*, this is "possibly the first time in history when the people with a disease are telling the doctors, scientists and politicians what they want." *Time* magazine put it another way: "the AIDS movement may have become the most effective disease lobby in the history of medicine."

The 1990 international AIDS conference in San Francisco coincided with Gay Pride Week. A U.S. Senator was denounced as a "homophobic pig" at the opening ceremonies, and the conference itself became a gay activists' forum. HHS Secretary Dr. Louis Sullivan's closing speech, in which he tried to say "We must learn to listen to each other . . . ," was drowned out by a thunder of shouts, whistles and air horn blasts, and he was pelted with condoms. About the time this was going on, the 21st annual Gay and Lesbian Pride March was taking place in New York, featuring, among other attractions, a contingent from the North American Man/Boy Love Association. This year's theme reportedly was "Family, Friends and Lovers."

Interestingly, the major pre-conference concern for the San Francisco meeting was the immigration ban on most AIDS-infected foreigners. The threat of "AIDS terrorists" to disrupt another medical forum raised no equivalent protest. However, AIDS activists and their medical soul mates may find themselves increasingly isolated at future gatherings. AIDS researchers have been extremely tolerant of gay barbarism. But many privately say they have just about had enough.

The "Safe Sex" Story

Implicit in almost all messages to the public about AIDS is the story that *safe sex*, including "protected" anal intercourse, is made possible by the use of condoms. This also is the message going to grade schoolers in the name of AIDS education. The problem is this information is just a "story," in fact it's pure baloney. The truth is that while the use of condoms makes the sexual transmission of the AIDS virus less likely, it does not always prevent it. And, for an infection that may be 100% fatal, that is important to know.

As birth control, latex condoms have a 10% to 15% chance of failure. But a woman is fertile only about 36 days a year; the AIDS virus from an infected person can be passed on 365 days a year. Commenting on a survey that showed a 17% condom failure rate for the prevention of HIV transmission, Dr. James Goedert of the National Cancer Institute said "the use of condoms will not eliminate the risk of transmission and must be viewed as a secondary strategy." The idea of a "lower" risk for HIV infection he described as "an inadequate goal and perhaps even a vacuous notion" (*New England Journal of Medicine* 316:1339, 1987).

A related piece of standard AIDS-education "safe sex" advice has been to ask potential sexual partners about their "risk history" for HIV. Based on the equally vacuous, idealistic notion that AIDS-educated persons are subject to new candor on matters sexual (an assumption equally misplaced in voluntary patient-based contact tracing schemes; see below), this counsel can prove dangerous.

In their report "Sex Lies and HIV" in *The New England Journal of Medicine* (March 15, 1990), two California researchers document "sizeable percentages" of lying for the purpose of having sex among a survey group of 18-to-25-year-old college students. Thirty-four percent of men and 10% of women had lied in order to have sex. Perhaps more revealing is that 20% of the men said they would lie about having a negative HIV-antibody test. And the authors suggest these reports of dishonesty are underestimates.

Obstructing Contact Tracing

Contact tracing—the effort to trace and notify persons possibly affected by a communicable disease—has been strongly resisted by AIDS activists as a public health measure to control the spread of the AIDS virus. The reason for fighting this standard procedure for a serious condition like AIDS has been that gay and bisexual men with HIV infection don't want their names known by health authorities.

There are, to be sure, arguments that can be offered against widespread contact tracing in the particular case of AIDS (long latent period, scarce resources, etc.), but the prime concern for AIDS activists appears to be anonymity for homosexuals. However, with women of childbearing age being infected unknowingly by sexual partners, and the further likely transfer of the virus to their children leading to the tragic situation described earlier, the need for tracing of some sort seems obvious.[13] One of the slogans of ACT UP has been "no tracking."

At the time of writing, contact tracing was only a requirement for HIV infection in about 11 states. In the two states with the biggest AIDS caseloads, tracing contacts is left largely up to the infected patient,

---

13   Confirming the value of this practice, the CDC reported that "Partner notification data from several states reveal a high seroprevalence rate, ranging from 11% to 39%, among persons identified as sex or needle-sharing partners, many of whom are themselves engaging in high risk behavior" (*Journal of the American Medical Association* 260:615, 1988).

although the physician may insist on following up. Public health statutes usually require or authorize contact tracing for sexually transmitted diseases, but HIV infection is not a sexually transmitted disease in most states. In New York, 1,800 surgeons and obstetricians sued colleagues at the state health department to have AIDS declared a sexually transmitted disease so that contact tracing of partners of HIV would be automatic. They were unsuccessful.

The prioritizing of the interests of gay and bisexual men over genuine public health concerns is an example of how AIDS has become the sacred cow of American politics and public health. When mainstream Americans begin to see more clearly what has been done and the overall framework within which it is happening (sex/AIDS education, etc.; see chapters 4, 5 and 6), they are liable to have quite different views on some of these matters than their political representatives.[14]

A lot of the problem concerning AIDS testing and partner notification is the desire on the part of gay and bisexual men for anonymity.[15] This has been the altar on which some common-sense measures on AIDS have been sacrificed. The reason advanced for *anonymous* AIDS-virus testing as opposed to *confidential* testing, which could involve reporting to public health authorities, is that high-risk persons would refuse testing altogether. The anonymous approach, however, frustrates traditional medical surveillance. It also ignores the fact that breaches of confidentiality by health departments almost never occur. And, it turns out, a comparison of procedures in two different states shows that gay men's fear of disclosure can be overcome with a well-run confidential testing program.[16]

What is needed, according to two physicians at the Oklahoma State Department of Health, is to address educational efforts to unwarranted fears regarding HIV reporting (*Journal of the American Medical Association* 263:36, 1990). What is not needed is the directing of public policy by what Dr. Stephen Joseph has called "street demonstrations by one self-interested group, or by sloganeering in political generalities."

The following are some silly consequences of placing anonymity for AIDS virus carriers above the wider public interest:

• As Dr. Lorraine Day, formerly chief of orthopedic surgery at the San Francisco General Hospital, told *60 Minutes*, "[Doctors] don't have the right to automatically test for AIDS, even though we have the right to test every patient for any other disease known to man, without a special consent. Why do I have to take care of a patient with a concealed weapon—AIDS— and not be allowed to know that the patient has a disease that can kill me, my nurses and my staff?"

14   A Media General-Associated Press poll, conducted May 1989, found that 72% of respondents felt that sexual partners of HIV-infected persons should be notified.
15   Strangely, some of the same gay activists who insist on anonymity for HIV-positive homosexuals are currently dragging other homosexuals "out of the closet," in a process called "outing."
16   See report by Dr. Richard E. Hoffman *et al.* of the Colorado Department of Health, *Western Journal of Medicine* 152:75, 1990.

•   In some states a physician risks a lawsuit if he alerts an HIV-positive person's sexual contacts against the patient's will (*Patient Care*, October 30, 1989).

•   Although it is documented that perforation of surgical gloves and blood-staining may occur in almost 50% of major operations,[17] surgeons are not allowed to routinely test for HIV status. The argument against testing in this situation, advanced usually by non-surgeons, is that maximum precautions should *always* be taken. This supposedly does away with the need for extra precautions in specific cases. Surgeons should be asking how they can comply with the most effective post exposure management—which, based on animal data, seems to be AZT started within one hour of HIV exposure[18]—when they don't know the HIV status, and it may take some time to find out.

•   There is no obligation on HIV-positive medical professionals to reveal their status to patients even though there may be a risk of AIDS-virus transmission in some circumstances.[19] A hospital in New Jersey is currently being sued for requiring a surgeon who carried the AIDS virus to get a patient consent form.

•   In most states, rape victims are not allowed to know their attackers' AIDS virus status. Furthermore, in most states convicted rapists cannot be compelled to undergo HIV testing.

Games With Blood Screening

Perhaps the most outrageous example of standing common sense on its head in the AIDS crisis was the gay activists' attempt to interfere with the introduction of blood-donor screening in 1983. This was before the identification of the AIDS virus, but after it had become clear that AIDS was being spread by blood transfusion and blood products. The CDC convened a meeting to discuss ways of preventing further spread of AIDS by this route. Clearly, high-risk persons—particularly homosexuals at that time—should have been asked not to donate blood (which homosexuals should not have been doing anyway, since it had been known from the early 1970s that hepatitis B was a homosexually transmitted blood-borne disease).

But incredibly, according to the report of the CDC meeting in the February 4, 1983, *Journal of the American Medical Association*, rep-

17   Writing in the *British Medical Journal* (295:392, 1987), Drs. Lafferty and Wyatt of the Brook General Hospital in London noted that "It is an everyday occurrence for surgeons to find at least one hand [after glove removal] stained with the patient's blood at the end of a major procedure. We were, however, surprised to find that the incidence is almost 50% and is not necessarily related to experience." While there is disagreement on the precise risk of AIDS to health-care workers, Columbia University public health specialist Vincent Covello gives a "worst case" estimate that over a working life 1 in 100 might become HIV infected, according to Craig Charney of the New York Hospital Workers Union (*In These Times*, January 24-30, 1990, p. 8).
18   See *Morbidity and Mortality Weekly Report*, January 26, 1990.
19   British surgeon Justin Cobb, in a humorous *British Medical Journal* (294:1668, 1987) paper "After Safe Sex, Safe Surgery?", advised (quite seriously), "I think we [surgeons] should all have mandatory annual blood tests for HIV state. . . . so that patients are not being operated on by the surgical equivalent of Typhoid Mary."

resentatives from the National Gay Task Force "called this 'scapegoating'"! Bruce Voeller of the NGTF claimed that excluding high-risk persons from donating blood would "stigmatize" homosexuals "at the time of a major civil rights movement." It was left to Dr. Louis Aledort, advisor to the National Hemophilia Foundation, to state the obvious: "They may want to protect their rights, but what about the hemophiliacs' right to life?"

To cater to the sensitivities of homosexuals, games with blood apparently still are going on in the Castro district of San Francisco, the area with the highest density of AIDS patients in the country, according to Dr. Lorraine Day. A blood bank still collects blood there so as not to offend gays, who believe their blood is just as safe as anyone else's. When Day objected, "They had all sorts of bad press about me. The Mayor came out against me. The University came out against me. The Centers for Disease Control advisor to the Mayor came out against me. All were calling me bigoted because I didn't want blood for my patients collected from the highest density AIDS district in the country" (*New Dimensions*, March 1990).

Federal Homophobia

A measure of the level of fear felt by officialdom in the face of AIDS activism is the unusual and uncharacteristic behavior of the Food and Drug Administration. The pharmaceutical industry newsletter *Scrip* recently reported on some of the "radical changes" brought about at the FDA as a result of the AIDS crisis.

According to the newsletter, Peter Barton Hutt, a former FDA chief counsel, claimed that as a result of the militancy of AIDS activists the agency has developed "a whole new series of rules that have never existed before, even for cancer patients." Hutt noted the contrast between AIDS patients being allowed to import any drug for their personal use (unless it raised a safety concern) with the former bitter fight by the FDA against the use of laetrile by cancer patients. He gave the example of the agency permitting AL-721 to be sold as a food when it was clearly being used as a drug (for AIDS treatment). He also noted that the FDA strangely had not taken action against the AIDS group which ran its own trial on the potential AIDS treatment tricosanthin (compound Q) without formal permission: "If this had been any other drug by any other group, there would have been criminal prosecution in six months" (*Scrip*, September 29, 1989, p. 19).

In fact, six months later the FDA authorized this group to conduct new trials with compound Q, putting the agency in the position of approving a study that was illegally conducted. Dr. Paul Meier, a University of Chicago statistician who often advises the agency, reportedly said: "My picture of all this is that the FDA is running scared" (*New York Times*, March 9, 1990).

ORIGINS AND FUTURE DIRECTIONS

The average American would be totally shocked if he or she really knew what certain influential leaders in academic sexology (who, by the way, have a powerful influence on the development of school sex education programs; see next chapter) saw as the desired future direction of the sexual revolution. However, as ten years of the AIDS epidemic have shown, public opinions on sexual matters can be shifted fairly quickly. To understand what might be ahead, it is necessary first to step back to the beginning, to the acknowledged greatest sex researcher of them all—Alfred C. Kinsey.

Evident throughout Kinsey's books is the view that sex is to be enjoyed as early in life as possible, more frequently, with a greater variety of partners of the same or opposite gender, and without the guilt of Judeo-Christian cultural restraints. There is no genuine science behind these views, just as there is no science behind Kinsey's lesser known but more dangerous claim that children can enjoy and benefit from sexual interaction with adults.

It is this last notion that looms sinisterly on the horizon of the future path of the sexual revolution, for it is a doctrine held closely but dearly by Kinsey's philosophical disciples, who today have some control over the future of sex education. In a 1977 *Forum* publication, *Variations*, following two letters extolling the joys of father-daughter incest, Kinsey co-author Wardell Pomeroy told readers that "incest can be a satisfying, non-threatening, and even an enriching emotional experience." Pomeroy was formerly academic dean of the Institute for the Advanced Study of Human Sexuality in California, one of the handful of institutions that grant advanced degrees in human sexuality to sex educators.

The sex establishment has a number of other figures with favorable attitudes toward incest. Several of them, such as John Money of Johns Hopkins and Floyd Martinson of Gustavus Adolphus College, are quoted in two revealing *Time* magazine articles featuring the "disturbing idea . . . gaining currency within the sex establishment [that] very young children should be allowed, and perhaps encouraged, to conduct a full sex life without interference from parents and the law" (*Time*, September 7, 1981 and April 14, 1980; see Appendix C). Similarly, Mary S. Calderone, co-founder of the Sex Information and Education Council of the United States (SIECUS), reportedly told the 1980 annual meeting of the Association of Planned Parenthood Physicians that providing today's society "very broadly and deeply with awareness of the vital importance of infant and childhood sexuality" is now the primary goal of SIECUS (*Ob.Gyn.News*, December 1, 1980, p. 10).

By 1983 Calderone was writing that the child's sexual capacities should "be developed in the same way as the child's inborn human capacity to talk or to walk, and that [the parents'] role should relate only to teaching the child the appropriateness of privacy, place, and person— in a word, socialization" (*SIECUS Report*, May-July 1983, p. 9).

What then lies ahead for sex education? Will the sex revolution receive a boost from the future advocacy in schools of the once-taboo notion of adult-child sex? Will this most unscientific of Kinsey's "research" findings be embraced as a valid concept to be discussed/taught in classrooms? The answer to the last question could be yes, unless the process is stopped, as is very possible, at the grass roots level. As revealed in the following chapter, sex education experts believe sex education programs of the future will tackle the subject of adult-child sex "with a diminished sense of guilt" as the artificial barriers between normal and abnormal begin to disappear.

Of course cross-generational sex could hardly be taught without some validation of pedophilia taking place. This would require pedophilia being viewed as an "orientation" rather than an abnormality. Far-fetched, you might think. But in 1988 in the publication *Behavior Today* (December 5, p. 5) it was reported that "a nationally recognized expert on sex offenders . . . stated that pedophilia . . . may be a sexual orientation rather than a sexual deviation. [This] raised the question as to whether pedophiles may have rights."

With views like the above on the back burner in academe, developments in the area of "AIDS education" in the lower grades have to be monitored with some concern. A former SIECUS executive director has noted that AIDS education provides a "time of rare opportunity" for educating the public about what sex education is *really* all about (*SIECUS Report*, January 1987). What exactly does this mean? Certainly the opportunity to teach young children how to have intercourse (vaginal and anal) and other sexual contacts in a way that minimizes the risk of HIV-virus infection is hardly likely to discourage early sexual activity any more than teaching kids about hangover prevention would discourage underage drinking.

"LIKE IT IS"

"Like it is" today is not how "like it is" was supposed to be in the promised brave new world of sexual "honesty" and "freedom." What we have now is a society of technological sophistication and ecological ignorance; the latter includes an unwillingness to recognize basic essential codes of human behavior. The sexual revolution is not the *fault* of youth; on the contrary, they are its victims. It is, according to Dr. Klein, the result of a society in which "we profess chastity as an ideal, but sex for profit and fun is flaunted everywhere. . . . We exhibit, stimulate and excite youth, and deny and criticize the response" (*Clinical Obstetrics and Gynecology* 21(4):1151, 1978). And full intellectual vindication of the response—called moral relativism—is, in any event, comfortingly available. This has been an era of "messages," and a hedonistic message has gotten through.

It is not just the fault of the profiteers, however. One of the aims of "progressive" sex educators has been to promote "sexual alternatives," sex without guilt, the pursuit of orgasm, and recreational sex. To that end, sex education in some schools employs as teaching aids what would have been called pornography a few years ago. Dr. Vernon Mark, a Harvard surgeon and author of the book *The Pied Pipers of Sex*, has accurately pointed out that this strategy of eliminating guilt has actually eliminated morality: "If you don't feel guilty about anything you have no morality" (*The Pied Pipers of Sex*, Haven Books, 1981).

Does the development of a sexual amorality in young people have consequences beyond venereal disease, single parenthood, inability to relate, insecurity and poverty? Common sense would dictate that it does. To say that it was not connected in some way to the type of event illustrated by the infamous "wilding" attack in New York's Central Park in 1989, for example, would be stupid. (Although it is noteworthy that in all the hand-wringing analysis that followed that tragedy the only "cause" that some commentators were prepared definitively to rule out was "moral relativism.")

Several destructive cycles are operative in society. The cycles of abused-child-to-child-abuser[20] and child-of-alcoholics-to-alcoholic are well known. To these can be added other cause-and-effect pathologies connected in some way to a breakdown in what used to be regarded as norms of male-female relating. There is a cycle involving promiscuity, teenage pregnancy, single parenthood and welfare dependency. There is the cycle of divorce, children of divorce, and more divorce. The relationship of premarital sex to extra-marital infidelity has already been mentioned. It appears there may even be a cycle of sex education leading to increased teenage sexual activity leading to the perceived need for more sex education. The commonly proposed solution for all of this is better access to contraceptives—a band-aid approach that is truly simplistic and naive when viewed in the context of the total social pathology involved.

It is to be hoped that the sex revolution will eventually come to be viewed as the drug revolution and that some kind of U-turn toward balance can be attempted. But that won't happen till society has reached a consensus that it is time to "bottom out." Progressively more shocking revelations are going to be required—like the fact, revealed in an April 1989 CBS *Face the Nation* broadcast by New York juvenile prosecutor Peter Reinharz, that 8- and 9-year-olds are now engaging in rape, sodomy and sexual assault of 3- and 4-year-olds. According to Reinharz, were it not for the preoccupation with the city's drug war, this would be his No. 1 concern.

The current concern of Hollywood with some aspects of ecology is quite heartening. If some of the same people could make the connection to the human end of the ecology spectrum, then perhaps something constructive could be done about the mass pollution of the young that has taken place these past 20 years or so by the selling of sexual narcissism. However, it may be easier to get aroused about toxins produced by others than by oneself. Interestingly, the new word "eco-porn" began to appear around the time of Earth Day, 1990. Perhaps the penny will drop eventually.

In 1985, CDC epidemiologist Dr. Donald Francis offered the opinion that "[AIDS] certainly will end the sexual revolution" (*Newsweek*, August 12, 1985). It hasn't, yet. And in the homosexual community, where the modal form of sexual behavior seems always to have been promiscuity, reports of behavior change in response to AIDS may be premature. According to *Newsweek* (March 12, 1990), a new

---

20 Some experts are attributing at least some of the recent upsurge in violent crime statistics to the emergence of growing numbers of abused children as violent criminals.

"pro-sex" movement is developing among younger gays tired of restraints on their night life and sexual freedom.

The 1967 *Newsweek* writers posed a key question in concluding their update on the "permissive society":

Whether the new freedom produces good or ill depends on man himself. "Is man essentially a hedonistic, pleasure-loving, self-indulgent type?" asks theologian Martin Marty. "Or is he essentially a purposeful, work-oriented, self-denying creature? We simply don't know."

Well, if the intervening years have taught us anything about the human condition, it is that purposefulness, hard work and the capacity for self-denial in the interests of others are not inborn. They come through training and the example of others.

In a society where there is no consensus on teaching the young behavioral codes and moral guidelines (and where efforts to this end are seen as odd—eg, the *New York Times* editorial "Quaint Counsel for Teenagers"), a self-indulgent, self-destructive culture will develop. And yet, paradoxically, there is evidence teenagers would welcome strong, consistent moral guidance to help them realize ideals of behavior which are placed nearly out of their reach in this society by almost every pressure they face.

In his article "Teenage Pregnancy in the United States" (*Family Planning Perspectives* 20:262, 1988), James Trussell, professor of economics and public affairs at Princeton University, writes of some insights on teenage sexuality based on research principally on black adolescent mothers:

First, there is a discrepancy between the values adolescents express and their actual behavior. Their "ideal" sexual code places emphasis on waiting until marriage to have sex and on the practical dangers of becoming pregnant. These values, however, must be "stretched" because of the dangers of everyday life.

As if to corroborate this, an abstinence-oriented, school/community-based sex education program in South Carolina has been shown effective in achieving a remarkable decline in pregnancies in comparison with a control population where there was an increase. Among the objectives of the program were the enhancement of self-esteem and alignment of personal values with those of family, church and community (*Journal of the American Medical Association* 257:3382, 1987).

Many voices are raised about the imperative to get back to teaching "values." New York Governor Mario Cuomo told columnists Rowland Evans and Robert Novak that drugs are not America's biggest problem, "I think the biggest problem is values." He also said, "We have to find a better word for it" (*Washington Post*, June 19, 1989). Of course, there are dissenting voices on values. A recent major report on the AIDS epidemic by the National Academy of Sciences was critical of government programs as "imposing values" and thereby making the programs less effective.

Finding a better word for values is not the only problem. As Irving Kristol, a senior fellow of the American Enterprise Institute, pointed out in a *Wall Street Journal* editorial-page piece a few years ago (September 15, 1987),

> One might think that knowing right from wrong is not so remarkable as to merit comment. But, in fact, there are two major institutions in our society where such knowledge is regarded with suspicion and distrust. The first consists of the media. . . . The other is our universities, which cheerfully allow that they are much too sophisticated to know right from wrong, and regard any claim to such knowledge with disdain.

Kristol went on to point out that great universities in the past have always taught some form of moral philosophy. It was usually—as in Adam Smith's case, a professor of moral philosophy—"an intellectual effort to justify, by philosophical analysis alone and without reference to divine revelation, the traditional tenets of our Judeo-Christian moral code." Today, however, it has become fashionable in academe to be "value-free" and, as Kristol says, "committed to radical, rationalist and supposedly scientific skepticism." This kind of thing let loose in the school system has the potential to "provoke severe moral disorientation among the young and immature." As will be seen in future chapters, a whole philosophy of sex education has been designed with that very intention.

If education in the art of healthy living is still possible, however, then finding a better word for "values" makes sense, as too often this expression is seen as the property of the religious Right. This is highly unfortunate because the concept belongs to all of society and is integral to its health and survival. It belongs to the Left and the Center also, to the non-religious as well as the religious. The stumbling block may be that the most successful social codes in history are those handed down in the Judeo-Christian heritage. But they are not unique to that heritage. As Will and Ariel Durant point out in their book *The Lessons of History* (Simon and Schuster, 1968), a larger knowledge of history stresses the universality of these codes and "concludes to their necessity." They are actually matters of health more than "morality," which is another way of saying that health and real morality are much the same thing.

Historian and anthropologist J.D. Unwin examined comprehensively the relationship between sexual mores and the future of societies. He concluded that no society or culture can prevent decline and eventual eclipse once it has abandoned itself to sexual license (*Sex and Culture*, Oxford University Press, 1934). Specifically, Unwin found that pre- and post-nuptial chastity were the greatest predictors of energy, productivity and cultural achievement. However, this situation was difficult to maintain—even before cable television and home videos.

CHAPTER FOUR

HETEROPHOBIA [1]

THE KINSEY AGENDA IN SEX EDUCATION

Edward W. Eichel

Chapter Overview

The previous chapter provided a glimpse of how former Kinsey coworkers and their academic disciples have begun to insinuate a theory of indiscriminate sexuality into sex education materials. This is a direct result of the original Kinsey child sex experiments—the "scientific" justification, in particular, derives from that research foundation.

In this chapter it will become clear that a sex education "establishment" in the United States is well on the way to introducing fullblown Kinseyan philosophy into the nation's schools, via control of sex education programming. (The distillate of Kinsey philosophy—as noted earlier—is that every type of sexual activity is natural and thus normal, and should begin as early in life as possible.)

How has this control been achieved? Quite simply, by gaining the power to set the accreditation guidelines for the only formal university-based degree programs for human sexuality educators. In other words, many, if not most, of today's professional sex educators are schooled and graduated in Kinsey's philosophy. Thus, schoolchildren are now being taught the "Kinsey Scale," that heterosexuality is only one "option"; and there is the underlying assumption—at the highest echelon

---

1   "Heterophobia" is a term coined here to refer to those who have an irrational fear of, and hostility toward, heterosexuality. Heterophobia is often evidenced by gay activists, radical feminists and pedophiles in active campaigning against societal norms of heterosexual relating, the institution of marriage and the basic structure of the nuclear family. This new word counters the "gayspeak" expression *homophobia*, which was originally coined to imply an irrational fear of homosexuality and which has come to be used commonly as a smear term to intimidate those who oppose the agendas of homosexual activists.

of sex educators—that children are sexual and should be sexually active.

This is the implementation of what former Kinsey coworker Wardell Pomeroy seemingly innocuously called Kinsey's "grand scheme." Its development has been greatly accelerated by the AIDS epidemic and the resulting rush to educate children, even at the lowest grade levels, in "the facts" of human sexuality—a perfect situation for widespread dissemination of the original Kinsey philosophy.

The American Psychiatric Association's decision to remove homosexuality from its Diagnostic Manual is also reviewed. This was a major step forward for the Kinsey Agenda in general.

Kinsey's research was carried out on a non-representative group of Americans—including disproportionately large numbers of sex offenders, prostitutes, prison inmates and exhibitionists—and involved illegal sex experimentation upon several hundred children, masturbated to orgasm by "trained" pederasts. It has become the "scientific" basis for *the* official doctrine of sex education in the United States. Shocking? Yes. True? Demonstrably. Details of this "research" have been dealt with earlier.

THE KINSEY PHILOSOPHY OF SEXUALITY

Those who have read through the previous chapters will be somewhat familiar with Kinsey's sexual philosophy. But it is worth reviewing at this point.

Kinsey believed that all sexual activity is natural. This is what led him to say in his Female Report, "It is . . . difficult to explain why each and every individual is not involved in every type of sexual activity" (Female Report, p. 451). Actually, Kinsey provided the explanation himself: children were not actively sexual and adults tended to be heterosexual only because "cultural restraints" and "societal inhibitions" decrease their natural sexual proclivities and condition them toward an "acceptable" form of sexuality (heterosexuality). At the end of his Male Report, Kinsey pronounced the following basic conclusion about all types of sexual activity—including heterosexual intercourse, homosexual contacts and animal contacts:

> [They] may *seem* to fall into categories that are as far apart as right and wrong, licit and illicit, normal and abnormal, acceptable and unacceptable in our social organization. In actuality, they all *prove* to originate in the relatively simple mechanisms which provide for erotic response when there are sufficient physical or psychic stimuli [Male Report, p. 678; emphasis added].

He added:

> But the scientific data which are accumulating make it appear that, if circumstances had been propitious, most individuals might have become conditioned in any direction, even into activities which they now consider quite unacceptable [*ibid.*].

As noted previously, it follows from this ideology that Kinsey viewed bisexuality as normal (indeed superior) in uninhibited people[2] and considered cross-generational sex necessary for full development of sexuality. The Kinsey Reports themselves, it appears, were attempts to be part of the "scientific data" that would obsolete the cultural restraints and inhibitions that conditioned society to apply terms such as "acceptable" and "unacceptable" (moral and immoral) to types of human sexual behavior. In this respect, they were a basis for a new theory of sexuality—an ideology of indiscriminate sex.

SEX EDUCATION PHILOSOPHY

In an article titled "Truth in Sex Ed" (*National Review*, July 3, 1987), former Secretary of Education William Bennett postulated that the education provided in public schools could indeed be an improvement over the sex education received in the street and on television. Bennett described sex as "inextricably connected to the psyche, to the soul, to personality at its deepest levels," emphasizing that sexual intimacy "affects feelings, attitudes, one's self-image, one's image of another." He concluded that "Sex involves men and women in all their complexity" and "may be among the most value-loaded of human activities." From this perspective, if sex education could help to prepare children for the challenge of committed relationships in adult life, it would indeed render a profound human service.

However, there is strong evidence that the basic ideology of sex education has been dominated by a handful of individuals who have the goal of programming young minds by teaching children beliefs and values far different than their parents ever envisioned.

At the present time, the future direction of sex education in the United States is in some doubt. The teachers who teach tomorrow's teachers—and who have recently drawn up the guidelines for accreditation of degree programs for sex educators—are largely committed to a Kinseyan view of sex. Is this important? It is when the sexual tenets of Alfred Kinsey are fully understood and when it is realized that the Kinsey view of "normal" human sexuality is based on "research" on a population sample wholly non-representative of society. Unethical experimentation on infants and children also has been a basis for reaching profound conclusions on human sexual behavior (chapters 1 and 2).

The Kinsey childhood sexuality research may be the most egregious example in this century of an attempt to gather scientific information from the misuse of human research subjects. Thus, in the current anxiety to develop sex education programs appropriate to the AIDS era, it should be a matter of serious concern that Kinsey's research and Kinsey's concept of human sexuality and behavior norms are the guiding principles of leaders in sex education and the foundation on which many sex education programs are based.

---

2   See also Kinsey, Pomeroy, Martin and Gebhard, in Hoch and Zubin: *Psychosexual Development in Health and Disease*, Grune & Stratton, 1949, pp. 24-27.

ACCREDITATION   FOR   HUMAN   SEXUALITY
PROGRAMS

Standardization of the Kinsey Ideology

In 1983 the Society for the Scientific Study of Sex (SSSS, or "Quad S") announced the forming of a committee that had been "charged with developing guidelines for an accrediting body for university-based degree programs in human sexuality."[3] This society—one of the oldest sexological organizations in the U.S.—counts among its members most of the nation's leading academic sexologists, including Kinsey co-authors Wardell Pomeroy and Paul Gebhard. Heavily represented on its original accreditation committee were academicians from institutions that developed the only three human sexuality programs designed to educate sex educators. All three programs (New York University, University of Pennsylvania and the Institute for the Advanced Study of Human Sexuality [California]),[4] and members of the accreditation committee mentioned below, have been committed to the homosexual-oriented Kinsey-school ideology.

The SSSS committee originally included Deryck Calderwood from New York University, Kenneth D. George (an avowed homosexual[5]) from the University of Pennsylvania, and Wardell Pomeroy, then Dean of the Institute for the Advanced Study of Human Sexuality in San Francisco. Another committee member was Paul Gebhard, who in 1982 retired from his post as director of the Kinsey Institute for Research in Sex, Gender and Reproduction (current name).

What were the ideologic goals of the SSSS accreditation body? A 1978 presentation by committee member Wardell Pomeroy to the *Third International Congress of Medical Sexology* in Rome may help to answer this question.[6] Pomeroy noted progress, though slow, in the evolution of what the public considered to be "normal" human sexuality. The greatest development had been the recognition of homosexuality as a "variation" rather than a sickness. This allowed "[m]ore attention [to be] given now to bisexuality, which may ease the confrontation between good and bad, healthy and unhealthy."

According to Pomeroy, the late 1960s and '70s saw a flood of "serious" books about sex (such as *The Hite Report*) and an acceptance of "sexual science." These two developments brought "implicit recommendations about ideal sexuality: both male and female are now expected to be sensuous, sexually fantasizing, always ready-to-do-it no matter what the outlet or choice of partners." The "emphasis on abnormality and illness" was "gone."

---

3   Announcement in *The Society Newsletter* (SSSS), May 1984, under the caption "National Committees 1983-84." Names of committee members listed. Accreditation process commenced in 1986.

4   In Canada, the University of Montreal offers a degree in sexuality eduction.

5   "How to Successfully Treat Male Couples." An interview with Kenneth D. George in *Sexuality Today*, November 4, 1985, p. 4.

6   Pomeroy's presentation is reproduced in Forleo and Pasini (eds.), *Medical Sexology*, PSG Publishing Co., 1980, pp. 72-78.

Moving on from this point, Pomeroy saw a new "exciting concept" emerging—a "fresher way of viewing our sexuality"—the idea that "to broaden our concept of what *is* sexuality" we may consider that "there is not only one way to *be* in sex but many, and that how we are is not so much a product of how we are born but rather how we are raised and oriented socially and taught to perceive psychologically and experientially." An important belief, held by Kinsey and most sexologists, is stated here: how we *are* sexually depends to some extent on what we are *taught*. Pomeroy also noted that the "idea of *childhood* sexuality" is one "that [has] forever affected our conception of human sexual development and thoughts about sex education."

One member of the original SSSS accreditation committee was Vern L. Bullough, a historian of the gay movement. In the *Chronicle of Higher Education* (Vol. XXXIV, November 18, 1987), Dr. Bullough declared: "The big issue in the field now is how people become sexual," and he added, "maybe we're coming at it from the wrong direction. We've long asked the question, 'Why are some people homosexual?' when we should actually be asking, 'Why are people heterosexual?'"

Dr. Bullough's radical approach to sexuality has an even wider dimension. He provided a foreword for Dutch pedophile Edward Brongersma's book *Loving Boys (Volume I): A Multidisciplinary Study of Sexual Relations Between Adult and Minor Males* (Global Academic Publishers, 1986), stressing the viewpoint that pedophilia is "a subject that too often has been ignored entirely or been subject to hysterical statements" (pp. 10-11). The issues raised by Bullough are relevant to a Kinseyan agenda that has been promoted in sex education, and their true meaning will become increasingly clear in this chapter.

Bullough reportedly has advocated that "activism" should play a role in what is believed (and presumably taught) about sexuality. At an international conference on homosexuality held in The Netherlands in 1987, he stressed that "Gay people have to set the terms of research into homosexuality." He elaborated, "Politics and science go hand in hand. In the end it is Gay activism which determines what researchers say about Gay people" (Mark Schoofs, "International Forum Debates Treatment of Homosexuality," *Washington Blade*, December 1987, p. 19). As in science, so in education.

Many educators have actually been unaware of the subtle—sometimes not-so-subtle—indoctrination that may have affected their own thinking. They have been inundated in their training with terms such as "diversity" and "pluralistic society," but would probably be surprised to learn the scope of the agenda that might be implicit in those words.

A constant struggle now is being waged by community school boards and religious organizations to prevent basic and traditional concepts of marriage, family, and humanistic values from being eliminated from sex education programming in public schools. From this standpoint, it is important to be mindful that parents have been supportive of sex education because of the fearful consequences of unintended pregnancies and sexually transmitted diseases upon the lives of children.

Parents never gave educators license to downplay or eliminate heterosexual norms. But that kind of indoctrination now is occurring in sex education programming, supposedly with the intent of dispelling "homophobia."

The term *homophobia* may be more than a little self-serving. In the article "Male Homophobia" (*Journal of Social Issues*, vol. 34(1), 1978), authors Stephen F. Morin and Ellen M. Garfinkle view it as an irrational and pathologic hostility toward homosexuals by heterosexual men. But the authors reveal an aggressive gay agenda. In their treatise they propose that the "experiences of gay men [be] used as a basis to suggest possible creative role violation for all men."

In a second article, "The Gay Movement and the Rights of Children" (*Journal of Social Issues*, vol. 34(2), 1978), Morin and Stephen J. Schultz get more explicit about their agenda and demands. They submit that "social systems must support and facilitate the development of a gay identity and life style, by informing children about the existence of gay-identified adults and their life styles, by providing positive gay role models, and by allowing the opportunity for exploring gay feelings and life styles."[7]

Under the guise of programming focused on the protection of homosexual *rights*, homosexual "options" and lifestyles are being recommended to heterosexual children in schools. This is a breach of the confidence that parents place in educators.

THE SIECUS PRINCIPLES FOR SEX EDUCATION

A Declaration of Abnormality?

It is possible to deduce from a host of current medico-social problems such as venereal disease, teenage pregnancy, child sex abuse, AIDS, divorce, childhood suicide, etc., that society is experiencing a crisis in human values (see previous chapter). It is becoming clear that "errors" in sex research and misconceptions about sexuality have contributed to the current problems. Hopefully, it also will become clear that the need for accurate sex education is coupled with the need to put facts about physical function within the context of societal values.

One organization in the vanguard of human sexuality education, whose leaders have their own ideas of what healthy societal values should be, is SIECUS (the Sex Information and Education Council of the United States).

---

7   Gay activist groups, like the Gay Media Task Force, similarly have tried to make sure (successfully, for the most part) that homosexuality is portrayed only in a "positive" way in movies and television. Prohibitions apparently include representations of homosexuals as promiscuous or anything other than regular, "mainstream" people (see *Target: Prime Time*, by Kathryn C. Montgomery, Oxford University Press, 1989). Mistakes can require "re-education," CBS News has learned: In the wake of the Andy Rooney fiasco, the news division president reportedly met with members of the Gay & Lesbian Alliance Against Defamation (GLAAD) "and agreed to a program of internal education about homosexuality at CBS News" (*TV Guide*, February 17, 1990).

According to Mary Breasted in her book *Oh! Sex Education* (Praeger, 1970), SIECUS, established in 1964, is "a voluntary health organization with a rather broad and ambitious purpose—to establish 'sexual sanity' in America" (p. 11). SIECUS is described in its own literature as "the *only* organization in the United States that acts as an advocate for human sexuality and provides information and education in sexual matters through a clearing house and resource center" (emphasis in original).

SIECUS has had a fruitful relationship with New York University, as will be seen. Since 1978 the organization has been affiliated with NYU's Department of Health Education and has worked closely with its graduate program in human sexuality—one of only three in the country, as mentioned earlier. This graduate program has sponsored human sexuality symposia at which well-known European pedophiles have been among the featured speakers.

SIECUS' idea of current needs in sex education has led to the basic conflict that is coming to a boil in the field today. Primarily this conflict concerns opposing views about the nature of human sexuality in a civilized society and whether traditional Judeo-Christian beliefs about sexuality (considered a religious and cultural artifact by many sexologists) are repressive and unhealthy.

The opposing viewpoints and their implication for values and sexual behavior are represented in two conflicting statements of purpose. *The Interfaith Statement on Sex Education by the United States Catholic Conference, National Council of Churches, and Synagogue Council of America,*[8] a document drafted by the Interfaith Commission on Marriage and Family Life, dated June 8, 1968, specifies that sex educators "should teach that sexual intercourse within marriage offers the greatest possibility for personal fulfillment and social growth."

In contrast, a document titled *SIECUS/NYU Principles Basic to Education for Sexuality*, published in the January 1980 *SIECUS Report*, advocates "acceptance of the wide range of possible expressions of sexuality." This statement is consistent with the document's claim that "the majority of individuals have some elements of both homosexuality and heterosexuality in their makeup that may or may not be expressed by the individual throughout his or her life." The document was drafted "first, to provide a position base broad enough to be acceptable to health workers everywhere, and second, to enlist official support for the document by organizations in the health field throughout the United States and elsewhere in the world."

Seen as representative of two opposing ideological directions, the *Interfaith Commission Statement* and the *SIECUS/NYU Principles* provide some insight into the politics of the sex education field. The underlying issues are: Is *heterosexuality* the basic scheme of sexual

8   *The Interfaith Statement on Sex Education*, drafted by the Interfaith Commission on Marriage and Family Life. Approved June 8, 1968, by the National Council of Churches, The Synagogue Council of America, and the United States Catholic Conference. Cited in *Family Living Including Sex Education, Curriculum Guide of the New York City Board of Education*, 1985.

gender, and is sexual intercourse between a man and woman the natural and most complete form of sexual expression? Or, should *bisexuality* be considered a more advanced state of human sexual development— as implied in the Kinsey research—because it includes homosexual erotic behaviors?

In view of the above disagreement about the nature and course of human sexuality, it is necessary to bring up a matter that should be of concern to the public. Has there been a hidden agenda in sex education? Are some sex educators promoting one view at the expense of the other? Are they proselytizing against heterosexuality, in the name of dispelling "homophobia," and—wittingly or unwittingly—encouraging homosexual experimentation? Is the compromise of the heterosexual criterion of normality the beginning of a domino effect on human values?

THE KINSEY LEGACY

Programming Sexual Orientation

Sexologists have long criticized religious moralizing, calling it repressive and saying that it inhibits the natural expression of sexuality—even within the bond of marriage. There has been, however, too little public awareness of abuses and coercive practices within the academic community in relation to sex education. A reverse moralizing has begun under which children are indoctrinated with a philosophy of sexuality totally foreign to mainstream society. Of particular concern is the attempt to teach children "scientific" "facts" (as in Kinsey usage) about sexuality that contradict traditional values, but which have not— in actuality—been validated by genuine scientific research.

Numerous texts and learning materials substantiate this allegation. An example is the publication *What's Happening* (produced by the Emory University Family Planning Program), which was distributed at a National Boys Club of America conference in Washington, D.C., in 1984, for boys 14 to 18 years of age. It states: *"Experts* do agree . . . that homosexuality and heterosexuality are not 'either/or' choices. It is a matter of degree. *Many of us*, when you stop to think about it, are *'bisexual'*—we find people of both sexes attractive." It continues: "Attraction to both sexes seems natural. But as we grow up, we are *taught* that we are supposed to be turned on only by the opposite sex" (emphasis added).[9]

"About Your Sexuality"

Another example of programming that introduces young people to orientations other than heterosexuality is the instruction kit *About Your Sexuality*,[10] which includes filmstrips that depict explicitly erotic acts between homosexuals and between lesbians. The material is directed toward teens and preteens, an age when children are inexperienced and suggestible.

9   "Homosexuality . . . Gay or Straight." In: *What's Happening*, a publication of Emory University Family Planning Program, Atlanta, Georgia 1979, p. 42.

10   Deryck Calderwood's *About Your Sexuality* (1983 revised edition); instruction program kit created under the auspices of the Unitarian Universalist Association, Boston.

The late Professor Deryck Calderwood of New York University, who developed the program under the auspices of the Unitarian Universalist Association, stated his rationale for the revised 1983 edition: "There has . . . been a change in the way 'Love Making' is approached." He elaborated: "In the present version all lovemaking is placed in one unit." (Previously there were separate units on heterosexuality and homosexuality.) "Now, however, the material focuses on the human experience of making love first, and looks at the choice of partner as a secondary one."[11]

Calderwood stated that the revision of his instruction kit "demonstrates the spirit of acceptance that we wished to present right from the start" and fulfills the "underlying philosophy of the program" because it is "more strongly aligned against homophobia and more supportive of the ability of young people to make well informed decisions about their . . . sexual relationships" (Preface to *About Your Sexuality*, 1983).

Educating the Educators

SIECUS, and individuals associated with it, have been pivotal in charting a course for the future of sex education and also in determining how the sex educators of tomorrow are themselves educated today. Under the SIECUS banner, sex education has been linked to a gay agenda.

SIECUS founder Dr. Mary S. Calderone, formerly medical director for the Planned Parenthood Federation of America, has been called "The High Priestess of sex education." In recent years, she has been stressing the need for teaching about childhood sexuality. Her view on the importance of this need apparently is shared by her colleague and SIECUS co-founder Dr. Lester Kirkendall, an emeritus professor in the Department of Family Life at Oregon State University, who has been described (by a SIECUS publication) as a "pioneer not only in SIECUS but in the entire field of human sexuality concerns" and as one who helped set the stage "in the early and middle years of this century for the expansion of the sexuality frontier . . . " (*SIECUS Report*, March 1984, p. 1).

Just where Kirkendall would locate the boundaries of the new frontier was not made clear in the 1984 *SIECUS Report* article, where he said his desire was to help in "stabilizing marriage and the family" (*ibid.,* p. 3). However, Kirkendall is on record one year later as wanting to see cross-generational sex as a legitimate topic of discussion in the classroom (see below).

Dr. Kirkendall was the academic mentor of another "outstanding educator in the field of sex education," Deryck Calderwood of *About Your Sexuality* fame. Calderwood, a former board member of the Society for the Scientific Study of Sex and chairperson of the SIECUS board, conducted an innovative workshop at a New York University

11   "Explicit Sexual Materials—Useful Tool for Education of Teenagers." An interview with Deryck Calderwood in *Sexuality Today*, October 1, 1984.

international seminar in Holland (attended by E. Eichel), where the students explored each other's genitals (see below).

The connection between another famous sex educator, Kinsey co-author Wardell Pomeroy (a founding board member of SIECUS), and Calderone, Kirkendall and Calderwood is indicative of the connection between the Kinsey Institute, SIECUS and the Human Sexuality Program at New York University. The Kinsey Institute provided the research base for the Kinsey agenda; SIECUS was to become the primary database for the area of sexuality education (see below); and New York University educated the educators to teach the Kinsey model of sexuality.

Shortly after founding SIECUS in 1964, Drs. Calderone and Kirkendall became closely associated with Kirkendall's former student Deryck Calderwood in the implementation of SIECUS objectives. *Sex* education became "sexuality" education. There was a significant shift of focus "beyond" traditional heterosexual concerns, such as "body-part identification, health and function, and the relationships within the nuclear family structure," to education focused on the Kinsey ideology of sexual "orientation" (Ina A. Luadtke, "Practical Application of the SIECUS/Uppsala Basic Principles," *SIECUS Report*, January 1980, p. 3).

The 1982 SIECUS publication *Winning the Battle for Sex Education*, by Irving Dickman, denied the charge that there was a "sex education plot" or "a SIECUS curriculum," but specified that for a period they did have a *consultant* on staff "who worked with committees wishing to develop sex education programs" (p. 29). Dickman failed to point out, however, that this consultant was none other than Deryck Calderwood, one of the core group of individuals in SIECUS who can be clearly identified as having a gay-oriented, Kinseyan view of human sexuality.

Reviewing his professional development as a sexologist at a conference in 1983, Professor Calderwood recounted that he began his career as the first male staff member at SIECUS, and thanked those who made his progress in the field "tremendously easy," namely, others of the SIECUS core group—Mary Calderone, Lester Kirkendall and Wardell Pomeroy.[12]

When New York University instituted a sex education fellowship program for elementary school teachers back in 1968, it was Professor Calderwood who "educated the educators."[13] The graduate student newspaper relates, "in 1970 the New York State Education Department approved the curriculum for a Marriage, Family Life, and Sex Education Program within the Department of Health Education at New York

12   "An Assemblage of Personal Histories: The Pentimento of a Sexologist." Proceedings from presentation at Eastern Regional Conference of the Society for the Scientific Study of Sex, *Sexology: Retrospective and Prospective,* Philadelphia, April 17, 1983. Audio and video recordings.

13   See Calderwood D: "Educating the Educators." In Lorna Brown (ed.); *Sex Education in the Eighties,* Plenum, 1981, pp. 191-201.

University, making it the first such specialization program in the nation—and possibly the world."[14]

Calderwood developed the program at New York University with a concentration upon the issue of *homophobia*, emphasizing the societal biases against homosexuality. This may have created an effective facade for an agenda and goals that are inconsistent with the implied objectives of a "Marriage and Family Life" program. The learning strategies employed in the Calderwood program have included a battery of personal sex history questionnaires and a nude body workshop.[15] The questionnaires probe explicit details of the student's past sexual experiences. In the workshop, students of the same gender have been assigned tasks that include the physical exploration of each other's genitals. Bisexuality has been presented as an unbiased sexual orientation. Considering the content of Calderwood's course, a legitimate concern would appear to be the incursion of *heterophobia*—a campaign against heterosexuality—into sex education.

After Calderone retired from SIECUS in 1982, she joined Calderwood as an adjunct professor in his Human Sexuality Program at New York University. The SIECUS offices have since moved to NYU. At a memorial service for Calderwood in August of 1986, a former executive director of SIECUS related that after finishing his term as SIECUS chairman in 1984, Calderwood (in failing health) headed the Nominating and Personnel Committees to "bring in new people" to carry on in the organization in ways that were "specifically significant."[16]

Another institution involved in the task of educating tomorrow's sex educators is the University of Pennsylvania, where Professor Kenneth George, a homosexual, heads the Human Sexuality Education Program. In a *SIECUS Report* article, "Homophobia: Let's Deal With It In Our Classes!" George listed a series of questions which he has posed to his heterosexual students:

> How would you feel if you learned your best friend is gay? How would you feel if you were gay? How did you feel when you *first* had a same-sex experience? [*SIECUS Report*, July 1978, pp. 6, 9; emphasis added].

Professor George's interviewing technique is obviously derived from the original Kinsey model. The principle of the method was termed by Kinsey, "placing the burden of denial on the subject." Kinsey explained the strategy behind the technique: "The interviewer should not make it easy for a subject to deny his participation in any form of sexual activity. . . . We always assume that everyone has engaged in every type of activity. Consequently we always begin by asking when they first engaged in such activity" (Male Report, p. 53).

14   "Human Sexuality Program: Not Just for Educators," *Grad Tidings*, New York University Graduate Students Organization newsletter, Spring 1984.

15   Observations based on the experience of Edward Eichel in the NYU Human Sexuality Program druing a summer colloquium in Maastricht, The Netherlands, 1983 (see also chapter 5).

16   "Deryck and SIECUS." Eulogy by Ann Welbourne-Moglia, executive director of SIECUS, at Judson Memorial Church, New York City, September 26, 1986.

In the case of Kinsey's research, this technique had the intent of increasing the numbers of people reporting homosexual experiences. In the classroom setting it will encourage heterosexual students to think that there are homosexual elements in their own sexuality, a seeming confirmation of Kinsey's sexual continuum theory.

Referring to the Kinsey spectrum ranging from exclusive heterosexuality to exclusive homosexuality, George claimed in his *SIECUS Report* article that "Significantly, in sexually nonrepressive societies only one or two percent fall at either extreme of the continuum" (p. 6). What he is saying is that, in an uninhibited society, only 1% or 2% of the population would not be having homosexual relationships.

THE SIECUS/NYU PROGRAMMING

From Bisexuality to Pedophilia

SIECUS founder Mary Calderone has helped to define "what sex education is really all about" from SIECUS' point of view. According to a 1980 report in a medical newspaper (*Ob.Gyn.News*, December 1, 1980, p. 10), Dr. Calderone pronounced at the annual meeting of the Association of Planned Parenthood Physicians that "awareness of the vital importance of infant and childhood sexuality" is now the primary goal of SIECUS.

Dr. Calderone's personal viewpoint about the nature of child sexuality was somewhat clarified in a dispute with sociologist John H. Gagnon at an SSSS conference in 1981. Dr. Gagnon was reluctant to define children as "sexual," stressing that "young children do not conceptualize a set of experiences, attitudes, and motives which adults might label as sexual." In contrast, Dr. Calderone asserted that children are sexual from birth, basing her definition of "sexual" upon the lowest possible denominator of *physical* response—children "can feel sensation from touching and from genital stimulation from infancy on."[17] (Calderone's observation begs an absurd question. Since she has support from Kinsey's research for saying that infants and children are capable of sexual pleasure, does the fact that a baby can feel sensation when its genitals are touched implicate the infant as the "partner" in a sex act?)

By 1983 Mary Calderone was writing that the child's sexual capacities should "be developed in the same way as the child's inborn human capacity to talk or to walk, and that *[the parents'] role should relate only to teaching the child the appropriateness of privacy, place, and person—in a word socialization"* (*SIECUS Report*, May-July 1983, p. 9; emphasis added). What Calderone appears to be saying is that children should be sexually active and parents should help them.

In her *SIECUS Report* article "Parents and the Sexuality of Their Children in the 'Year of the Child'" (November 1979), Dr. Calderone lifted the veil a little on what she is trying to insinuate about childhood

---

17   Elizabeth Rice Allgeier, "Children's Interpretations of Sexuality," *SIECUS Report*, May-July 1982, p. 8. Comments by Calderone and Gagnon are paraphrased by Allgeier, who is recounting a discussion at an SSSS meeting, November 1981.

sexuality. (It should be noted that sexologists who believe in the benefits to young children of early sexual activity always leave themselves wriggle room. They never want to appear to be advocating what they are presenting evidence for.) She pointed out that parents were wrong in thinking that puberty signaled the onset of sexual feelings and responsiveness. These have been present since before birth, and parents should be teaching young children all the facts about their capacity for sexual pleasure and response. How this capacity should be used is conspicuously not addressed. The first task is to educate parents that the capacity exists.

Calderone likened this task to the spreading of a "new religion":

> Every new religion, every new political doctrine has had first to make its adults convert in order to create a small nuclear culture within whose guiding walls its children will flourish [*SIECUS Report*, November 1979, p. 6].

The arrival of mandated sex education for young children—lauded by SIECUS—is of concern in relation to a heavy pedophile participation and advocacy in SIECUS-affiliated NYU training programs for educators and health professionals (see below). Fears of a pedophile agenda are further aroused by Mary Calderone's use of a new "scientific" prop—an ultrasound picture of penile erection in a 29-week-old fetus. First shown at the Sixth World Congress of Sexology, Washington, D.C., May 1983, this finding is being touted as further evidence of child sexuality[18]—and will probably be used as support material for the proposition that it makes sense for young children to be sexually active.

In a 1985 "Quad S" panel discussion on the topic of child sexual abuse, it is notable that Mary Calderone interjected at one point: "I . . . have a question that is . . . almost the reverse of what we've been talking about. What do we know about situations in which young children and older people, stronger people, have had a sexual relationship of one kind or another that has been pleasant, and the child feels good about it because it's warm and *seductive* [referring to the adult seducing the child], and tender?" (emphasis added). Calderone pressed her case with a note of pathos: "If the child really enjoys this, it may be the only time the child ever gets a loving touch."[19]

SIECUS' pedophile sympathies were evident 20 years ago in the 1970 SIECUS Study Guide publication (No. 11) *Sexual Encounters Between Adults and Children*. Here, authors John Gagnon and William Simon describe the results of sexual contacts between adults and children in language that seems to have come straight out of Kinsey:

> All individuals involved in the drama of [adult-child sexual contact] can be scarred by it, but except in rare instances where violence is

18   Mary S. Calderone, "Fetal Erection and Its Message to Us," *SIECUS Report*, May-July 1983, pp. 9-10. This is becoming a common, naive misinterpretation by sexologists of a normal reflexive and vascular reaction.

19   Mary S. Calderone on panel, "Childhood, the First Season: Nurturing Sexual Awakening—A Panel Discussion of Masturbation, Sex Play, Sexual Abuse, Nudity and Body Image Issues." SSSS Eastern Region Conference, *The Seasons of Sexology: Cycles of Time*, April 20, 1985.

involved, the scarring is more likely to come from various adult reactions to the event itself; these usually are the result of unresolved sexual conflicts and account for the reaction of parent and police . . . (p. 23).

Calderone's awe of the "sexuality" of the fetus is also reminiscent of Kinsey; in this case his enthusiasm about the erectile responses of infants in his illegal child sex experiments—and his defense of pedophilia (Male Report, pp. 177, 178, 50l). The connection between Kinsey and Calderone must be taken literally. Dr. Calderone several years ago described the plan for a division of labor between SIECUS and the Kinsey Institute in which SIECUS was designated to have taken on the role of educational organ for the Kinsey philosophy:

> Few people realize that the great library collection of what is now known as the Kinsey Institute in Bloomington, Indiana, was formed very specifically with one major field omitted: sex education. This was because it seemed appropriate, not only to the Institute but to its major funding source, the National Institute of Mental Health, to leave this area for SIECUS to fill. Thus we applied and were approved for a highly important grant from the National Institute for Mental Health[20] that was designed to implement a planned role for SIECUS— to become the primary data base for the area of education for sexuality [*SIECUS Report*, May-July 1982, p. 6].

Calderone's role in advancing a Kinseyesque vision of sexuality has been profound. Like Kinsey, she has assumed a messianic posture. In her 20-year-old article "Sex Education and the Roles of School and Church," in *The Annals of the American Academy of Political and Social Sciences* (Vol. 376 [March 1968], pp. 53-60), Calderone expressed concern that sex education has not equipped society to progress sexually at the same rate it has advanced technologically. She lamented, "man himself is not changing as fast as are his institutions and his world, and one is left to speculate about the obsolescence of man in relation to the technology that he himself has developed" (p. 57).

Calderone also asked, "If man as he is [is] obsolescent, then *what kind do we want to produce* in his place and *how do we design the production line*? In essence, that is the real question facing those who are concerned with sex education—what is it, how to do it, who does it" (p. 57; emphasis added). As far as Calderone and an academic elite are concerned, how sex education should be redesigned to reprogram society sexually has become quite clear. The public at large was not consulted. When they find out what's been going on (and what some of the future plans are—see below), they'll likely have something to say.

---

20   Because of insufficient funds the NIMH reportedly did not implement the funding for SIECUS. However, it is evident—for example, in the *SIECUS Principles Basic to Education for Human Sexuality*—that SIECUS has been an educational organ for the Kinsey philosophy and ideologic goals. SIECUS was formally affiliated with New York University in 1978.

FUTURE DIRECTIONS IN SEX EDUCATION

What then is on the sex education horizon? With the credentialling of sex educators in the control of academics who largely espouse Kinsey's philosophy of sexuality, what kind of developments in the teaching of human sexuality can be expected in the years ahead?

In their article "Sex Education in the Future," in the *Journal of Sex Education and Therapy* (Spring/Summer 1985), Lester Kirkendall and Dr. Roger Libby (of the University of Massachusetts and founding editor of the journal *Alternative Lifestyles*) predict that sex education programs of the future "will probe sexual expression . . . with same-sex [partners]" and "even across . . . generational lines." They proclaim that with "a diminished sense of guilt . . . these patterns will become legitimate" and "[t]he emphasis on . . . normality and abnormality will be much diminished with these future trends."

If the protective bond that exists between parent and child could be broken down, the boundless vision of changing sexuality presented by Kirkendall and Libby indeed might be more likely to become a reality. Although Kirkendall and Libby imply that the "future trends" which they describe are a natural development, it appears that little has been left to chance. There is evidence of a tactical focus on young people and an attempt to *direct* their sexual choices independently of parental influence and societal norms.

The above-stated scheme is consistent with the North American Man/Boy Love Association (NAMBLA) document *Resolution on the Liberation of Children and Youth*, which advocates that children "must have the unhindered right to have sex with members of any age of the same or opposite sex . . . ."[21] In pursuing this agenda, the pedophile movement has attempted to capitalize upon the period of parental conflict that inevitably occurs as youths enter the difficult stage of their adolescent development.

As reportedly proclaimed by a founder of NAMBLA, David Thorstad, "Man-boy love relationships are . . . a happy feature of the rebellion of youth, and of its irrepressible search for self-discovery. . . . [M]ost of us, *given the opportunity and the assurance of safety*, would no doubt choose to share our sexuality with someone under the age of consent" (emphasis added).[22]

Such views are finding currency outside what would formerly have been considered the looney confines of organizations such as NAMBLA. According to reports in *Time* magazine, there are a growing number of figures in the sexology establishment venturing the view that adult-child sex is not harmful. For example, Tufts University psychiatrist and family therapist Larry Constantine is quoted as saying, "Children really are a disenfranchised minority. They should have the right to express themselves sexually, which means that they may or may

21 *Resolution on the Liberation of Children and Youth*, adopted by the North American Man/Boy Love Association at the NAMBLA Seventh Conference, Boston, December 4, 1983.
22 Richard Goldstein, "The Future of Gay Liberation: Sex on Parole," *The Village Voice*, August 20-26, 1980.

not have contact with people older than themselves." And Harvard Health Service psychologist Douglas Powell reportedly has said: "I have not seen anyone harmed by this [adult-child sexual contact] so long as it occurs in a relationship with somebody who really cares about the Child" (Time, April 14, 1980 and September 7, 1981; see Appendix C for reproduction of former article).

In the New York University summer seminar conducted by Professor Calderwood in The Netherlands in 1983 (personally attended by author E. Eichel), the class noticed a disproportionate number of speakers focusing on—and presenting material in support of—pedophile relations. One speaker was Dr. Theo Sandfort (currently of the gay and lesbian studies department, University of Utrecht), whose 1982 book (English edition), The Sexual Aspect of Paedophile Relations (Pan/Spartacus), had been banned in the United States.

Sandfort's opus, which is a report on his research, stressed that sexual contacts between pedophiles and young males did not have a negative influence upon the boys' "well-being" (p. 84),[23] and that problems arose because of the reactions of parents and the legal authorities (p. 85). His report concluded: "It can be expected that when the boundaries around the nuclear family disappear, children will more readily accept emotional ties with adults other than their parents" (p. 83). In his presentation at the seminar, Dr. Sandfort coyly deflected a question as to whether he was a pedophile himself, insisting that it was an irrelevant issue in relation to his research.

At the same NYU seminar, Dutch law advocate and legislator Edward Brongersma discussed the sensibilities of pedophiles and the benefits of pedophiliac relationships for children. He assured the student body that it was only a matter of time before legislation would be passed in The Netherlands—and throughout the world—which would be more liberal toward such relationships. Biographical information shows that he has more than a casual interest in the topic of pedophilia.[24] He is founder of the Dr. Edward Brongersma Foundation which was established "to advance scientific research into the development of the sexual lives of children . . . with special emphasis upon the phenomenon of erotic and sexual relationships between children and adults . . . ."

It is evident that Dr. Brongersma has dedicated a good part of his political career to the "reform" of sex laws in an attempt to legitimize pedophile relationships. In a 1980 British Journal of Criminology

23 In their book Human Sexuality— Second Edition, William Masters, Virginia Johnson and Robert Kolodny wrote of Sandfort's research: "[U]nbelievably, each boy was interviewed in the home of 'his' pedophile with the pedophile present, without any apparent regard for the fact that the adult's presence would have almost assuredly prevented the boy from voicing complaints about the way he was treated because of fear of punishment."

24 From a statement of objectives published by the Edward Brongersma Foundation, Tetterodeweg 1, 2051 EE Overveen, The Netherlands. According to Vern Bullough, in the Introduction to Brongersma's book Loving Boys, Brongersma is "a distinguished Dutch lawyer, a retired member of the Dutch Parliament who in 1950 was arrested, tried and convicted for having sex with a 16-year-old boy. He spent 11 months in prison. . . .[but since has won] reinstatement to the bar, re-election to the Dutch Parliament, and in 1975 as a reward for his services, the Queen made him a Knight of the Order of the Dutch Lion. He is, however, still a pedophile . . . ."

article, "The Meaning of 'Indecency' with Respect to Moral Offences Involving Children" (*British Journal of Criminology* 20:20, 1980), he asserted that it was on his "insistence" (he was a member of the Upper House of the Dutch Parliament at the time) that the Dutch Minister of Justice announced in 1977 that priority would be given to a review of proposed legislation to modify laws regarding "indecency with children." In his plea to change penal laws regarding pedophilia, Brongersma proposed that sexual "[c]ontacts which are . . . freely consented to by . . . the child . . . should not be forbidden by law." Also, the same statute would protect the pedophile in contacts "solicited by the child" (*ibid.*, p. 21).

However, the opinion of Dutch legislators opposing the change of penal laws on pedophilia prevailed. In response to a renewed effort to change sex laws in 1985, Adriaan Kaland, speaking for the Christian Democrat Party, proclaimed, "Children are a vulnerable group to whom the government may not stop affording its protection."[25]

[A noteworthy update on the activities of Dutch pedophilia proponents Sandfort and Brongersma appears in the Hayworth Press (Binghampton, NY) catalogue announcing a new book they are editing, titled *Intergenerational Intimacy*.[26] This is described as a "ground breaking book" that "presents new historical, legal, sociological, psychological, and cross-disciplinary research on male intergenerational intimacy." This work apparently will be published simultaneously as the *Journal of Homosexuality* (Vol. 20, Nos. 1/2; available summer 1990). Articles advertised include "Man-Boy Love and the American Gay Movement," by David Thorstad of NAMBLA.]

It is clear that there has been an attempt on many levels to condition educators and acclimate the public toward the acceptance of pedophilia. When an NYU/SIECUS colloquium was held in Sweden in 1979 to formulate an international code of principles for sex education programming, the issue of adult-child sexual relations was broached. As director of the NYU Human Sexuality Program, Deryck Calderwood had a central role in the proceedings. SIECUS President Mary Calderone also was in attendance. She had prepared the first draft of the code of principles in 1976.[27]

25   "Sex at Age 12?—Youth Will Be Served," New York *Daily News*, November 8, 1985. From the Associated Press, The Hague, The Netherlands.

26   A third author/editor of this book is Alex X. van Naerssen, Ph.D., research coordinator of social sexology, Vakgroep Klinische Psychologie, University of Utrecht, The Netherlands. Dr. van Naerssen also was a guest lecturer in the New York University international seminar coordinated by Deryck Calderwood.

27   Robert O. Hawkins, Jr., "The Uppsala Connection: The Development of Principles Basic to Education for Sexuality," *SIECUS Report*, January 1980, p.1.

A participant in the colloquium, Robert O. Hawkins, reported on the proceedings in an article which appeared in the *SIECUS Report*, titled "The Uppsala Connection: The Development of Principles Basic to Education for Sexuality" (*SIECUS Report*, January 1980). According to Hawkins, discussion on the topic of pedophilia concluded:

Most pedophiliacs (people who are sexually interested in minor children). . . .are gentle and affectionate, and are not dangerous in the way childmolesters are stereotypically considered to be.[28]

The SIECUS principle that was derived from this discussion (Principle 17) did not mention the issue of pedophilia specifically. It stated: "A rational understanding of the range of sexual expressions is a goal of education for sexuality." The final published version of the principle advocated the same basic objective, with a few specific words added (added words italicized):

Rational understanding *and acceptance* of the *wide* range of *possible* expressions of sexuality constitute one goal of education for sexuality [*SIECUS Report*, January 1980, p. 15].

THE SAR (SEXUAL ATTITUDE REASSESSMENT) SEMINAR FOR PROFESSIONAL CERTIFICATION

Sex educators may feel that the overview of the sex education field that has been presented is overstated. However, many seem unaware of the intent and possible impact of what is, in effect, gay programming directed at professionals.

Consider, however, that the major organization for professional certification—the American Association of Sex Educators, Counselors and Therapists (AASECT)—for more than a decade has required a Sexual Attitude Reassessment (SAR) seminar as part of the criteria for certification. The SAR training has included a media event to provide participants with "meaningful exposure to a wide range of human sexual behavior that extends outside their own area of experience" (*Glide In/Out Newsletter*, February 1971, unnumbered p. 2).

---

28 "In a thorough study of police records, probation presentencing reports, courtroom transcripts, and medical reports, Christie, Marshall, and Lanthier in 1978 reported on 150 incarcerated sex offenders. They found that 58 percent of the child molesters were violent during the commission of the crime and 42 percent of the child victims were physically injured" (Christie M, Marshall W, Lanthier R, "A Descriptive Study of Incarcerated Rapists and Pedophiles," Report to the Solicitor General of Canada, Ottawa, 1979. Cited in Sheldon Travin, Harvey Bluestone, Emily Coleman, Ken Cullen, John Melella, "Pedophilia: An Update on Theory and Practice," *Psychiatric Quarterly* 57[2]:89-103, 1985).

Wardell Pomeroy has described the SAR-type media "bombardment" programming at the Institute for the Advanced Study of Human Sexuality (IASHS) as follows:[29]

As part of our intensive courses we project several films on to a series of screens simultaneously. They vary in content from "hard porn" homosexuality to milder loving themes. . . . [T]he results are very interesting and useful [Eric Trimmer speaks to Wardell B. Pomeroy, "Sexology—Therapy or Titillation?" *British Journal of Sexual Medicine*, January 1982, pp. 37-39].

Mary Calderone has related how an SAR seminar helped her to get over "sexual hangups, particularly about homosexuality." In the SAR program,

she viewed a homosexual couple keeping house and then engaging in homosexual lovemaking (ie, mutual masturbation and sodomy). 'I went out walking on air, because now I knew what homosexuals did, and they did all the same things I like to do, and it was fine. I felt good about them from that moment on' *[U.S. Catholic*, October 1982, p. 26. Cited by Randy Engel in "The Pivotal Role of SIECUS," *The Wanderer*, June 22, 1989, p. 9].

Most SAR participants may not promote homosexual behaviors themselves, but as professionals they will have been desensitized to such behaviors and encouraged to be non-judgmental and to have a pluralistic outlook. How will they react in the face of an increasingly aggressive gay agenda designed to take advantage of the AIDS crisis?

THE AIDS WINDFALL

GAY PROGRAMMING FOR CHILDREN

As incredible as it may seem—in spite of the fearful prospect of venereal disease associated with a gay lifestyle—gay activists continue to work for the teaching of the equality of non-traditional sexual lifestyles (what some have called a pansexual ideology) in education and the health sciences.

Programming for school children that brings attention to homosexuality and gay sexual behaviors has been a long-term goal.

29   The SAR media technique was instifued by the Reverend Robert T. McIlvenna, founder and president of IASHS. McIlvenna organized the fight for homosexual law reform in Great Britain. He is founder in the U.S. of the Council on Religion and the Homosexual ("National Sex Week," *The Review of the News*, June 9, 1971, p. 3). SAR orginally stood for "Sexual Attitude Restructuring," and was apparently modified by changing "Restructuring" to "Reassessment" to make the intent to influence thinking less obvious. (See Calderwood: "Educating the Educators." In *Sex Education in the Eighties*, Plenum, 1981, p. 193). Paul Fleming, M.D., chair of AASECT's SAR Committee, recently has suggested that "SARs must be constantly revised so that one discusses 'things which are hot in the field—AIDS, sexual oppression in today's world.'" Cited in "Should SARs Be Part of The Certification Process for All Sexologists?" *Sexuality Today*, November 16, 1987, p. 3.

This is undoubtedly based on the Kinseyan logic that people would be more likely to engage in homosexual behaviors if they are exposed to such behaviors at a young age.[30] From this standpoint, the AIDS programming mandated in 1986 for the New York City public schools may have been a major breakthrough for gay activists, who turned the programming into a gay lobby forum. At one of the first teacher-training sessions held in a Manhattan-based high school, the following list of "do's" and "don'ts" was presented:[31]

• Homosexuals should not be blamed for the spread of AIDS.

• Infants infected with AIDS should not be referred to as "innocent" children as that implies that somebody is guilty.

• Teachers should not be squeamish about using explicit terms to describe gay sexual behaviors.

• Stress safe-sex behaviors. Don't make an issue about the number of sex partners.

• Teachers should stress to children that they should take a civic stand on issues to protect the civil rights of homosexuals.

In the winter of 1986, the Board of Education delayed the release of a $97,000 AIDS videotape for the public schools and called for a $46,000 editing job because it over-played the theme of "tolerance toward homosexuals" in relation to lifestyle. Spokesperson Jean Hernandez asserted, "This is not an attitude film. This is supposed to be an educational film."[32] The film, *Sex, Drugs and AIDS*, was circulated around the country before the editing was implemented.[33]

In the January 1987 *SIECUS Report*, executive director Ann Welbourne-Moglia referred to the AIDS crisis in her article "A Time of Rare Opportunity" (pp. 15, 16). In counting the major gains of the last year, she listed mandatory sex education in the New York City public schools and the support of [then] Surgeon General C. Everett Koop, who made the recommendation "to begin teaching about AIDS at the lowest grade possible." She ended on this note: "Let us hope that as we are doing everything we can to stop AIDS, we are also educating the public about what sex education is *really* all about" (emphasis added).

BASIC ERRORS IN SEX RESEARCH

Some fundamentally wrong conclusions from "sex research" appear to be responsible for the *content* and *objectives* of sex education

---

30   For example, Kinsey's statement, "Whether exclusively heterosexual patterns are followed, or whether both heterosexual and homosexual outlets are utilized in his history, depends in part upon the circumstances of early experience" (Male Report, p. 204).

31   High School AIDS Education Workshop. Presentation by Bruce Schutte and Rebecca Porper, program facilitaors from the New York City Department of Health. Attended by Edward Eichel at a New York City high school, January 1986.

32   "Movie Star's AIDS Video Faces Board of Ed's Knife," *New York Post*, November 19, 1986.

33   Mitchell Halberstadt, "AIDS Film Controversy Continues," *New York Advocate*, March 9, 1987, p. 17.

programming. The errors involve misconceptions about 1) the nature of sexual gender, and 2) the nature of the sex act.

THE NATURE OF GENDER

When the late Alfred C. Kinsey of the Institute for Sex Research published his revolutionary Male (1948) and Female (1953) Reports on sexual behavior, he argued that *no one is truly heterosexual* (Male Report, p. 639; Female Report, pp. 450, 451). His data did not support his theory.[34] There was no scientific basis for his assumption that the pattern of heterosexual behavior comes "as a result of social pressures which tend to force an individual into an exclusive pattern..." (Female Report, p. 450). Kinsey seemed to be implying that heterosexuality was an unnatural, socially imposed condition. He polemicized that "only the human mind invents categories [like heterosexuality or homosexuality] and tries to force facts into separated pigeon-holes" (Male Report, p. 639). However, he set his own categories and agenda.

Kinsey created a seven-point scale to judge the sexual normality of interviewees according to his own personal criterion of sexual health. The scale represented *bisexuality* as a natural "balanced" sexual orientation midway between heterosexuality and homosexuality (Male Report, p. 638, Figure 161). Where a person was placed on this scale was entirely decided by the subjective judgment of Dr. Kinsey and a few personally trained staff.[35]

(Kinsey associate Paul Gebhard expressed ambiguity about Kinsey's coding method for assessing and placing interviewees on his heterosexual-homosexual rating scale; particularly, he criticized the manner in which Kinsey added together *thoughts* about sex with actual sex acts to classify people [In Karlen A: *Sexuality and Homosexuality*, W. W. Norton & Co., 1971, p. 282].)[36]

The Kinsey group (which included Wardell B. Pomeroy, Clyde E. Martin, and Paul H. Gebhard) defined their concept of sexual normality as follows:

[W]e suggest that sexuality, in its biologic origins, is a capacity to respond to any sufficient stimulus. . . . This is the picture of sexual response in the child and in most other younger mammals. For a few uninhibited adults, sex continues to remain sex, however they have it [Kinsey, *et al.* In Hoch and Zubin, 1949, p. 27].

Kinsey advocated that the sexuality of the young infant was "unspoiled" since the child could respond to any form of stimulus without judging the source. According to one-time Kinsey Institute researcher John H. Gagnon, the later development of diverse forms of sexual "preference" indicates a variety of human "sexualities" which are based upon learning experience and none are to be considered unnatural

---

34 See Male Report: p. 652, Table 148; p. 656, Figure 169; p. 658, Figure 170; Female Report: p. 499, Table 142.

35 Personal communication from Gwenn Pershing, Head of Information Services, Kinsey Institute for Research in Sex, Gender and Reproduction, May 13, 1986.

36 The relevance of this observation to Kinsey's homosexuality figures is covered briefly in chapter 6.

(Gagnon JH. "Science and the Politics of Pathology." *Journal of Sex Research* 23[1]:120-123, 1987).

In his 1977 book *Human Sexualities* (Scott Foresman & Co.), Gagnon advocates a process of social engineering that in practice combines his and Kinsey's models of sexuality. He sums up the problem of child sexual development from his own viewpoint: "[T]here does appear to be something that could be called a competence for orgasm that can be realized at a very early age. What is more important is determining what activities or social circumstances might sustain the interest or contribute to the desire of young boys or girls to continue the activity" (p. 84). Gagnon suggests, "We may have to change the ways in which [children] learn about sex. We may have to become more directive, more informative, more positive—we may have to promote sexual activity—if we want to change the current processes of sexual learning and their outcome" (p. 381).

(Indeed, those in the highest echelon of sex educators have designed sex education programming with an agenda based on this ideologic foundation. We can begin to understand why recent studies indicate that sex education has been unable to curtail teenage sexual activity and reduce teenage pregnancy [see Stout and Rivera: "Schools and Sex Education: Does it Work?" *Pediatrics* 83(3):375-379, 1989].)

Gagnon makes an important qualifying remark in relation to Kinsey's findings on the orgasmic potential of children. He cautions, "much of [Kinsey's] information comes from adults who were in active sexual contact with . . . boys and who were interested in producing orgasms in them" (p. 84). He further concedes, "A less neutral observer than Kinsey would have described these events as sex crimes . . ." (p. 84).

For Kinsey, the blurring of sexual identity—elevating and stressing *bisexuality* (as opposed to heterosexuality)—was an essential step in opening an unlimited range of sexual options. Kinsey supported an ideology that might be called pansexuality—"anything goes" that provides excitement and pleasure. But in fact, it is an ideology that frowns upon monogamy and traditional concepts of sexual normality.[37] It also considers intercourse between a man and woman a limited form of sexual expression. (Pomeroy, in a 1972 article, "The Now of the Kinsey Findings," uses the term "addiction" to explain the primacy of heterosexual intercourse [*SIECUS Report*, September 1972, p. 1].)

Finally, there is the issue of Kinsey's lack of concern for the emotional implication of sex acts as reflected in a comment he made in response to criticism about his research: "Now they want us to consider love. If we started in on that, we'd never finish" (Pomeroy WB: *Dr. Kinsey and the Institute for Sex Research*, Harper & Row, 1972, p. 195).

But Kinsey team member Paul Gebhard contradicted Pomeroy's remembrance about Kinsey's omission of data on the topic of love.

---

37   Wardell B. Pomeroy: "The Masters-Johnson Report and the Kinsey Tradition." In: Brecher and Brecher, 1967, p. 117.

Gebhard noted, "There were no questions as to how many heterosexual love affairs a person experienced nor what attributes were found sexually appealing in a partner, yet these questions were asked of homosexuals" (Gebhard P. Johnson A: *The Kinsey Data*, W. B. Saunders, 1979, p. 16).

THE NATURE OF THE SEX ACT

Beyond Kinsey's view of heterosexuality as a culturally imposed artifact, a second major error that has colored the thinking of health professionals and sex educators concerns the pioneering research on sexual response by William H. Masters and Virginia E. Johnson. The impression has been created that Masters and Johnson researched and defined *the nature of the sex act.*

In *Human Sexual Response*, published in 1966 (Little, Brown), the husband-and-wife research team concluded that orgasm had the same basic response pattern regardless of whether the stimulation was human or mechanical (pp. 133, 134). The theme was expanded in *Homosexuality in Perspective* (Little, Brown, 1979), in which they proclaimed that "the inherent facility for orgasmic attainment" is identical "regardless of whether the sexual partner is of the *same* or *opposite* gender" (pp. 404, 405; authors' emphasis). These findings appeared to provide physiological support for Kinsey's belief in the equality of all sexual activity.

But the Masters and Johnson conclusions were invalid. Their findings were based not on the reality of actual intercourse but on physical responses generated in the female by an electric-powered plastic phallus—a procedure they called "artificial coition." The use of this mechanical equipment for stimulating and photographing intra-vaginal response gave the *impression* of objective research, but it was totally naive to suppose that this sexual robotry could monitor the complexities of human sexual union (McGrady M: *The Love Doctors*, Macmillan, 1972, pp. 307, 308).[38]

Consequently, the research of Masters and Johnson is now being challenged by a number of sex researchers. There is strong evidence that heterosexual intercourse is unique and has the potential for more complete and satisfying levels of response than Masters and Johnson documented in their laboratory experiments.[39] (The attempted suppression of these research findings is, as yet, an untold story.)

Unfortunately, the claim that sexual response is identical in any type of sexual activity has given the impression that a preference for indiscriminate behavior is consistent with our physical nature. And, it

---

38   See also: "Reexamination of Masters and Johnson's Findings on Physical Alignment," an interview with E. Eichel, *Sexuality Today*, June 27, 1983.

39   See: 1. Fox CA, *et al.*: Measurement of intra-vaginal and intra-uterine pressures during human coitus by radiotelemetry. *Journal of Reproduction and Fertility* 22:243-251, 1970. 2. Perry JD, Whipple B: Pelvic muscle strength of female ejaculators: evidence in support of a new theory of orgasm. *Journal of Sex Research* 17:22-39, 1981. 3. Singer J, Singer I: Types of female orgasm. *Journal of Sex Research* 8:255-267, 1972. 4. Eichel E, Eichel J, Kule S: The technique of coital alignment and its relationship to female orgasmic response and simultaneous orgasm. *Journal of Sex & Marital Therapy* 14:129-141, 1988.

has inclined many people toward sexual experimentation and a romance with promiscuity that has been a disaster physically and emotionally. These errors in sex research, by Kinsey and by Masters and Johnson, have been harmful because they have created an ambiguous image of sexual gender, a depersonalized attitude toward sex and a pessimistic vision of the most fundamental expression of sexual relating.

FURTHER RESEARCH ON HOMOSEXUALITY

The research data on homosexuality generated by Kinsey and his followers at the Kinsey Institute have been employed *both* to weaken resistance against, and to muster support for gay lobby objectives. They have been used to influence the psychiatric assessment of homosexuality, and for the promotion of gay rights legislation. Also, "a significant part of the legal profession took [Kinsey's] work seriously," proclaimed C. A. Tripp,[40] a close Kinsey associate, and "[a] good many judges read his books, which influenced their handling of cases involving sex" (Pomeroy, 1972, p. 464). Hence, the scientific objectivity of such studies is an important matter in relation to a wide range of social issues—including criminal justice policy on sex crimes.

A follow-up of the early Kinsey studies was initiated in 1969 by the Kinsey Institute to "supplement (and partially to correct)" the original Kinsey data on homosexuality (Harold Lief, *SIECUS Report*, November 1978, p. 1). It was the first large-scale study on homosexuality since the original Kinsey reports. The project began with a pilot study funded by a $375,000 grant from the National Institute for Mental Health, and was completed and published in 1978.

This report, *Homosexualities: A Study of Diversity Among Men and Women*, by researchers Alan P. Bell and Martin S. Weinberg (Simon & Schuster), was claimed by the authors to "amply demonstrate that few homosexual men and women conform to the hideous stereotype most people have of them." However, it did not succeed in demonstrating that homosexual and heterosexual sexuality are similar and equal entities.

The Bell and Weinberg study was reviewed in the *SIECUS Report* by Harold I. Lief, founder of the Center for Sex Education in Medicine at the University of Pennsylvania. Dr. Lief was selected by SIECUS to review the study because of his reputation as "a psychiatrist sympathetic to human rights but also an objective scientist" (*SIECUS Report*, November 1978).

In his review, Dr. Lief made a number of observations about "a common feature of homosexual life, namely, the extremely large number of [sex] partners of the majority of homosexual men and the frequency with which partners are complete strangers..." (*ibid.*, p. 14). His critique of the Bell-Weinberg study was insightful and revealing in a number of ways. He commented:

40   Author of *The Homosexual Matrix*, McGraw-Hill, 1975.

So intent are the authors at demonstrating that except for the obvious difference in sexual orientation, homosexuals really are not different from heterosexuals, that they seemingly gloss over the difference [p. 14].

Lief made the distinction that

Casual sex is frequent enough in heterosexual life, but it does not have the overwhelming intensity, compulsivity, and sex-only orientation of so much of homosexual behavior [p. 14].

Lief identified an underlying agenda in the Bell-Weinberg study:

They (Bell and Weinberg) want their findings to be helpful in the political arena. They would like to do everything they can do to enhance the civil rights of people with homosexual behaviors [p. 13; emphasis added].

THE "DENORMALIZATION" OF HETEROSEXUALITY

POLITICS OF THE AMERICAN PSYCHIATRIC ASSOCIATION'S DECISION ON HOMOSEXUALITY

The Kinsey Reports were an important consideration underlying the American Psychiatric Association's (APA) decision to "normalize" homosexuality by eliminating it as a pathology from the organization's *Diagnostic and Statistical Manual* in 1973. The Introduction of the *National Institute of Mental Health Task Force on Homosexuality Final Report* in 1972—a report influential in the APA decision—led with a declaration of what is recognizably the Kinsey bisexuality credo.[41]

It began: "Human sexuality encompasses a broad range of behaviors within which lie both the *exclusive heterosexual* and the exclusive confirmed homosexual. Between these two *extremes* . . . " (p. 2, emphasis added).

The report included a recommendation for "*[b]roader programs in sex education*" and specified that "[i]nformation about homosexuality should be included in . . . the schools as well as for the public at large" to alleviate "condemnatory and punitive attitudes." The report also recommended "[s]pecial training for *all law enforcement personnel* . . . teachers, ministers, lawyers, health educators, and youth group counselors" to "replace judgmental and condemnatory attitudes . . . " (p. 4; emphases in original).

An appendix to the report, titled "Detailed Reservations Regarding the Task Force Recommendations on Social Policy," included the following comment by APA member Dr. Henry W. Riecken:

It is as if they [the Task Force] said, "here is a phenomenon about which we know almost nothing and about which there is a great deal of anxiety and concern; *therefore*, let us suggest a major revision in public policy for dealing with this phenomenon." I cannot escape the

---

41   *National Institute of Mental Health Task Force on Homosexuality: Final Report and Background Papers*, edited by John M. Livergood, M.D., U.S. Government Printing Office, 1972, p. 2.

belief that this is an utterly unreasonable conclusion to draw from the sea of ignorance and misinformation in which we find ourselves [p. 71; emphasis in original].

Around this time, the Masters and Johnson research, mentioned earlier, was getting publicity. According to psychiatrist Charles W. Socarides in his book *Beyond Sexual Freedom* (Quadrangle, 1977),

Early in 1972, when Dr. William H. Masters of St. Louis announced to the nation's press that homosexuality is a "natural" and by direct implication normal sexual act or sexual condition, he raised the status of the anus to the level of the vagina (*New York Times*, November 18, 1971). What was until then a purely excretory organ had become a genital one—by decree [p. 121].

Shortly thereafter, the American Psychiatric Association declared homosexuality to be normal. Dr. Socarides summed up the implication of the APA decision on homosexuality with the following statement:

A movement within the APA had accomplished what every society, with rare exceptions, would have trembled to tamper with, namely, the revision of a basic code and concept of life and biology: that men and women normally mate with the opposite sex, not with each other [Socarides' review of *Homosexuality and American Psychiatry: The Politics of Diagnosis*, by Ronald Bayer (Basic Books, 1981); reviewed in *Review of Psychoanalytic Books* 2:87, 1984].

In *Beyond Sexual Freedom*, Dr. Socarides gives a fascinating account of how homosexuality itself came "out of the closet"— progressing from pathology to alternative lifestyle. At the very time when a number of psychiatrists were beginning to believe that this disorder involving a "serious change in human relationships" could be reversed, at least in some cases, an unfortunate train of events went into motion.

In the 1960s, in response to legal and social persecution, homosexual groups began to form and turn against their oppressors, and before long against those in the medical profession who believed homosexuality was a treatable condition. In 1964, the New York Academy of Medicine's Committee on Public Health said that "homosexuals have gone beyond the plane of defensiveness and now argue that their deviancy is a 'desirable, noble, preferable way of life.'" Homosexual groups—constituting a vocal but very small minority of homosexuals—reacted increasingly by proclaiming their "normality" and attacking any opposition to this view (Socarides, 1977, p. 83).

Socarides vainly tried to do something about this situation by proposing to the Director of the National Institute of Mental Health the establishing of a national program for the prevention and treatment of homosexuality and other sexual disorders. The aim was to try and alleviate suffering to the individual and his family and address a problem that affected the whole nation. The Federal Government decided it did not want to get involved.

Instead the NIMH task force came out with its report, which prepared the way for the APA decision. Prior to the APA decision, another Task Force on Homosexuality (of the New York County District Branch of the APA), composed of psychiatrists affiliated with the major medical centers in New York City, came out with its findings on this subject. This report "documented the fact that exclusive homosexuality was a disorder of psychosexual development, and simultaneously asked for civil rights for those suffering from the disorder." It was considered "not acceptable," however. As Dr. Socarides observed, "The message was coming through loud and clear: the only report acceptable would have been one which was not only in favor of civil rights but one which declared homosexuality *not* a psychosexual disorder (Socarides, 1977, pp. 87, 88; emphasis in original).

The APA decision on homosexuality was basically one in favor of the Kinseyan (homosexual) model of sexuality and against the Freudian (heterosexual) model. Sigmund Freud believed that intercourse between a man and a woman was the natural objective of the sex drive. He considered homosexuality to be "an arrest of sexual development."[42] Also—unlike Kinsey—he classified certain sexual behaviors as abnormal, referring to adult-child sex, for example, as "cowardly" and a "substitute" form of outlet for "impotent" people.[43]

Understandably, homosexual activists had a heavy stake in the APA's decision. As Socarides tells it in *Beyond Sexual Freedom*, the movement to get the APA nomenclature committee to delete *homosexuality* was "first spearheaded by Vice President [Dr. Judd] Marmor of the APA and other psychiatrists in league with the Gay Activists Alliance, the Mattachine Society, and the Daughters of Bilitis (the women's arm of the Mattachine Society)" (p. 88).

In the period leading up to the APA's decision, according to Socarides, "militant homosexual groups continued to attack any psychiatrist or psychoanalyst who dared to present his findings as to the psychopathology of homosexuality before national or local meetings of psychiatrists or in public forums" (*ibid.*, p. 87).

Former Kinsey colleague Paul Gebhard was on the NIMH Task Force committee, representing what Socarides calls "the Kinsey-Hopkins faction." In his review of Ronald Bayer's *Homosexuality and American Psychiatry: The Politics of Diagnosis*, Socarides states:

> Whatever conspiracy may have existed had its early origins in the National Institute of Mental Health Task Force on Homosexuality established in the late 1960s. . . . I was personally informed by Paul Gebhard, a member of this commission, that . . . psychoanalytic clinicians were purposefully left out of this committee because of our "bias"—a "bias" based on our "Freudian background" [*Ibid.*, p. 90].

Wardell Pomeroy, like Gebhard, showed his contempt for Freudian thinking. Dr. Bayer related the following account of Pomeroy's testimony before the APA Nomenclature Committee (February 3, 1973) regarding the decision to "normalize" homosexuality:

---

42   Sigmund Freud's letter to the mother of a homosexual (April 9, 1935); reproduced in *Medial Aspects of Human Sexuality*, December 1968, p. 40.
43   Sigmund Freud: *Three Essays on the Theory of Sexuality*, Strachey J (ed. and trans.), Basic Books, 1962, pp. 14, 15. Originally published in 1905.

He (Pomeroy) called upon the . . . Committee to acknowledge homosexuality as a normal variant, suggesting with only thinly disguised contempt that psychiatry would have done well to accept the conclusions he and Kinsey had put forth twenty-five years earlier [Bayer, 1981, p. 117].

According to Bayer, Pomeroy proclaimed:

I have high hopes that even psychiatry can profit by its mistakes and can proudly enter the last quarter of the twentieth century [*ibid.*].

On December 14, 1973, the APA Board of Trustees declared homosexuality normal. This decision was ratified by a small majority of APA members following a letter urging this course signed by candidates for the APA presidency. As Ronald Bayer relates in his book *Homosexuality and American Psychiatry*, what the letter did *not* indicate was "that it was written, at least in part, by the [National] Gay Task Force . . . and funded by contributions the Task Force had raised." Bayer added: "Though each [signer] publicly denied any role in the dissimulation, at least one . . . had warned privately that to acknowledge the organizational role of the gay community would have been the 'kiss of death'" (p. 146).

Four years after the APA decision, the journal *Medical Aspects of Human Sexuality* (November 1977) published the results of a survey taken among 2,500 psychiatrists on the subject "current thinking on homosexuality." By 69% to 18% (13% uncertain), respondents answered that "homosexuality was usually a pathological adaptation as opposed to a normal variation." This result suggests that the political component of the APA decision process led that body to a position not supported by the majority of the psychiatric profession.

A number of eminent figures in the medical profession were apprehensive of the impact of the APA decision on society. Abram Kardiner, former professor of psychiatry at Columbia University, recipient of the Humanities Prize of *The New York Times* in 1966 and an expert in the area of psychoanalytic investigation of cultures, wrote in a 1973 personal letter to Dr. Socarides:

A powerful lobby of "gay" organizations has brought pressure on the American Psychiatric Association to remove homosexuality from the category of aberrancy. This is only one facet of the tidal wave of egalitarianism and divisiveness that is sweeping the country. . . . But this egalitarianism is bound to exact a high price from the community . . . [for it is a] symptom of a social distress syndrome. . . . Above all it militates against the family and destroys the function of the latter as the last place in our society where affectivity can still be cultivated [Socarides, 1977, pp. 89, 90].

Kardiner also warned of

. . . an *epidemic* form of homosexuality, which is more than the usual incidence, which generally occurs in social crises or in declining cultures when license and boundless permissiveness dulls the pain of ceaseless anxiety, universal hostility and divisiveness. Thus in Betsileo the incidence of homosexuality was visibly increased at a time when the society was in a state of collapse [*ibid.*; emphasis in original].

A decade later, several years into the AIDS epidemic, Pomeroy continued to lobby for and defend the Kinsey scheme for sexual *evolution*. Nowhere was the Kinseyan ideal of multiple sexual contacts and outlets acted out more than in the gay bathhouses, where AIDS-virus spread was a serious danger. When finally a group of homosexual physicians advocated closure of these establishments in San Francisco, Wardell Pomeroy intervened, according to Ronald Bayer in his book *Private Acts, Social Consequences: AIDS and the Politics of Public Health* (The Free Press, 1989).

Bayer recounts, "From the faculty of the Institute for the Advanced Study of Human Sexuality, a group that included Wardell B. Pomeroy, a well-known former colleague of Alfred Kinsey, a letter was sent to [Mervyn] Silverman [director, San Francisco Department of Health] warning of the consequences of closure [of the gay bathhouses]. Sexual activity driven from the bathhouses would shift to other locations and would hinder any 'scientific and professional' approaches to the problem. Without rational justification, bathhouse closure could only be viewed as 'short-sighted, simplistic, and obvious in its political rather than humanitarian motivation'" (pp. 35, 36). "Political" as applied to bathhouses presumably has a different meaning than when applied to the APA decision on homosexuality!

Pomeroy's qualifications for directing the "evolution" (his own term; see *SIECUS Report*, September 1972, p. 1) of human sexuality were recognized by Kinsey himself. At a scientific conference in 1983, Dr. Pomeroy related that Kinsey had hired him on the basis of his personal sex history, deducing that he "had not picked up all the taboos, and the inhibitions, and the guilts that . . . [his] colleagues had . . ." (source, footnote 12).

From the Kinseyan point of view, the APA decision on homosexuality was perceived as more than an act of compassion, it was an important *evolutionary* step in the "denormalization" of heterosexuality.

One member of the NIMH Task Force on homosexuality, Dr. John Money (professor of medical psychology and associate professor of pediatrics at Johns Hopkins University School of Medicine), has in successive years more pointedly expressed the Kinsey view of bisexuality as the new norm of sexual health.

In Money's article "Bisexual, Homosexual, and Heterosexual: Society, Law, and Medicine," in the *Journal of Homosexuality* (Spring 1977, pp. 229-233), he applies the term "obligative heterosexuals" to men and women without homosexual experience. This label qualifies exclusive heterosexuality as a quasi-psychopathology.

Money proclaims that "condemnation of homosexuality induces impairment of all sexuality rather than an increase of heterosexuality."

Dr. Money has more recently carried his theory of sexuality a dramatic step further. Discussing the topic "Homosexuality: Nature or

Nurture" on the WNET, New York, program *Innovation* (May 19, 1987), Money suggested that homosexuals are a chosen people—a kind of super race. He theorized that nature wanted some individuals to achieve scientific feats such as going to the moon or creating great works of art. To do this she had to "loosen up" their sexuality.

Referring to the statues and paintings of Michelangelo (assumed to have been a homosexual), Money concluded that "nature was happy to let one man not make babies as long as he could do all of that."

Money qualified his statement with the assurance, "I don't think nature would ever turn everyone into a Michelangelo."

GAY RIGHTS

THE VICTIM STRATEGY

In conclusion, a basic issue must be brought to the attention of the public: are gay activists waging a campaign against heterosexuality *per se*? And, indeed against the long held societal taboo on adult-child sex?

A one-dimensional picture has been presented to the public that homosexuals are victims of discrimination and their civil rights are constantly being threatened. There is little or no attention given to the possibility of transgressions against heterosexuals—and particularly children. The strategy underlying much of the rhetoric about gay rights has been defined clearly enough by a historian of the gay movement, Dennis Altman, in his 1982 book *The Homosexualization of America* (Beacon press):

> The greatest single victory of the gay movement over the past decade has been to shift the debate from behavior to identity, thus *forcing opponents into a position where they can be seen as attacking the civil rights of homosexual citizens* rather than attacking specific and (as they see it) antisocial behavior [p. 9; emphasis added].

Gay activists may claim that it is absurd to suspect there is any scheme to promote homosexuality because it is impossible to really change anyone's sexual orientation—adult or child. But that disclaimer masks certain beliefs—consistent with the basic tenets of the Kinsey research—that might explain why gays are so unrelenting in their effort to influence the content and ideology of sex education for children. Since Kinsey implied that *heterosexuality is abnormal*—simply a symptom of cultural repression—there would be no need to "change" the orientation of children. A hidden gay agenda in sex education would reach boys and girls before they are affected by societal "restraints" and rescue them from the supposedly pathologic norms of exclusive male-female relating.

Could this be the rationale behind the effort by special interest groups to eliminate non-gay concepts like "marriage," "monogamy," the "nuclear family" and "normality" from the sex education curricula for public schools?

Certainly, the mainstream American view that a stable traditional family unit (ie, female mother/male father) constitutes the best environment for healthy rearing of children is under attack in what used to be traditional academia. According to two editors at the sometimes irreverent *Dartmouth Review* (January 31, 1990), that Ivy-League Mecca of learning's only course on marriage and the family uses as its basic text *The Marriage and the Family Experience* (by Bryan Strong and Christine DeVault), which "continually denigrates the traditional family in the United States as overly restrictive and oppressive."

This book, the Dartmouth writers declare, advocates that "homosexual families represent legitimate—and perhaps more desirable—alternatives to traditional family structures. According to the text, gay and lesbian families are often healthier than normal families because they eliminate the constraining gender roles frequently imposed upon family members by society. 'Freedom from such roles [as husband and wife],' assert Strong and DeVault, 'is often regarded as one of the major advantages of the gay lifestyle.'" [Note: a previously touted "advantage" was a swinging, multiple partner lifestyle, until the gay bowel syndrome, AIDS *et al.* put an end to the ecological legitimacy of that concept; see chapter 3.] The Dartmouth authors see in courses like this an attempt to impart "the value of valuelessness" and to create "the illusion of moral equivalency" for the aberrant.

Harry Hay and the Marxist founders of the Mattachine Society—forerunner of the modern gay and lesbian movement—early on pinpointed the identification of most members of society with heterosexual nuclear families as the cause of society's hostility to same-sex love and sexuality, according to John D'Emilio in the June 27, 1990, issue of *OutWeek*. It follows that if gays saw the heterosexual nuclear family as a source of some of their problems, the hostility might be mutual.

To some extent the shoe is now on the other foot. The gay movement has acquired considerable political and academic power. Currently, proponents of the Kinseyan (and gay) view of human sexuality have put themselves in a position to influence the content, teaching methodology and ideology of any new training programs for sex educators. By setting themselves up as the accrediting body for university-based Human Sexuality Programs, they now have the potential to control the future of sex education.

In July of 1985, the Commission on Accreditation of Human Sexuality Programs of the Society for the Scientific Study of Sex published its *Manual for Accreditation*. Predictably, academic topics recommended for course work include "Homosexuality (and bisexuality)," "Sexual variations," and "Alternate lifestyles." The topic of "Abnormal sexuality" is nowhere to be found. One particularly noteworthy item is the mandated topic "History of Sexual Behavior." This is an apparent attempt to validate Kinsey's research and have his agenda considered part of the logical, historical progression of human sexual behavior.

It remains to be seen whether the academic community will recognize and challenge the influence of the Kinsey school at this point in time, or whether the reaction must come at a grass-roots level.

CHAPTER FIVE

THE KINSEY AGENDA IN ACTION

Compiled by Edward W. Eichel and Dr. J. Gordon Muir

Chapter Overview

Many parents around the country are unaware of the degree to which the Kinsey philosophy of human sexuality already is part of the sex education programming received by their children, although, certainly, there are areas where such programming has not yet made inroads into the educational system.

However, even when the Kinsey agenda is not spelled out in an obvious way, it is important to realize that it is the standard ideology of those in academia who educate the sex educators. There is no degree-granting human sexuality education program that teaches anything else. *Educators trained in Kinsey ideology are the "experts" who more and more will influence the content of—and even design—the specific sex instruction materials used in public schools.*

*Examples follow of the attempted implementation of two sex education programs—*Mutual Caring, Mutual Sharing *and* About Your Sexuality *(reportedly also a mail order item in some pornography catalogues).* The contents of several sex education textbooks are reviewed, including two by Kinsey co-author Wardell Pomeroy that advocate premarital intercourse and encourage teenage promiscuity, and another by sex-ed author Gary Kelly that describes how to have anal intercourse, and "non-harmful" sex with animals. Kelly's book was reportedly voted onto the "Best Books for Young Adults List" by the American Library Association and comes recommended by Mary Calderone of SIECUS.*

What is confusing about the prevalence of the Kinsey teaching is that, thus far, it is least obvious at the lowest or more generalized level of education because, at this level, many non-specialists are still teach-

ing from a grass-roots, common-sense, traditional, value-oriented point
of view. However, under the aegis of private and federally funded
AIDS-education programs, a mandated curriculum embodying the
Kinsey philosophy of human sexuality may ultimately be in place at all
levels.

If parents wish to find out if a Kinsey-type sex education curriculum
is in place in their children's schools, they may contact the school
principal and obtain the curriculum guidelines and text being used in
courses such as "Family Life Education," "Health Education," "Male-
Female Studies," etc. They may also request to see films and videos
used in these classes. And it is useful to ask children what they are
being taught about gender roles and human sexuality and if they have
been advised that classroom discussions be treated as "confidential."
After reading this book, it should be easy to discern the features of the
underlying ideology—for present or future recognition in such classes.

OBJECTIVES OF THE KINSEY CURRICULUM

These have been described in their academic and research
framework in the previous chapters. Essentially, they boil down to
three basic goals:

1. To get heterosexuals to engage in homosexual experiences.

2. To progress toward the ultimate extension of Kinseyan
philosophy—acceptance of the possibility of adult sexual relations with
children.

3. To encourage sexual activity in children (the great paradox of
"AIDS education")—the prelude to and basis for the previous point.
This pressure is not coming from the children. It is being initiated by
adults, even though there is a total absence of evidence (and strong
evidence to the contrary) that premature sexual activity correlates with
mature, effective and fulfilling male-female sexual relating. It does
correlate, however, with a number of disease conditions, including
cancer of the cervix.

Parents today should be alert to any education program that
promotes, however subtly, homosexual experience to heterosexual
children.

The following documentation indicates how in practical reality the
above-stated agenda is being advanced through the education of sex
educators and implemented in some school systems. The main points
of a letter from author Eichel to the ethics committee of the American
Association of Sex Educators Counselors and Therapists (AASECT)
are summarized below. The contention is that the training of sex
educators in human sexuality programs is a conditioning process to
influence personal ideology, teaching methods and goals:

. An agenda hostile to the concept of a heterosexual norm is being
promoted within the sex education profession by gay activists. This
agenda has no foundation in science.

. The teaching of this view of human sexuality to educators has
been prominent in Dr. Deryck Calderwood's Human Sexuality Pro-

gram at New York University. Also a core group at SIECUS [Sex Information and Education Council of the U.S.], particularly founders Lester Kirkendall and Mary Calderone, has been trying to introduce Kinseyan philosophy to the entire field of education.

. In some cases the indoctrination is quite unsubtle. At an NYU-sponsored summer colloquium in Maastricht, Holland, Dr. Calderwood directed his class in exercises designed to get heterosexuals to explore homosexual experiences. Although he explained that bisexuality—as depicted in his video *Kinsey Three: The Bisexual Experience*—was "an unbiased point of view," his program seemed designed to move students in one direction—same sex experiences. In one exercise—a "nude body workshop"—students took turns at observing each other's genitals. This was followed by manual exploration of others' genitals while blindfolded, with attempts to identify each individual. In the same workshop, students were instructed to trade prostate exams with a partner. Although a brochure for a Calderwood video showing a young man examining his own prostate claims that he is using instructional pamphlets from the American Cancer Society, this organization, when contacted, disclaimed having such pamphlets or recommending such techniques.

. The involvement of pedophiles in training sessions for sex educators is disturbing. In Calderwood's seminar in Holland there were presentations by Dutch pedophiles in which it was stressed that child sex is not harmful. Students were not informed that one lecturer had spent time in prison.

. There is a disquieting degree of *control* exercised over students in programs such as Calderwood's. For example: 1) a requirement to attend the Gay Day Parade; 2) the photographing of students in embarrassing and sexually explicit situations [a common defensive tactic of pedophiles]; and 3) debriefing following seminar activities/sessions to ensure maintenance of confidentiality of methods and agenda.

Calderwood has been a highly influential figure in SIECUS and in professional sex education circles in the United States. Thus far, no action has been taken on the basis of the Eichel complaint.

"MUTUAL CARING, MUTUAL SHARING: A SEXUALITY EDUCATION UNIT FOR ADOLESCENTS"

Mutual Caring, Mutual Sharing is a sex education program that recently came to public attention when it surfaced in New Hampshire amid considerable controversy. This program is the Kinsey agenda in action. Developed by a disciple of the late Deryck Calderwood, *Mutual Caring* promotes homosexuality above heterosexuality. It cropped up in the Strafford County Prenatal and Family Planning Program as a result of what appears to be networking by gay activists in the State Health Department. A $161,000 grant was obtained for design and implementation of the program.

Below are reprinted a series of articles from *The New York Times* and the *Manchester Union Leader* describing the controversy surrounding the attempt to initiate this education effort.

Sex Education Manual Prompts Moral Outra

(*Rod Paul*, New York Times, *April 24, 1988*)

(*Copyright 1988 by The New York Times Company. Reprinted by permission*)

CONCORD, N.H., April 22—A federally financed manual outlining a curriculum of sex education for teenagers has touched off a political firestorm in this conservative state because it describes homosexuality as normal.

Since January more than 200 copies of the 60-page manual, which also discusses such issues as pregnancy, rape, contraception and sexual abuse, have been distributed to medical, family planning and government agencies around the state, and school districts have requested copies of it.

The manual has been criticized by county, state and Federal officials, including Gov.John H. Sununu. The Federal Government has begun action to try to block its distribution.

Program 'Should Be Expelled'

Senator Gordon J. Humphrey, a Republican, has asked Federal officials to investigate how the manual came to be produced with taxpayers' money, saying: "The program deserves an F. It should be expelled from New Hampshire."

The manual, "Mutual Caring, Mutual Sharing: a Sexuality Education Unit for Adolescents," was prepared for the Strafford County Prenatal and Family Planning Clinic in Dover with a $161,000 Federal grant. Cooper Thompson, an educator who is a member of the Campaign to End Homophobia, based in Cambridge, Mass., spent more than three years developing it, working with community groups, schools and youth organizations to test the curriculum.

The manual is intended for discussions about sex issues by groups of about a dozen teenagers and a teacher.

According to the manual, "Gay and lesbian adolescents are perfectly normal and their sexual attraction to members of the same sex is healthy."

"Homophobia Is the Problem"

Chuck Rhoades, the Dover clinic's executive director, defended the manual, saying: "It recognizes that there are some young people who are homosexual and that these young people are often the targets of hatred, prejudice and violence. Those are the types of attitudes labeled homophobia. The manual, in part, seeks to address homophobia. Our position is consistent with every mainstream medical psychological, educational and legal group in the country. We say that homophobia is the problem."

He said critics should be aware that the manual did not call for specific discussion sessions on homosexuality or homophobia. "What exists in the manual are comments in the introduction which are intended to help teachers give support to homosexual teenagers in the classroom," he said. "Also, there are ways the teacher might respond firmly to disparaging remarks against homosexual teenagers."

The reaction to the manual has been unrelenting since its distribution became publicly known two weeks ago. Now, the Federal Department of Health and Human Services has moved to block the clinic from distributing the manual.

Nabers Cabanis, a Deputy Assistant Secretary, has asked public health officials to "take whatever action is necessary to suspend dissemination" of the curriculum, "pending a review."

Clinic Funds in Jeopardy

Ms. Cabanis questioned whether the curriculum complied with Federal regulations on family planning grants like the one that paid for the manual.

Governor Sununu said: "It is not the kind of document that I would like governing any kind of programs that my kids are exposed to." He asked the State Attorney General to see if distribution of the manual could be blocked.

Strafford County commissioners voted to cut off financial support to the clinic but later backed off, offering to reinstate the financing if the clinic agreed to stop distributing the manual. The county provides $39,000 of the clinic's $580,000 annual budget. State lawmakers from the county have scheduled an April 29 meeting to discuss the matter.

"I'm not against sex education, but when teachers start telling kids if you are lesbian or homosexual then you are all right, normal and healthy," said Roland Roberge, a Commissioner, "That's not O.K."

The New Hampshire chapter of the National Organization for Women has threatened a lawsuit unless county officials keep financing the clinic.

Mr. Rhoades says a cutoff of funds by the county could jeopardize the family planning services the clinic provides to as many as 300 pregnant women, mothers and infants each year.

"It will hurt a lot, especially the low income women and girls," he said. "But as far as I am concerned I stand by what was written in the curriculum."

- - - - - - - - - - - - - - - -

"Inside Job"

(*Jim Finnegan*, Manchester Union Leader, *May 3, 1988*)

(*Copyright 1988 by the Union Leader Corporation. Reprinted by permission*)

It is becoming increasingly apparent that that controversial three-year sex education project of The Clinic in Dover was an "inside job" and that the Governor and Council were just plain conned into approving three annual contracts totaling $156,843 in federal family planning funds used to pay for the "New Directions for Young Men" project that developed the sex education curriculum portraying homosexuality as normal and healthy.

But what of the state employees who supposedly watched over the sex education project in intimate detail?

The Governor and Council need not wait for state Public Health Director William T. Wallace Jr.'s May 10th report on his agency's oversight of the project to conclude that this was strictly an "inside job" pulled off without the governor's and the executive councilors' knowledge and most assuredly without their consent. Research into relevant documents by *Union Leader* staff reporter Roger Talbot reveals that certain Bureau of Maternal and Child Health personnel were aware of the controversial sex curriculum as it was developed, tested and written.

Documents provided the *Union Leader* upon request to bureau chief Charles S. Albano show that certain state officials were in on it from the beginning, helping four years ago to select the project's so-called Male Involvement theme, drafting the outline in pursuit of the federal money and well aware of the inclusion in the project of the controversial sex education manual "Mutual Caring, Mutual Sharing." By 1985, The Clinic was referring to development of the teaching manual as a primary objective of its project.

But while this may have been an "inside job," in terms of its implementation, there are indications that the amoral (some would say immoral) concept was imported to New Hampshire. When The Clinic's New Jersey-to-Dover based executive director, Chuck Rhoades, submitted his final report to the highly cooperative Ruth Abad, health promotion adviser in the state maternal health bureau, he concluded his letter:

"Thanks for your support during this project and for bringing me up here in the first place."

We submit that the Governor and Council should be extremely interested in determining the philosophical underpinnings of this project and precisely where and under whose auspices they and it originated.

- - - - - - - - - - - - - - - - - - -

Clinic's Sex Manual Philosophy Rooted in Director's Education

(*Roger Talbot*, Manchester Union Leader, *May 16, 1988*)

(*Copyright 1988 by the Union Leader Corporation. Reprinted by permission*)

The administrator of a project that developed the sex teaching manual "Mutual Caring, Mutual Sharing" has held membership in a homosexual advocacy group and studied with Deryck Calderwood, whose sexuality program at New York University favored homosexuality.

Charles K. "Chuck" Rhoades, executive director of the Strafford County Prenatal and Family Planning Program (The Clinic), is a 1982 graduate of NYU's master's degree program in health education/human sexuality.

Calderwood, 63 when he died in 1986, developed and presided over NYU's "Marriage, Family Life, and Sex Education Program" since it was approved as the first graduate-level sexuality curriculum in the country in 1970.

Rhoades, now 34, was listed in a memorial service program as among those who eulogized Calderwood—as "Deryck the Teacher"—on Sept. 26, 1986, at the Judson Memorial Church in New York City's Greenwich Village.

Calderwood's program at NYU included nude body workshops and the use of questionnaires that probed the sexual history of his students.

Edward E. Eichel, who completed the NYU human sexuality master's program in 1984, participated in a nude workshop during the program's summer seminar in Maastricht, The Netherlands, in 1983.

"The workshop required students of the same gender to engage in physical exploration of each other's genitals," Eichel said.

Eichel said Calderwood led the male student group while female students met with a woman teacher. "Then both groups got together," he said of the nude workshop he attended in Holland.

Eichel, a New York City psychotherapist with 20 years experience, has challenged Calderwood's theories of sexuality education and written critically of his teaching methods.

He said he enrolled in the NYU program to understand it.

"I went through it and it's all bull. . . . It's manipulative and shallow—not science, just propaganda," Eichel said.

Eichel did not know whether Rhoades' course of study had included any encounter sessions similar to the nude workshop.

On Friday, Rhoades declined to be interviewed about his educational background. He said his graduate work at NYU was "irrelevant to the issue."

Earlier, he had said lawyers for the American Civil Liberties Union had advised him not to comment on The Clinic's dispute with the state pending resolution of the question of control over the teaching manual. The Clinic's directors have refused to turn over their mailing list and copies of the manual to the state commissioner of health and human services.

Eichel, Calderwood's former student, said the NYU program was developed "with a concentration on the issue of homophobia, emphasizing the societal biases against homosexuality."

A similar emphasis on homophobia is evident in "Mutual Caring, Mutual Sharing," which defines it as "the fear and hatred of gays and lesbians."

Among Calderwood's works is an instructional kit for teenagers, titled "About Your Sexuality." He developed it in the late 1960s under the auspices of the Unitarian Universalist Association. It was revised four times, most recently in 1983.

On page 1 of "Mutual Caring, Mutual Sharing," Rhoades and project coordinator Doug Cooper Thompson credited Calderwood's "About Your Sexuality" as the source of some of the activities they included in their 62-page teaching manual.

The 1983 edition of "About Your Sexuality" includes explicit filmstrips showing couples of the same and opposite sexes engaged in masturbation and intercourse. The program is flexible, however, allowing teachers to use the material with or without the filmstrips and tailor their presentations for groups ranging from fifth graders, to adolescents or adults.

Calderwood described the 1983 edition as an attempt to convey the program's underlying philosophy: That the experience of making love is important—not the choice of partners.

In his preface to the 1983 edition, Calderwood wrote:

"The consideration of all styles of lovemaking within one unit, rather than separating out homosexual and bisexual forms, is likely to be as confronting and unacceptable to some as the original visuals were at first. The format demonstrates the spirit of acceptance that we wished to present right from the start . . . .

"(The program) is more strongly aligned against sexism and homophobia and more supportive of the ability of young people to make well-informed decisions about their affectional and sexual relationships," wrote Calderwood.

Rhoades has been executive director of The Clinic since 1985.

He came to Dover in 1984 to coordinate "New Directions for Young Men," the federally funded project The Clinic conducted under contract with the state's Bureau of Maternal and Child Health.

The sex education teaching manual which evolved from that project states in its introduction:

"We wanted this curriculum to take what is often regarded as a radical approach to sexuality: that sexual expression is, in its purest sense, a healthy and basic aspect of being human and multi-variant in terms of individual differences. This would mean that we would strive to affirm the sexual feelings of young men and women, that we would help them sort through these sexual feelings, and that we would help them choose responsible ways of expressing their emerging sexuality."

Calderwood was long affiliated with the Sex Information and Education Council of the U.S. as a consultant, director and chairman of the board. SIECUS, which has no government ties, disseminates information on sexuality issues and provides training in areas such as curriculum development, said Eichel.

Rhoades listed SIECUS among his professional affiliations.

Rhoades also listed the National Organization for Changing Men.

Also a member of that organization was Thompson, the Cambridge, Mass., educational consultant hired when Rhoades became The Clinic's executive director. Thompson pilot-tested the curriculum with several groups of adolescents, wrote the sex education manual and trained teachers to use it.

In the manual, the National Organization for Changing Men is described as a group with nationwide membership "committed to [a] pro-feminist, gay-affirmative, male-supportive agenda."

The organization's research on homophobia is cited in the manual.

The manual includes a full-page report from the Homophobia Task Group of the National Organization for Changing Men. It states, in part:

"On average, one person in 10 is gay. Amongst your family members, your friends, your coworkers, the public figures you admire—one in every 10 is gay. While some have been embittered by society's prejudices, the vast majority of gay people lead diverse, well adjusted, satisfying lives. Gay people are proud to be gay. They are proud of having learned the truth about themselves despite societal oppression and lies . . . ."

Rhoades came to Dover after working as a health educator and director of education for Planned Parenthood of Northwest New Jersey in Morristown, N.J. He also was an instructor at a family planning project in Harlem and conducted sexuality education workshops at the University of North Carolina's Center for Early Adolescence.

While in New Jersey, Rhoades wrote "New Methods for Puberty Education," a 177-page teaching manual about puberty-related topics for use in grades four through nine.

His past work included the planning of more than 160 sexuality education programs for parent groups. He conducted more than 400 "educational programs for school students in coeducational and sex-segregated settings on a variety of reproductive health education topics."

On Friday, M. Mary Mongan, commissioner of health and human services, gave The Clinic 30 days to surrender all remaining copies of the "Mutual Caring, Mutual Sharing" manual. She declared The Clinic in default of its contract and said failure to comply with her order may result in the state reassigning to other agencies about $300,000 it now provides annually to support clinic programs.

The manual—in which homosexuals are described as "a very natural presence in our society"—has been criticized by the governor, the Executive Council, Strafford County commissioners, state officials, clergy and educators.

Typical of the comments was that of the state's commissioner of education, John T MacDonald.

MacDonald, after reading the manual from cover to cover, said he concluded, "It is neither age- nor content-appropriate for public school use."

- - - - - - - - - - - - - - - - - -

NETWORKING INSIDE SEXOLOGICAL ORGANIZATIONS

Recently, the American Association of Sex Educators Counselors and Therapists reversed a long-standing policy and decided to make public advocacy statements. One of the first to come out was a defense of the *Mutual Caring* sex education program. A handful of people within AASECT, without consulting the membership, announced that body's support of Rhoades' New Hampshire program, declaring it to be "well within the guidelines of competent sex education." This example, according to author Eichel, illustrates how a small group of activists working within an organization can produce a policy statement erroneously purporting to represent not only the entire membership but the whole profession.

As a member of SIECUS (The Sex Information and Education Council of the U.S.), the SSSS (Society for the Scientific Study of Sex) and AASECT (The American Association of Sex Educators, Counselors and Therapists), Eichel penned a further letter to AASECT in which the following points were made about this practice in general and AASECT's defense of the *Mutual Caring* program in particular:

. Gay activists within the sexological organizations have progressively gotten control of administrative positions and key committees and have networked to create the illusion that they represent entire organizations, the entire field—the opinion of experts in the field. In recent months, the SSSS and AASECT have issued position statements put together by a handful of individuals—networking for special interest groups—and made public pronouncements as though their advocacy represented the organizations. No vote is ever taken of the entire organization. They appear to have moved on the premise that there is really no policing force to monitor or counter such activity.

. An example of the manipulation occurring by means of advocacy statements is the announcement of support for Chuck Rhoades and the program *Mutual Caring, Mutual Sharing* (by Doug Cooper Thompson), which is under investigation in New Hampshire. This program was apparently maneuvered through the public health department without proper procedural input and administrative surveillance.

. This program refers to heterosexual children as "more accurately those. . . . who believe that they are heterosexual" (p. 11). This is an attempt to promote the Kinsey ideology and agenda that heterosexuality is pathologic, whereas uninhibited people are really bisexual—and that is normality. The attempt is to get heterosexual children to have homosexual experiences. The promotion of gay behaviors and polemicizing against heterosexuality *per se* is thematic throughout the program. It is suggested that anal intercourse is safe with a condom (p. 42). Experts do not agree. A 1981 book, *Anal Pleasure and Health,* is recommended as a resource material. (That book was written before the high-risk factor of anal intercourse associated with AIDS was well known and publicized.) The program developers recount that in developing and testing the program it was "casually assumed, without judgment, that any of the group [of children] might be sexually active now or in the future with an [AIDS] infected partner . . ." (p. 42).

. The self-appointed AASECT advocacy committee informed the general membership—which would have little or no familiarity with the Rhoades-Thompson program—that "[t]he Board reviewed the sex education program which had been criticized, and found that it was well within the guidelines of competent sex education. It [the advocacy group] then issued a statement that it objected to the withdrawal of funds [for the program] on the grounds that the program was within professional guidelines . . . ."

. The attempt by gay activists to push heterosexual children into high-risk AIDS categories of sexual "orientation" and sexual behavior should be a felony at this point in time. It should certainly never have been federally funded.

No action has been forthcoming on the basis of this complaint.

"ABOUT YOUR SEXUALITY"

This Deryck Calderwood sex education instruction kit for preadolescent and adolescent children has become a state-of-the-art model for Kinsey-type programming. In 1988, in one district in Connecticut, parents objecting to the introduction of this type of instruction into a school system began some networking of their own in defense of their children. In this case the battle was over Calderwood's classic sex education piece, which, reportedly, also is a mail-order item in some pornography catalogues.

The story of the Connecticut parents and the battle over "About Your Sexuality" are well described below in an article from the *New York City Tribune.* An editorial about this instruction kit by Richard Neuhaus of *The Religion & Society Report*—inspired by the Connecticut incident—is also reproduced.

A Church-Backed Sex-Ed Program Stirs Furor Among Parents, Clergy

(*Chris Corcoran*, New York City Tribune, *July 18, 1988*)

(*Copyright 1988 by News World Communications Inc. Reprinted by permission*)

A church-founded sex education curriculum entitled *About Your Sexuality* is at the center of a storm of controversy roused by parents and clergy who claim that the syllabus contains outright pornography that encourages sexual permissiveness and experimentation.

Published by the Unitarian Universalist Association and written by the late Deryck Calderwood, who was one of the first sex educators and who believed in the moral legitimacy of all aspects of free sex, the film strip and audio cassette program is designed for children as young as 12.

Among other things, youngsters viewing the film strip are exposed to graphic color pictures of male actors engaging in anal intercourse and oral sex, lesbian sex scenes and a male transvestite preparing himself in his female attire.

The *About Your Sexuality* program, which costs $275 to purchase, has come under attack recently by syndicated columnist Michael Mc-Manus, Episcopal clergymen—who resent it being recommended reading in their own new and controversial sex education curriculum—and parents, who condemn it as a deceptive attempt to promote homosexuality.

The Unitarians, who by their own admission comprise the most liberal church in America, say the program is socially advanced because it focuses first on lovemaking and second on who one's partner is.

The Rev. Eugene B. Navias, director of the department of religious education for the Unitarian Universalists, is responsible for the distribution of *About Your Sexuality*. He said the program, which was first published in 1970 and which is now in its fourth revision, is widely used in his denomination and seeks to answer for teenagers all sex related questions they might have, even if it sometimes offends people.

Navias said that 3,086 *About Your Sexuality* kits have been sold since the curriculum was first issued. He was unable to report the number of participants over the years, but guessed that roughly 100 people have been taught from each kit—totaling over 300,000.

"When we began addressing the sex education issue in the late '60s," Navias said, "we found that the teachers of teens in our church were bringing us questions that they didn't know how to answer.

"The public schools' education programs skirted controversial questions," he continued.

This motivated the denomination to develop its own program, under the guidance of sex educator Calderwood, who was for years a professor at New York University's graduate sexuality program.

'The Jefferson Tradition'

"We come out of the tradition of [Thomas] Jefferson, who encouraged open inquiry," Navias said.

Calderwood, who died in 1986 at age 63, was a disciple of sex pioneer Alfred Kinsey and believed, with Kinsey, that no type of sexual behavior is abnormal or pathological. He crafted the ideology of the NYU program, which has been called by one former student, Edward W. Eichel, "a gay studies program for heterosexuals."

Eichel, a married man who graduated from the program because he needed the credentials and who is now a New York psychotherapist, said: "Marriage was never discussed, not even as a category. Our textbook had a chapter on [heterosexual] intercourse, but we skipped it."

The *About Your Sexuality* program, which suggests participation in 30 to 40 sessions of 90 minutes each, is geared to "clarify [children's] values so they will become responsible for their own sexuality," Navias said.

But critics of the program claim that the values imparted by the program are ones of heterosexual and homosexual experimentation, medically unsafe sexual practices and deviant behavior such as transvestism.

Referring to the film sequence on homosexual sex, the manual instructs the group leader: "You might compare any negative responses concerning the difficulty of accepting same-sex lovemaking with the difficulty some people experience in watching a birth film for the first time.... It is a natural part of life.... It may take some time to appreciate and enjoy the beauty of the experience."

If parents wish to preview the material before allowing their children to see it, the program recommends they sit through 16 hours of sessions that are an encapsulation of the regular program.

"We do not feel that this is a program that can be quickly surveyed," Navias said.

But critics of the program say a conscious effort is made by program directors to withhold from parents the more sexually graphic pictures when parents do agree to go through the time-consuming process of screening the material for their children. Furthermore, there is a recurring chorus in the curriculum's text that directs adolescent participants not to share what goes on in the program with their parents or people outside of the group.

Navias confirmed that the program forbids the children to speak to their parents about what is said by others in the groups or what is revealed in the questionnaires. But this practice, he said, protects the sense of group trust that is essential if the children are going to be able to share honestly.

One sex therapist, the Rev. Fred Ward, a Unitarian minister who practices in New Jersey and a former student of Calderwood's at NYU, has since 1970 trained hundreds of people to be teachers of the *About Your Sexuality* program. He gives it high marks.

"We've trained people from the Catholic faith, every Protestant denomination, Judaism, the Boy and Girl Scouts, the YM- and YWCA, the Department of Corrections, private and public schools," Ward said.

"We're trying to help young people discover their own values and attitudes about human sexuality rather than trying to teach a specific set of values. We teach a valuing process.

"For instance, we teach values and attitudes about homosexual relationships, and then what [program participants] decide is very much up to them," Ward said.

Critics of the program, however, say a systematic methodology is employed that teaches young people that all types of sexual experiences are common and equally morally acceptable. And worse, they say, the program is actually designed to encourage homosexual experimentation.

For example, pictures in one filmstrip show young men having a pillow fight. They are followed by pictures of soldiers embracing in tears, of two men showering together, of two men lying naked in one another's arms with their genitals exposed and, finally, engaged in homosexual coupling.

Some parents have in the past reacted negatively to the material, Ward said, and forbidden their children to view it. The reason for this, he said, is that the parent usually "has not gone through the process," meaning he has not been thoroughly exposed to the program.

Ward said that some young people have kept in touch with him over the years, telling him how much they benefited from the course. Some of them, he said, asserted that they postponed sexual relationships after going through the course because "they don't have to experiment anymore to find out the truth about sex." Ward could not remember exactly how many such youths there were, saying only that they were "several" in number.

In answer to the criticism that the plethora of locker-room slang terms introduced early in the program is a method of desensitizing youths to the hard-core sexual material to come, Ward said it is merely the language of today's youth and gives students the necessary vocabulary to help them ask questions.

As for the explicit visuals of sodomy and fellatio, Ward said: "They are used at the discretion of the [group] leader if the group is mature enough to handle them. Originally, it was the kids who requested such explicit visuals."

One outspoken opponent of the program is the Rev. Kendell Harmon, an Episcopal priest who is outraged that his own church's sex education curriculum recommends *About Your Sexuality*.

"My most charitable description of the *About Your Sexuality* chapter labeled 'Lovemaking' is to call it pornography," Harmon said. "It systematically desensitizes the viewer. It presents the Kinseyan continuum of lovemaking, which is that some people are homosexual, some people are heterosexual and it's all OK.

"The material, as it's presented, is incredibly stimulating at a time of life when children's hormones are running wild," the priest said.

"In Christianity, marriage and heterosexual monogamy are held up as the ideal," he continued. "Marriage, however, never comes up in *About Your Sexuality*, even as a category.

"It's antithetical to the Christian ideal," he said.

"That my own church recognizes it and recommends it as a resource is a scandal," Harmon said.

Dr. Judith A. Reisman, author of a meticulously researched document on pornography for the U.S. government, lashed out at the Unitarian syllabus, saying it is both untruthful and harmful.

"The *About Your Sexuality* program is a highly dysfunctional corpus of information to deliver to anyone, much less young people," said Reisman.

"Calderwood produced highly misleading and fraudulent information regarding the nature of human sexuality. He was a Kinseyan and on that basis alone he was beginning on a framework of misrepresentation," she said.

To back up her charges, Reisman quoted from the preface to the 1983 edition of the manual for those who lead *About Your Sexuality* classes. It states, "To prepare students for including the bisexual and homosexual material, use the chart . . . that depicts the Heterosexual-Homosexual Scale as you read the following quote from the Kinsey report."

The quote reads, "[Human beings] do not represent two discrete populations, heterosexual and homosexual. . . . The living world is a continuum in each and every one of its aspects."

Reisman said that from a medical viewpoint the program encourages the spread of diseases.

"Calderwood explicitly promotes anal penetration without condoms in the filmstrips and states that washing well will enable males and females to enjoy anal intercourse without problems."

- - - - - - - - - - - - - - -

Indoctrinating the Children

(*Richard John Neuhaus*, The Religion & Society Report, *July 1988*)

(*Copyright 1988 by The Rockford Institute. Reprinted by permission*)

Indoctrination is a perfectly lovely word that gets a very bad press. Indoctrination is leading people into the doctrines or teachings by which a community desires to live. Thus, for example, we indoctrinate children that racial discrimination is wrong and that they shouldn't throw their chewing gum wrappers on the sidewalk. Yet the word "indoctrination" is piously eschewed by many educators. Indoctrination, they say, smacks of manipulation, of judgmentalism, of imposing our values on others. Education, they say, is not a matter of transmitting teachings but of eliciting the capacity of children to clarify the teachings by which *they* choose to live. In no area is this idea of the child as free agent to be more assiduously respected, such educators insist, than in the area of sexual behavior.

A good many other people, notably parents, are given to thinking that there are truths and falsehoods, even rights and wrongs—especially when it comes to sex. Not all parents think that way, of course. In fact, many of today's parents were educated not to think that way, and, therefore, all the greater is their embarrassment when they discover themselves thinking that way about the sexual behavior of their own thirteen- or sixteen-year-old children. As a result of their own indoctrination in guilt-free sexuality, they feel awfully guilty about their feeling that there are some things kids should not do and should not be encouraged to do. These conflicted feelings have everything to do with the confused reactions and seething resentments surrounding sex education in the schools. A common objection is that sexuality is too important and too morally laden to be left to the schools. That is a subject, we are told, that should be addressed by the home and the church. Educators respond that most parents are ill-equipped and disinclined to teach their children about sexuality and are just as glad to hand that job over to the schools. The educators are undoubtedly right in many instances. As for the church, it becomes increasingly evident that at least some churches have nothing to teach that is discernibly different from the pop-sexology disseminated by the schools.

Episcopal Indoctrination

For example, considerable controversy has been generated by *Sexuality, A Divine Gift*, a study guide put out by the Episcopal Church's Task Force on Human Sexuality and Family Life. Distancing itself from the usual adolescent pranks of such as Bishop John Spong of Newark, an Episcopal Church commission recently caught attention by urging that the "church should stand firm in its traditional moral principles." At the same time, however, it recommended *Sexuality, A Divine Gift* which, in the view of many, raises doubts about what those principles might be. The assumptions that inform *Sexuality* would seem to be made explicit in the program material that it recommends. "Highly recommended" by the task force is a curriculum titled *About Your Sexuality*, by the late Deryck Calderwood. Produced under the auspices of the Unitarian Universalists, the filmstrips and cassettes in *About Your Sexuality* are reportedly carried in pornography catalogs. Episcopalians who do not wish to get on distasteful mailing lists may now order directly from the church, which is no doubt a service of sorts. Whether the curriculum will help the adolescents for whom it is intended is another question.

The Calderwood curriculum makes for depressing reading. It is, of course, a sustained assault upon what perhaps most people still think of as elementary decency. But the assault is so earnest, so couched in jargon, so trivializing in detail that one finally succumbs to boredom. To be sure, it might be a quite different effect on a fourteen-year-old being introduced to the thrills of rutting, "same-sex enjoyment," and "self-discovery" through masturbation. Were parents aware of the contents of the curriculum, one may safely suppose that the reactions of most would range from uneasiness to outrage. Little wonder that those who serve as leaders in the Calderwood curriculum are repeatedly reminded to instruct the boys and girls that they must not tell others, they must most particularly not tell their parents, what went on in class. "Our society," they are told again and again, is sexually repressive, unenlightened, and naive, and parents who were educated before "this new age" just might not understand.

A Strange Orthodoxy

The teachings promulgated by the curriculum are troubling, but even more troubling are the intensively manipulative methods employed. But before getting to methodology, a few words on the orthodoxy that the curriculum seeks to advance. Norman O. Brown, a guru of the counterculture of the sixties, promoted "polymorphous perversity." Compared with Calderwood, there was something residually healthy about that, for it acknowledged, indeed exulted in, the category of the perverse. The present curriculum promotes what might be termed polymorphous naturalness. Anything that gives satisfaction is natural and good, the children are told. They are shown films illustrating myriad positions and improbable penetrations between and among people of varied sexes; boys and girls together are urged to "become comfortable" with handling tampons, jockstraps, and sundry contraceptive devices; one film has "Jeff" demonstrating the techniques of masturbation, including the pleasure of consuming his own semen, which it is suggested the boys might want to try; and so forth.

The curriculum is notably enthusiastic about "same-sex" experience and, despite the insistence that there are no rights or wrongs, it is forceful in its condemnation of "homophobia." Youngsters are encouraged to experiment homosexually and are assured—as the pedophilic have been assuring little boys from time immemorial—that it's harmless fun. In fact, the children are told and shown, homosexuality is all around us. This is illustrated by, among other things, a film of a father diapering his infant son, for, as we are told, baby boys also enjoy being masturbated. Anal intercourse is prominently featured, although there is no mention of AIDS, the mention of which might cast something of a pall over the excitements extolled by the curriculum.

The curriculum includes a listing of twenty-one questions about the "range of sexual experience," including, "Have you ever had sexual contact with an animal?" The question, the only question, that is asked about each of these experiences is, "Was this a satisfactory experience for you?" What is satisfactory is defined by whether it was or was not "ME." This is illustrated at one point by a chart which puts "ME" at the center, surrounded by the inhibiting pressures that must be resisted, such as "Church," "Parents," "Society," etc. The curriculum's enthusiasm for homosexuality is matched only by its devotion to contraception. The section on "Birth Control and Abortion" leaves no doubt that the latter is a dimension of the former. It is allowed that some people have moral qualms about abortion, but then it is confidently asserted: "Any assertion about when human life begins is arbitrary. . . . is necessary today for each person to arrive thoughtfully at a position which one believes is sound and in which one can have confidence."

Whether the subject is abortion or bestiality, it is presented in antiseptic language of clinical objectivity. But the full version of the course offers ample opportunities for the young people to "internalize" what they have learned about sexual possibilities and excitements by putting it into practice, also on weekend camping trips under the guidance of their leader.

The theme of *About Your Sexuality* is summed up in a gay manifesto recommended to the children. It declares, "We want to love ourselves." Nor, we are told, is this selfish or individualistic. On the contrary, it is part of a great and idealistic movement to overcome "our competitive, male-dominated, individualistic society" and establish a world "based on sharing . . . resources and skills." Loving ourselves is the "Human Liberation . . . that will create the basis for an all-embracing social change." In addition the curriculum is sensitive to "the great art and poetry" of our civilization and others that support its "holistic" view of sexuality. Walt Whitman is quoted on the joys of homophilia, and the editors show particular respect for a versifier named Rod McKuen, who apparently has also had some very satisfactory experiences. At points the curriculum suggests that conventional sensibilities should not be offended unnecessarily. For instance, it urges that children of a transvestite inclination be instructed in "appropriate cross-dressing."

A Manipulative Methodology

But enough on the dismal content of a curriculum that is recommended as part of the "ministry" of some churches. As sleazy as the attitudes and activities promoted is a teaching methodology that is manipulative, authoritarian, and, some may think, even cruel. Young children, adolescents, and teenagers are deliberately isolated in a semi-secretive environment where they are urged to distrust, even despise, family, parents, church, and societal norms. Nor, interestingly enough, are they even to trust their own sensibilities. Those sensibilities are to be reprogrammed in order to conform with what is repeatedly described as "enlightened understanding." If, for example, some children are at first repulsed by a film depicting homosexual intercourse, the leader is to encourage them to watch it again and again until they come to "appreciate the beauty of the experience."

What most people might think to be "normal" reactions to some ideas and practices are denigrated as "naive and unsophisticated." That follows, of course, once the category of normal has been eliminated, or, to put it differently, when the polymorphously perverse is declared to be the polymorphously normal. Reactions once described as normal are now deviant and vice versa. This curriculum for reprogramming human sexuality leaves no doubt that much must now be systematically repressed. Especially threatening to its purpose are ideas that children may have received from outside "the group," particularly from the family or the church. Perhaps at some point in the future a revised curriculum will be friendlier to the now despised traditional institutions of society, including the church, once those institutions have been appropriately reprogrammed.

In response to criticism, church officials have admitted that the curriculum is "extremely explicit." But that is not the problem at all, or at least it should not be. In the right context and at the right age, there need be no prudishness in teaching about the details of sexuality. In our culture it's an unusually sheltered teenager who has not been exposed to soft or hard porn. It is not clear, however, why he or she should be exposed to it in church. The problem with this material is what it communicates explicitly but, even more, what it says implicitly. Implicitly, it is a powerful denial of the very idea of *Sexuality, A Divine Gift*. Far from being a gift of God that can be directed toward great good or evil, sexuality is presented as nothing more than an appetite to be satisfied. Sex is divorced from interpersonal relationships, from procreative purpose, from the mysteries, obligations, and ambiguities of human loving. What is left is sex as appetite, whose imperious demands must be assuaged by whatever "lovemaking" one finds "satisfactory." In this view, sexuality is not a divine gift but a curse, and it is a wonder that this view is espoused by those who worry that the church has been identified in the past with a negative view of sexuality.

We do not wish to be unfair to the Episcopalians. *Sexuality, A Divine Gift*, together with the materials it recommends, has been subjected to vigorous criticism within the church. It is quite possible that the entire project will be formally repudiated by the church's General Convention in July.[1] There are similar programs in other churches, however, although perhaps none has gone quite so far in promoting materials exhibiting so thorough a disdain for Christian teaching about sexuality. Of course, many other teachings had to be set aside in order to prepare the way for a church to endorse the vulgarized paganism of *About Your Sexuality*. One does not get from Saint Paul to Rod McKuen in one leap. In addition, if this study is formally rejected, there will undoubtedly be some bishops and others who will explain the rejection by saying that the church was not mature enough, or sophisticated enough, or honest enough to deal with this "controversial" material. In our churches, old task forces typically do not die; they just come back with less egregiously offensive versions of the same message. The message is that, with respect to sexuality and much else, manipulative recruitment to the sad banalities of a debased culture is perhaps all that a church can do once it has lost its capacity to indoctrinate the young into the distinctive teachings of the community of faith.

- - - - - - - - - - - - - - - -

1   This sex education material was, in fact, repudiated at the July 1988 convention of the Episcopal Church, according to *The New York Times* (July 12, 1988, p. A22).

NEW YORK CITY BOARD OF EDUCATION FAMILY LIVING/SEX EDUCATION CURRICULUM

In 1986, concerns over sex education textbook content in New York City public schools inspired a strong letter of protest from a legal adviser of the Catholic Archdiocese of New York to the president of the New York City Board of Education. This letter speaks for itself. The full text is reproduced below.

Letter From John P. Hale to Robert F. Wagner, Jr., President, New York City Board of Education

(November 29, 1986)

I assume that you read the new curriculum on sex education before you mandated it on the Districts. In case you did not, I and several others thought it wise to read the books which your curriculum suggested be made available for reading by the children.

I plan in this series of letters to call your attention to certain material in those books. I recognize that we're both persons of sensitivity and certain matters are not discussed in public. I believe that in this case an exception must be made. Since your curriculum recommends a list of books as resources for children as low as the seventh grade (age twelve to thirteen), I feel that I can, indeed I must, quote the instructional material which those books contain.

Let me first direct your attention to the portion of your curriculum entitled "Resources for Students." At page 263 you cite "Learning About Sex—The Contemporary Guide for Young Adults" by Gary F. Kelly. Your short description says that Mr. Kelly's book helps teenagers "to clarify their sexual needs and values." You're correct. Mr. Kelly says at page 2:

I do not think it possible to write a book about sex without having many of my own values, opinions, and points of view showing through.

And he makes his values quite clear:

People differ greatly in their preferences for various forms of sexual behavior. I cannot judge the "rightness" or "wrongness" of any of these behaviors (p. 4).

Mr. Kelly is clearly an advocate of variety in sexual behavior. He says:

Most professionals in the field of human sexuality today seem to agree on one thing: That any individual's sexual orientations and behaviors need not be considered unhealthy unless they are causing physical or emotional harm to that individual or to others (p. 51).

Pornography?

. . . at least for most people, there does not seem to be any particular harm in the enjoyment of sexual pictures (p. 54).

What of looking at other people's naked bodies?

As much as many of us enjoy looking at other's [sic] bodies, it would be sensible to choose a method of doing so which is not frightening or embarrassing to others and not in violation of their right to privacy (p. 54).

Mr. Kelly recognizes that many children feel uneasy about getting started in sexual intercourse. Chapter 5 of his book is devoted to overcoming the natural reluctance to try something new. Mr. Kelly says:

... it makes sense to learn as much about the various forms of sexual activity as possible before deciding whether or not to engage in them (p. 67).

He describes how to engage in "petting"; he then moves to the next stage at page 66:

The term 'heavy petting' generally refers to deliberately stimulating the other person's sex organs. This is done not only with the hands but sometimes with the mouth. It may also refer to touching a girl's breasts. Sometimes, the touching is done through the clothing. Other times, one partner may reach inside the other's clothing or both may decide to remove their clothing. Of course, being in the nude with another person is often intensely pleasurable and highly sexually exciting. This represents a very deep level of sexual sharing which may carry with it strong emotions and the need for responsible decision-making.

Now I assume that your students may learn much from those two preliminary levels of sexual involvement. But Mr. Kelly will show your students how to move farther down the path. To really enjoy sex with your young partner, Mr. Kelly recommends against doing it in a car because of the cramped quarters (p. 68). (I'll show you in a later letter where it's suggested that a comfortable place to do it is at home when your parents are out.)

Mr. Kelly recognizes that many young people hesitate to engage in sexual activity because of "not knowing what happens during sexual activity" (p. 68). Mr. Kelly recognizes that inhibition and seeks to remedy it as he says:

I shall try, however, to describe what may happen as clearly as possible (p. 68).

In fact he describes it with such clarity and encouragement that I'm sure your students after reading it will no longer have any hesitation about becoming sexually active. Then, Mr. Kelly describes foreplay, mutual masturbation and sexual intercourse. Mr. Kelly recognizes that some young girls do not find sexual intercourse pleasurable. He advises perseverance. But Mr. Kelly does not stop at sexual intercourse. He suggests that the children try oral sex and says at page 70:

It would appear from the studies of sex researchers that a majority of people find oral sexual contact to be pleasurable and acceptable . . . *there seems to be no special medical dangers associated with oral sexual contact* [emphasis added].

Before commenting on the [italicized] section, I would point out that Mr. Kelly, consistent with his view of giving all of the variables, then says at pages 70-71:

Anal sex refers to the insertion of the male penis into the anus of his partner. . . . Unlike the vagina, the anus does not have its own source of lubrication, thus great gentleness and care must be taken, and a lubricating substance is often necessary for insertion. . . . Again, however, unless there are special medical problems, when cleanliness and care are observed, *there are no special medical dangers associated with anal sexual contact* [emphasis added].

Now Mr. Kelly may be correct that the way to overcome the natural reluctance of children to start engaging in sexual intercourse and other sexual behavior is to explain it carefully to them so they will know how to do it. But I must disagree rather strongly with his medical judgment that there are no special medical dangers associated with oral and anal sex. As a matter of fact, I thought what motivated you in issuing this curriculum was a concern with the level of sexual activity among the children in your schools and a special concern with the health hazards associated with oral and anal intercourse. I thought you knew that's how AIDS is spread. If you did, why would you recommend that your children read a book which encourages oral and anal intercourse and says there are no "special medical dangers" associated with such acts.

But there are other considerations. Oral or anal intercourse is sodomy. Under Penal Law, Section 130 *et seq.*, oral and anal intercourse are a crime in this state. You didn't know that is still the law? And you didn't know that there are special provisions of the Penal Law dealing with children under 17 engaging in sexual intercourse and sodomy?

How about having sex with more than two people? What would the Board teach the children about that? Mr. Kelly says:

The research studies on such sexual experiences are limited at this point. It may well be that some individuals find sex with more than one other person enjoyable and interesting (p. 77).

How about sadomasochism? Mr. Kelly says:

. . . sadomasochism may be very acceptable to sexual partners who agree on what they want from each other (p. 61).

What about having sex with animals? Mr. Kelly says:

There are no indications that such animal contacts are harmful, except for the obvious dangers of poor hygiene, injury by the animal or to the animal, or guilt on the part of the human (p. 61).

What about sex and marriage? Mr. Kelly says:

It is typical for people to think of sex when they think of marriage . . . . Currently, many people do not feel this to be true, and accept that sexual intercourse may be all right and meaningful in a loving, committed relationship, even without marriage (p. 128).

Is that what you plan to teach to the children in grades 7-12 in our schools? Lest you think that Mr. Kelly's book is an aberration, I plan to synopsize in further letters the other books which you have recommended to the children, books that say virginity makes no sense and that oral sex is a method of preventing pregnancy.

[Note: The recommended resource list for sex education in New York City schools was withdrawn].

SEX AND AIDS EDUCATION COURSES

The January 1988 edition of *FACT Report* gave a summary of some of the more egregious examples of the application of Kinseyan sex education philosophy around the nation. This summary was suitably prefaced by a statement from the 1972 Gay Rights Platform:

> We demand . . . Federal encouragement and support for sex education courses, prepared and taught by gay women and men, presenting homosexuality as a valid, healthy preference and lifestyle as a viable alternative to heterosexuality.

The text from here to the end of this chapter is from the *FACT Report* sex education review.

Sex and AIDS Education Courses

(FACT Report, *January 1988. Reprinted by permission*)

Prior to and along with the advent of the AIDS epidemic, sex education and "values clarification" courses have been subtly introduced in school systems throughout the United States and parts of Canada. In March 1984, the U.S. Department of Education conducted hearings in seven cities regarding the Protection of Pupils Rights Amendment, also known as the Hatch Amendment. Testimonies of concerned parents, civic and church leaders and others were given. The major media and press virtually ignored the hearings. The book *Child Abuse in the Classroom* (Crossway Books, 1985, Phyllis Schlafly, ed.) presents selected transcripts from those hearings. The following are several excerpts which vividly portray the type of indoctrination our nation's children are being subjected to:

· A parent of an eighth grader from Bellevue, Washington, testified that various questionnaires handed out to the children presupposed that all the children were already being promiscuous. "Of course, they constantly reminded the children to go to Planned Parenthood for their birth control.

"The parents have no idea the kids are being asked these things. There is one teacher in Bellevue who has all the boys say 'vagina'; he calls them individually and they have to all say this out loud in class. The boys say 'vagina' and the girls say 'penis'. One girl told me that she was so embarrassed that she could hardly bring out the word 'penis' because all these boys were sitting in the class. It just embarrassed her so. So he made her get up in front of the class and very loudly say it ten times.

"I feel what they are accomplishing is to embarrass them, to break down their natural sense of modesty, to just break down their barrier. . . . They say that they don't want the kids to have sex, but if they break down their natural defenses, those kids are going to have sex more easily."

    · A parent from Lincoln City, Oregon testified: "In my son's fifth grade Health class, all questions were answered without regard to a moral right or wrong. Homosexuality was presented as an alternative lifestyle. Sexual activity among fifth graders was not discouraged since it was feared that the students might be embarrassed and not ask additional questions.

    "I was present when a plastic model of female genitalia with a tampon insert was passed around so they might understand how tampons fit. Birth control pills were passed around and examined. Anal intercourse was described. At no time was there any mention of abstinence as a desirable alternative for 5th graders. The morality that was taught in the classroom that day was complete promiscuity."

    · Another parent from the same area stated that his daughter had been punished for being removed from this type of program. Emotionally, she was openly chided and ridiculed by other children in the school, without intervention from her teachers; physically she was detained and threatened with a pink slip if she did not attend, causing her to lose "free time" during school, unlike the students who attended the programs.

    · A father of three young boys from a town in Michigan delineated portions of a compulsory sex education curriculum for eighth graders which included the following questions:

One: Do you know why your parents and/or religion have taught that intercourse should wait until marriage? Do you accept these ideas? If so, then would you be creating a lot of inner turmoil to go against your own beliefs?

Two: Do you really feel comfortable and firm in your own beliefs? Try to imagine how you would feel about losing your virginity. Would it make you feel less valuable, less lovable, less good? If so it is a bad bargain . . . . [Note: this last line would be cited by education authorities as "encouraging abstinence."]

Five: What does intercourse mean to you—a permanent commitment for life, fidelity for both partners, love?

Six: However you answered question five, does your current relationship meet those criteria?

Seven: Is your current relationship emotionally open and intimate? . . . You are much more likely to have a satisfying experience if the relationship is on that level before you have intercourse.

Eight: Can you get effective contraception and will you both use it faithfully and correctly?

Nine: Are you prepared to face a pregnancy should your contraception fail?

Ten: Do you have the opportunity for uninterrupted privacy, free from fear of being heard or intruded upon?

"When the school boards are confronted by parents' objections [to this type of indoctrination] they say, 'Well, your children have a choice.' But when my sister-in-law refused to consent to having my niece enrolled in this type of program, the school authorities made the girl compile book report upon book report, an unreasonable amount of book reports, to be done each week. Not only that, she was separated from her schoolmates and completely isolated and made a social outcast, until enough pressure was exerted upon her mother that she finally consented for her daughter to become part of this sex education program.

"Is this not an attempt to change and subvert our children's way of thought and discredit parents who hold traditional values and beliefs?"

· From Phoenix, Arizona: "The need to protect pupils' rights is evident from 'health education' programs. One of the most objectionable sex questionnaires was published by the Federal Department of Health Education and Welfare in 1979. Consider some of the questions deemed to be appropriate for 'all adolescents of junior high age or older.'"

#12. How often do you normally masturbate (play with yourself sexually)?

#13. How often do you engage in light petting (playing with a girl's breasts)?

#14. How often do you normally engage in heavy petting (playing with a girl's vagina and the area around it)?

"Also consider these questions on page 150 from the 'Psychological Inventory.'"

#112. I think sexual activities like hand stimulation and oral sex are pleasurable ways to enjoy sex and not worry about getting pregnant. [Note: Mutual masturbation is now taught in AIDS education as "safe-sex." A latex "dental dam" is being recommended during oral sex.]

#119. For me, trying out different sexual activities is an important part of learning about what I enjoy.

"This type of questioning has to be regulated under the Hatch Amendment."

PARENT GETS OBJECTIONABLE CURRICULUM REMOVED

Mark Park Hiles, a leader in the fight for children's and parents' rights testified:

"My first introduction to how schools have changed occurred five years ago. I saw a movie which was shown to 8th graders in the kindergarten-through-12th-grade Human Development curriculum in their Human Sexuality Unit. The movie was 20 minutes long and depicted nude masturbation in detail. It showed how men do it, women do it, why they do it and where it feels best. Teenage actors were used.

"I determined to find out what was behind this K-12 curriculum. A teacher called me and said she had a copy of the 13-year curriculum guide and said she would leave it in her top desk drawer. I could come in when she was out, take it, and use it any way I wanted. I xeroxed 200 copies, spread it around the school, and both the program and the principal were removed from the school."

REPRESENTATIVE SAMPLINGS FROM PREMIER SEX-ED TEXTBOOKS

Learning About Sex: The Contemporary Guide for Young Adults, by Gary F. Kelly (Barron, Hauppauge, NY, 1986)

* Voted onto the Best Books for Young Adults List by the American Library Association.

* Dr. Mary S. Calderone, Co-founder and Former President, Sex Information and Education Council of the U.S. (SIECUS) asserts: "There isn't a person picking up this book who won't find something of special help and meaning in it. . . ."

Some sample quotes:

"A fair percentage of people probably have some sort of sexual contact with an animal during their lifetimes, particularly boys who live on farms. There are no indications that such animal contacts are harmful" (p. 61).

"Some people are now saying that partnerships—married or unmarried—should not be exclusive. They believe that while a primary relationship is maintained with one person, the freedom for both partners to love and share sex with others should always be present. . . . There is no general statement that can be made here about the 'best' or 'healthiest' way to be.

"Swinging or mate swapping . . . happens between couples who are friends and gradually become involved sexually" (pp. 136-7).

"Homosexuality is recognized to be a valid life-style which seems to be suitable for those who prefer to love and have sexual relationships with their own sex. . . . Most human beings have the potential for both heterosexual and homosexual attraction, and most of us learn to be heterosexual because our culture finds that pattern more acceptable" (pp. 56, 58).

"In the traditional marriage, however, it was sometimes impossible for the partners to be who they really were as individuals . . . but most gay men and women report that they have always felt themselves to be at an advantage in finding true equality in a relationship" (p. 133).

"There are, of course, many other double standards for males and females, many of them as equally absurd. Take, for example, the idea that it is all right for girls to touch and kiss each other as ways of showing tenderness and affection, but that is not all right for boys" (p. 73).

Changing Bodies, Changing Lives: A Book for Teens on Sex and Relationships, by Ruth Bell (Random House, New York, 1980), has been in use for eight years. Sample quotes:

"For you, 'exploring sex' might mean kissing and hugging someone you're attracted to. . . . Later, it might mean giving each other orgasms, or even making love. . . .

"Often this kind of sexual exploring is with a friend of your own sex. Lisa remembered:

"I had my first sexual experience when I was seven years old. It was with my best friend. We were constantly together. . . .Then one day we started fooling around and touching each other all over. For about a year, we'd sleep over at each other's houses and do this" (p. 85).

"You may think, as many people do, that we should stop thinking virginity is so special, and make our decisions about sex for other reasons" (p. 99).

"Most people are neither 'all straight' nor 'all gay'" (p. 112).

"Fear of gayness hurts straight people, too. Fear and prejudice go away quickest when you can meet some open homosexuals and know them as people. . . . The rest of this chapter may be a way for you to 'meet' some gay and lesbian teenagers indirectly and dispel some of the myths that contribute to the fear and discrimination against gay people" (pp. 112-114).

"Barry, seventeen is gay:

"I remember making out with a guy for the first time. We used to play basketball in the lot down the street and then come back to my place for a soda. This one time we were clowning around with towels drying off each other's sweat, and we started leaning up against each other. It was real exciting and real tender. We hugged and kissed for a while, then we went for a walk to get used to what had happened" (p. 95).

"Lesbians make love in lots of ways. Sometimes . . . [graphic positive description of lesbian acts were given].

"Gay men, too, have many ways of making love. One may . . ." [graphic positive description of oral and anal intercourse is given] (p. 122).

Boys and Sex and *Girls and Sex*, by Wardell Pomeroy, co-author of the Kinsey Reports (Delacorte, New York, 1981) have been in use for seven years. They are extremely graphic in their explicit, glowing descriptions of heavy petting, foreplay and a variety of positions for sexual intercourse. These books are recommended reading for 6th grade children (11-year-olds!) in the Milwaukee Public schools and elsewhere. A few of the statements excerpted from the narrative interspersed with these descriptions will suffice:

BOYS AND SEX

"Premarital intercourse does have its definite values as a training ground for marriage or some other committed relationship.

"In this sense, boys and girls who start having intercourse when they're adolescents, expecting to get married later on, will find that it's a big help in finding out whether they are really congenial or not; to make everyday-life comparisons again, it's like taking a car out on a test run before you buy it."

GIRLS AND SEX

"Petting is also extremely useful as a learning experience for later relationships, perhaps one that's better than intercourse itself. A boy ought to know how to stimulate a girl properly, and she ought to know what it's like to be stimulated . . . .

"There are many girls who regret after marriage that they didn't have pre-marital intercourse, because they've come to realize what a long, slow learning process it is after marriage. . . ."

The material presented in this issue is but a brief, highly edited overview of the values being instilled in children across the country. Educators, parents, physicians and others need to scrutinize curricula which are being rushed through in the name of AIDS education.

- - - - - - - - - - - - - -

CHAPTER SIX

FAILURE OF THE KINSEY DATA

Edward W. Eichel and Dr. J. Gordon Muir

Chapter Overview

The test of any theory— perhaps especially of human sexuality— is how it stacks up in the real world. By this yardstick, Kinsey's data on the prevalence of homosexuality in society— 10% of white males more or less exclusively homosexual (5 or 6 on Kinsey's scale) for at least three years between the ages of 16 and 55, and 4% exclusively homosexual (6 rating) throughout life after the onset of adolescence— now appear to be inaccurate.

The first test of the Kinsey data— a story of research dishonesty never fully told until now— was that conducted by the noted psychologist Abraham Maslow. Initially with Kinsey's cooperation, while Kinsey's research was still in progress, Maslow set out to find if there was bias in the composition of Kinsey's sample of interviewees. When Maslow was about to demonstrate to Kinsey that his study volunteers were sexually unconventional, Kinsey turned his back on this expert colleague, and his findings, and intentionally walked away from information that would undermine the credibility of his results. Kinsey's published work purposely misrepresents the Maslow story.

The second test is perhaps a more dramatic expose of the Kinsey homosexuality data. It is now coming to light that projections of AIDS cases based on Kinsey's 1940s— pre-sexual-revolution— estimates of the numbers of homosexuals may be off by several hundred percent, even when applied to a much more sexually "liberated" society 40 years later!

An examination of Kinsey's methods can help explain the discrepancy between AIDS prevalence and AIDS projections. His homosexuality rates, which have been applied to all of U.S. society, come from the overrepresentation of men with homosexual experience in his study sample and from faulty techniques of analysis. The homosexuality statistics derive from a group in which 20% to 25% had "prison experience" and 5% or more may have been male prostitutes.

Yet, using the same data and techniques by which he attempted to show that 13% of the male population was "predominantly homosexual," he could just as easily have shown that 100% was heterosexual.

And then there is the strange case of the grant that was made by the Russell Sage Foundation to have the original Kinsey data "cleaned" of its bias. This, of course, would have exposed the extent of the distortion in Kinsey's numbers. The project was botched. The individuals who negotiated the grant resigned from the Kinsey Institute. Kinsey co-author Paul Gebhard continued the project, but the original purpose was thwarted. Given the current use of the 1940s "unclean" Kinsey data even today in the matter of AIDS case projections, it is very curious that the Institute is not moving to restart this project.

Perhaps one reason for not wanting to clean up Kinsey's original data is fear of showing the extent to which his "homosexuality" figures have been in error. Two recently published sexual behavior studies— one conducted, ironically, for the Kinsey Institute in 1970 but only published in 1989—contain data suggesting that exclusive homosexuality is quite unusual in society.

INDICATIONS OF ERROR IN KINSEY'S RESEARCH

AIDS MISCALCULATIONS BASED ON KINSEY DATA

On July 19th, 1988, Health Commissioner Stephen C. Joseph announced that the New York City Department of Health had cut in half its estimate of city residents infected by the AIDS virus. The news was undoubtedly a shocking disclosure to the general public, and to many health professionals as well (Bruce Lambert: "Halving of Estimate on AIDS is Raising Doubts in New York." *New York Times*, July 20, 1988). Other nuances of this story demonstrated that the politics of AIDS is almost as complex and problematic as the characteristics of the AIDS virus itself.

AIDS activists from the gay community greeted with a somewhat bizarre ambivalence the good news that fewer people would die. They were upset that the revised statistics "suggested" the estimated number of homosexuals and bisexuals in the general population had been grossly exaggerated. It was specifically the over-estimation of the number of homosexuals in the New York City population that necessitated a downward revision of the AIDS projections for the city (estimates for other high-risk groups remained unchanged). The estimated gay male population among the 7.2 million residents of New York City was lowered from 500,000 to 100,000—an eighty percent drop (Lambert: "The Cool Reaction to New York's 'Good News' on AIDS." *New York Times*, July 21, 1988).

Health Commissioner Joseph told the story in his July 19, 1988 news release, "Health Department Revises Estimate of Human Immunodeficiency Virus Infection in New York City":

For some time . . . Health Department researchers have noted a disparity between the ratio of AIDS cases to the estimated number of gay men in New York City versus San Francisco: New York City, with a total population ten times that of San Francisco, has been estimated to have a population of gay men several times larger than San Francisco's, yet its AIDS caseload of homosexual men is less than twice that of San Francisco.

Recent San Francisco studies have produced more refined estimates of the number of HIV-infected gay men there, and have enabled New York City researchers to estimate anew the numbers of infected gay men in New York City, based upon the hypothesis that the ratio of the number of gay men with AIDS to the number of HIV-infected gay men is about the same in the two cities. That would produce an estimate of 50,000 HIV-infected gay men in New York City, rather than the previously estimated 200,000 to 250,000 [p. 3].

The erroneous New York City figures were based on statistics from the original 1948 Kinsey report on male sexual behavior, which projected, among other things, that one out of ten males in the general population was "more or less exclusively homosexual for at least three years between the ages of 16 and 55" and that 4% were exclusively homosexual throughout their adult lives.[1]

Kinsey's homosexuality statistics appear to be responsible for a further major error in estimates of AIDS virus infection rates—this time, nationally. The 4% exclusive homosexuality figure has been largely responsible for the Federal Government's claim—since 1986— that as many as 1.5 million Americans were infected with the human immunodeficiency virus (*Science* 243:304, 1989). Now, *four* years later, the figure may have to be revised down to around 1 million, and some Government officials suggest it should be as low as 650,000 (*Time*, January 22, 1990). The revised figure would be more in accord with recently published studies—one conducted, ironically, for the Kinsey Institute—indicating that predominant and exclusive homosexuality has been considerably overestimated in American and British society (see below).

The real-world refutation of the early Kinsey data will not come as a total surprise to some sexologists. The revision of the AIDS estimates—involving only the gay high-risk group—triggers an issue that has long been dormant in the sexuality field—the validity of the Kinsey data on homosexuality, based, as they are, on an unrepresentative sample of the population and an inappropriate statistical method for deriving prevalence figures.

[For a discussion of the error of using the accumulative incidence technique for calculating the prevalence of sexual behaviors, see chapter 1.]

---

1   See full text of former New York City Health Commissioner Stephen C. Joseph's news release, "Health Department Revises Estimate of Human Immunodeficiency Virus Infection in New York City," New York City Health Department, July 19, 1988. Kinsey's percentage figures are from his Male Report—see p. 651 and Figure 170, p. 658.

Some of the following material will shed more light on Kinsey's homosexuality figures and how they come to be the way they are. Like the AIDS statistics—to which they are related—they have been colored by political considerations.

THE AMERICAN STATISTICAL ASSOCIATION REPORT

Shortly after publication of the 1948 Kinsey report on male sexual behavior, a study to evaluate the report was undertaken by the American Statistical Association (ASA) at the request of the Committee for Research in Problems of Sex of the National Research Council (NRC). The ASA published *Statistical Problems of the Kinsey Report on Sexual Behavior in the Human Male* in 1954. The assessment concluded:

> Critics are justified in their objections that many of the most . . . provocative statements in the book are not based on the data presented therein, and it is not made clear to the reader on what evidence the statements are based. . . . [T]he conclusions drawn from data presented in the book are often stated by KPM [Kinsey, Pomeroy, and Martin] in much too bold and confident a manner. Taken cumulatively, these objections amount to saying that much of the writing in the book falls below the level of good scientific writing [Cochran W, *et al.*: *Statistical Problems of the Kinsey Report*. Washington D.C., the American Statistical Association, 1954, p. 152].

The ASA authors further specified, "In the case of homosexuality, we are chiefly concerned about possible bias in the sample . . . " (*ibid.*, p. 150).

Defenders of Kinsey's research will point to the fact that the ASA review was overall favorable. Indeed, in a section of the ASA report titled "Comparisons with Other Studies," Kinsey's 1948 work was rated first in a *methodological ranking*, based on "sample and sampling methods, interviewing methods, statistical methods, and checks," etc. (p. 219). However, some of the official correspondence cited in the ASA report hints of pressure to critique Kinsey kindly. In a letter to Dr. Isador Lubin, chairman of the ASA's Commission on Statistical Standards, Dr. George W. Corner, a member of the NRC's Committee for Research in Problems of Sex, made a strong appeal on Kinsey's behalf:

> I am writing to state to you the desire of the Committee for Research in Problems of Sex, of the National Research Council, that the Commission on Standards of the American Statistical Association will provide counsel regarding the research methods of the Institute for Sex Research of Indiana University, led by Dr. Alfred C. Kinsey [p. 4].

Dr. Corner, a long-time ardent supporter of Kinsey, related that the NRC had "been the major source of financial support of Dr. Kinsey's work, and at its annual meeting on April 27, 1950, again renewed the expression of its confidence in the importance and quality of the work by voting a very substantial grant for the next year" (p. 4). The letter further stressed:

Recognizing, however, that there has been some questioning in recently published articles, of the validity of the statistical analysis of the results of this investigation, *the [NRC] Committee, as well as Dr. Kinsey's group, is anxious to secure helpful evaluation* and advice *in order that the second volume* of the report, now in preparation, *may secure unquestioned acceptance* [p. 5; emphasis added].

The ASA report on Kinsey's 1948 study appears to have been something of a fence-straddling effort, noting that "it would have been possible to write two factually correct reports, one of which would leave the impression with the reader that KPM's [Kinsey, Pomeroy and Martin] work was of the highest quality, the other that the work was of poor quality and that the major issues were evaded." They concluded, "we have not written either of these extreme reports" (p. 1).

In their assessment of Kinsey's work, the ASA authors covered themselves with some powerful cautions. They stipulated that the Kinsey team's "[summarization of] what the data *appear* to show" might be valid "*assuming that the sample is representative, the measurements are unbiased,* and that their love for bold statements may be overlooked" (p. 150; emphasis added). And, of course, it is precisely these assumptions that have proven invalid in the light of information that has become available since the ASA statisticians wrote their review.

The ASA authors had no way of knowing the full extent of the participation of prisoners and sex offenders in Kinsey's sample. It seems that they also did not know of—or did not take account of—a second type of bias in the Kinsey data: the bias introduced by volunteering.[2]

THE KINSEY-MASLOW TEST FOR BIAS

Volunteer Error in the Kinsey Study

The following account reveals how a so-called great scientist hid information that he didn't like and turned his back on a colleague who was providing data that would undermine the credibility of his results. This is one of the clearest—if least known—examples in this century of dishonesty in a major scientific project. The lack of professional integrity demonstrated by this incident is supportive of the claim of fraud in Kinsey's research.

In his 1948 Male Report, Kinsey alluded to a little-known collaboration with the prominent psychologist Abraham H. Maslow[3] (Male Report, pp. 103, 104), whose sex research on animal behavior, and on the human female, had preceded Kinsey's work. Maslow, on the basis of his own findings about five years earlier (*Journal of Social*

---

2   Other contemporary statistical criticisms had been much more severe. Writing in *The American Journal of Psychiatry* (June, 1948), Hobbs and Lambert observed that "for some reason the authors are so thoroughly convinced that 'homosexuality' is highly prevalent that they are anxious to compound any possible errors in almost any way which will increase the apparent incidence." See also chapter 1.

3   Maslow was a cofounder of Humanistic Psychology and a leader of the Human Potential Movement.

Psychology 16:259-294, 1942), warned Kinsey about the probability of bias in the personality type and sexual behavior of his volunteers. Maslow had concluded in his 1942 paper on female sexuality that "any study in which data are obtained from volunteers will always have a preponderance of [aggressive] high dominance people and therefore will show a falsely high percentage of non-virginity, masturbation, promiscuity, homosexuality, etc., in the population" (*ibid.*, pp. 266, 267). Kinsey at first agreed to a joint project with Maslow to test for the degree of this volunteer bias in his own study.[4]

Maslow recruited students for Kinsey's research from his classes at Brooklyn College. As he already had personality assessments for these students, he was able to show that the type of person volunteering for the Kinsey project displayed the characteristic bias that he called "volunteer-error." This error meant that Kinsey was collecting a greater number of unconventional sex histories than would have been obtained from a truly random sample of the population.

Maslow provided Kinsey with the personality assessment data for the students that volunteered for his study. Kinsey had the matching sex-history data. At this point *Kinsey ceased to cooperate with Maslow, refused to give him the matching sex data and refused to continue their joint project to determine the exact extent of the bias in the Kinsey sample.* Maslow, without Kinsey's participation, published a paper on his part of the joint study. In this he refers to the fact that Kinsey still had not published his own portion of the results ("Volunteer-error in the Kinsey study." *Journal of Abnormal and Social Psychology* 47:259, 1952). Maslow did not make an outright accusation in his article, but 18 years later he all but admitted this was a Kinsey cover-up. Six weeks before his death in 1970, Maslow recounted the entire affair in a letter to a colleague:[5]

> [W]hen I warned him [Kinsey] about "volunteer error" . . . he disagreed with me and was sure that his random selection would be okay. So what we did was to cook up a joint crucial test. I put the heat on all my five classes at Brooklyn College and made a real effort to get them all to sign up to be interviewed by Kinsey. We had my dominance test scores for all of them and then Kinsey gave me the names of the students who actually showed up for the interviews. *As I expected, the volunteer error was proven and the whole basis for Kinsey's statistics was proven to be shaky.* But then he refused to publish it and refused even to mention it in his books, or to mention anything else that I had written. *All my work was excluded from his bibliography.* So after a couple of years I just went ahead and published it myself [emphasis added].

---

4   Maslow AH, Sokoda JM: Volunteer-error in the Kinsey study. *Journal of Abnormal and Social Psychology* 47:259, 1952. This affair was recently brought to light by Edward Hoffman in *The Right to be Human: A Biography of Abraham Maslow*, New York Tarcher/St. Martin's, 1988, pp. 167-170.

5   Letter from Abraham H. Maslow to Amram Scheinfeld, April 29, 1970. (Located in Archives of the History of American Psychology [NB Box M424], University of Akron, Akron, Ohio 44304.) Reproduced in full in Appendix A.

Kinsey did, in fact, allude to the Maslow collaboration (Male Report, pp. 103, 104). But he presented a totally different impression than was given in Maslow's 1952 paper. Kinsey implied that the matter of volunteer error was minor and may only have involved having some more "extrovert" and "assured" individuals in his sample. And Kinsey clearly misled his readers when he said, "how [these results] affect a sexual history is not yet clear." It *was* clear, and Kinsey withheld the details and never referred to the Maslow study again—even in his Female Report five years later, and one year after Maslow had drawn attention to the issue by publishing his part of their two-part study.

It is remarkable that this research "giant" so quickly turned his back on data that did not fit his thesis. It is perhaps not so surprising that Kinsey's co-researcher Wardell Pomeroy, who assisted him in the aborted collaboration with Maslow, did not mention Maslow's name in his 1972 Kinsey biography.[6] It is as if the event had never taken place.

In effect, the volunteer bias in Kinsey's study exaggerated the kind of sexual behavior and attitudes about sex that Kinsey idealized thematically in his reports. And if former Kinsey Institute employee Gershon Legman is correct in saying that the purpose of Kinsey's research was to "respectabilize" unconventional behavior [see chapter 1], then volunteer error served Kinsey's purposes well.

Kinsey's breaking of his agreement with Maslow and his concealment of his part of their results is better understood in this light. Also better understood is Kinsey's conspicuous failure even to mention the Maslow collaboration in his Female Report, despite publication of Maslow's article discussing Kinsey's sample just one year earlier.

In fact, there was a second very good reason Kinsey *should* have acknowledged Maslow in his 1953 book: Lewis Terman's 1948 review of Kinsey's male research pointed out that *volunteer error was detectable in Kinsey's male sample from internal statistical evidence alone*. Kinsey, who was familiar with Terman's criticisms of his Male Report, was thus aware of independent confirmation of what Maslow had been telling him.

The Maslow affair, which has just come to light, is one of the most clear-cut examples of deceit in science that the authors of this book have ever seen. Why did Kinsey do this? Apart from his preset agenda, discussed elsewhere in this volume, another motive is identified by Maslow's friend, Dr. Amram Scheinfeld, to whom Maslow had confessed his disillusionment with Kinsey. Maslow's letter to Scheinfeld was actually a response to an earlier letter to Maslow in which Scheinfeld said of the Kinsey research: "Al [Kinsey] was setting out then to be the world's No. 1 sexology (*sic*)—and, by gosh, he succeeded, though by means which we'd hardly endorse."[7]

6   *Dr. Kinsey and the Institute for Sex Research*, Harper & Row, 1972.
7   Source: Archives of the History of American Psychology; see footnote 5.

DISSEMBLING IN A MEDICAL JOURNAL

Another clear-cut example of deceit in science is purposeful mis-representation in a professional publication. This also is a fairly good indication of data problems, and of problems with the ethics of those handling the data. The following account helps to explain how Kinsey could have dealt with Dr. Maslow the way he did.

In 1941, an article by Kinsey on homosexuality appeared in a reputable medical publication, the *Journal of Clinical Endocrinology* (Vol. 1, pp. 424-428, 1941). Noting that there was a lack of acceptable data on the subject because "the best of the published studies are based on the select homosexual population which is found in prisons," Kinsey went on to present some of his own data, which, he implied, were not from a *select* population. He wrote, "Elaborate analyses of these data suggest that they provide a fair basis for estimating the frequency [of homosexual experience] in our American population as a whole. . . ." But he *concealed* the fact that his own data were from the same type of select sample that he had just described as being unsuitable for use in drawing conclusions about the general population.

Kinsey noted in the same article that he already had 300 of the high school histories contributed by a colleague, Glenn Ramsey, in Peoria, Ill. As we later learn, these were from a high school group described by a Kinsey co-author as "aberrant" because of a very high rate of homosexuality (see below).

Given this propensity for deceit so early in his career, what followed later perhaps is not so surprising.

[Details of the prisoner content of Kinsey's male interviewees are given below and in chapter 1.]

MISLEADING DATA ON HOMOSEXUALITY

It was shown earlier (chapter 1) that Mengele-like "scientific" experiments on infants and children were the basis for Kinsey's con-clusions—largely accepted and taught in academia today—on childhood sexuality. Similar uncritical acceptance of Kinsey's "science" has led to the widespread assumption, heard somewhere almost every day, that 10% of the population is gay. These false assumptions remain popular scientific lore, perpetuated through con-stant repetition in a so-called skeptical media and through appropriation as givens in medical and psychological journals.[8]

It is quite obvious from the text and tables of the Male Report itself that Kinsey and co-authors set about to discover a high incidence of homosexuality in society.

From a totally unrepresentative interview sample, the Kinsey team *"generalized"* that 1) "37 per cent of *the total male population* [of the United States] has at least some overt homosexual experience to the

---

8   Commentator Pat Buchanan has written several columns—beginning in 1983—pointing
     to ethical violations and deception in Kinsey's research. He even challenged journalists
     to investigate the matter, but no one picked up the ball.

point of orgasm between adolescence and old age . . . nearly 2 males out of every 5 that one may meet"; 2) one out of every four males has "distinct and continued homosexual experience" for at least three years between ages 16 and 55; 3) one in eight males "has more of the homosexual than the heterosexual," while 10% are "more or less exclusively homosexual" for the same period; and 4) "4% of . . . white males are exclusively homosexual throughout their lives, after the onset of adolescence"(Male Report, pp. 650, 651; emphasis added).

It is a considerable P.R. achievement that Kinsey got the public, the media and most (but not all) of his peers to be duped by this collection of statistics from a sample in which up to 25% of persons had a prison or sex-offender history (see chapter 1). And Kinsey would no doubt smile broadly if he could know that today "the government's guess that between 945,000 and 1.4 million Americans are currently infected with the [AIDS] virus . . . [is] based largely on [his] contention that 4% of all Americans are 'exclusively homosexual' throughout life," according to William Booth in the January 20, 1989, issue of *Science*.

To make matters even more confusing (or embarrassing!), it turns out that what the Kinsey authors implied to be "homosexual *activity*" or "homosexual *experience*" may not have been correctly described. They state in the Male Report that "the statistics given throughout this volume on the incidence of homosexual activity . . . are based on those persons who have had physical contacts with other males, and who were brought to orgasm as a result of such contacts" (Male Report, p. 623). This is deceptive because some of Kinsey's statistics—like his famous 10% figure—appear to derive from his homosexual-heterosexual ratings data, which are based on "psychologic reactions" as well as "overt experience" and do not require contact to orgasm.

It was noted in chapter 4 that Female Report co-author Paul Gebhard had expressed ambiguity about the manner in which Kinsey added together *thoughts about sex* with actual sex acts to classify people on his rating scale. The rating a person received on this scale (his degree of homosexuality) was entirely decided by Dr. Kinsey and a few personally trained staff, whose subjective judgment included weighing the relative importance of thoughts and dreams.

The two most incisive critics of Kinsey's Male Report statistics were Dr. Albert Hobbs and R.D. Lambert of the sociology department at the University of Pennsylvania. In their June 1948 review in *The American Journal of Psychiatry*, they pointed out another definitional problem with Kinsey's use of the words "homosexual" and "homosexuality." They showed from Kinsey's own data that what he loosely referred to as "homosexuality" was, "in the main . . . 'homosexual play' among preadolescents and adolescents . . . rather than a pattern of life" (p. 763).

"By age sixteen," noted Hobbs and Lambert, "31.6% of the population, according to [Kinsey's] data (Table 139, p. 624), has had some homosexual experience . . . [but the] peak incidence is only 37.5%, which is reached at age 19"! They added, kindly (giving the Kinsey team the benefit of the doubt): "[the Kinsey authors] apparently *forgot* that the percentages referred to an activity which may have occurred no more than once during a lifetime and *assumed that it was occurring throughout the life of the individual*" (*ibid.*, p. 762; emphasis added). (A third definitional problem was the probable classification of male prostitutes—of whom there may have been a minimum of 200 in the Kinsey sample—as homosexuals. See next section.)

Using the same techniques of analysis, Hobbs and Lambert commented, the Kinsey team could have shown that "almost 100% of the population had more of the heterosexual than the homosexual in their histories," instead of emphasizing that 13% of the population had more of the homosexual than the heterosexual. "This is an apparent paradox which is not faced by the authors" (*ibid.*, p. 762).

Quite apart, then, from the Kinsey authors' deception in concealing the true composition of their sample, there is a second major deception in the *presentation* of the homosexuality statistics. An age category ("between . . . 16 and 55") was invented and two totally different types of homosexual experience were added together as if they were one and the same thing. Incidental adolescent homosexual experiences of heterosexuals (the most common type of same-sex experience recorded by Kinsey) were combined with the adult experiences of true homosexuals. This created the illusion that a significant percentage of males were genuinely homosexual.

This maneuver is essentially confirmed by John Gagnon and William Simon in their 1973 book *Sexual Conduct: The Social Sources of Human Sexuality* (Aldine Publishing Co.), where they describe a reanalysis of 2,900 college students in the Kinsey data. They found that 30% had had same-sex experience. However, in all but 5% these experiences consisted of a single or few contacts between the ages of puberty and 18, "but nothing after that" (pp. 71, 72).

Basic disproportions in Kinsey's male sample were discussed in chapter 1. Serious disproportions might therefore be expected among the sample from which Kinsey derived his homosexuality statistics. This turns out to be the case. Hobbs and Lambert highlighted the problem:

> *Two-thirds of the males in the United States [in 1948] who are 16 years of age or over have been married, and almost 85% of those over 30 years of age have been married. In the sample from which the percentage of "homosexuality" among all "adult" (16 years[9] of age or over) males is derived, less than 15% of those over 15 have been married and over 35% are still single at 30 years of age. In the educational group with the highest incidence (those who entered high school, but did not go beyond) 46% are still single at age 30, and those married are so few that they cannot be included in any age group [ibid., p. 762; emphasis added].*

9 Kinsey's definition of "adulthood" beginning at age 16 is purely arbitrary and helps to obscure the fact the "homosexual" behavior being discussed is chiefly adolescent sex play.

They added another significant observation: "Over 80% of the incidence of all categories of homosexuality from 'at least incidental homosexual experience' to 'exclusively homosexual throughout their lives' is derived from 'inactive' Protestants, one of 6 religious categories" (*ibid.*, p. 762).

In the 40-odd years since the Kinsey homosexuality statistics were presented, bits and pieces of additional information on these data have trickled out from various sources, including the published works of former Kinsey associates. It is amazing, however, that in all that time no one has provided an accurate demographic accounting of the males from whom Kinsey derived homosexuality and other sexual behavior statistics that were applied to the entire U.S. white male population.

Even an attempt by Kinsey Institute staff to reanalyze the data failed (see below). Our own efforts to further clarify the composition of Kinsey's male sample—including telephone interviews (by E.E.) with Kinsey co-authors Pomeroy and Gebhard and former Kinsey Institute staff member John Gagnon—lead us to believe that it is purposeful that the full truth about Kinsey's interviewees has not been revealed.

Although there were supposedly 5,300 white males in Kinsey's total male sample, of whom up to a quarter, as noted previously, were sex offenders and/or had prison experience, it appears that only 4,301 were used as the basis for his homosexuality statistics.[10] (Actually, it is difficult to find the other 1,000 anywhere in Kinsey's data.) However, it seems that about 20% to 25% of the 4,301 also had prison backgrounds.

In his 1977 book *Human Sexualities* (Scott Foresman & Co.), John Gagnon gave some information on a group of interviewees that approximated Kinsey's homosexuality sample. He related that about 950 of the non-college population had "prison experience" (p. 253). This fits with a warning by Paul Gebhard in the *National Institute of Mental Health Task Force on Homosexuality: Final Report and background papers* that "[homosexuality] figures for the grade school educated and high school educated [in the 1948 Kinsey Report] are distorted by the inclusion of substantial numbers of individuals with prison experience" (p. 24).[11]

This leads to a final mystery about the Kinsey homosexuality data. In a telephone interview, January 1988, Paul Gebhard told E. Eichel about the contribution to the Kinsey data of an "aberrant" high school group—the only high school in the study—where the homosexuality rate was "running something like 50%"—higher even than among prisoners in that educational category!

In a telephone conversation (March 1990) with former Kinsey colleague C.A. Tripp (author of *The Homosexual Matrix*), Eichel further learned that this high school "had a very big homosexual component," but nevertheless was included in the 1948 Kinsey Report.

10   See Male Report, Table 140, p. 628; also Gagnon *et al.* in the National Research Council's advisory report, *AIDS: Sexual Behavior and Intravenous Drug Use*, National Academy Press, Washington, D.C., 1989, p. 118.
11   U.S. Government Printing Office, Washington, D.C., 1972.

It transpires that the location was Woodruff Senior High in Peoria, Ill., and that the contributor of data was Kinsey disciple, and Woodruff teacher, Glenn Ramsey, who conducted sex surveys of children (coordinated with the Kinsey research) without the consent of parents or, it appears, the school. Ramsey was fired in connection with this effort, but he managed to contribute about 350 histories to the Kinsey research, according to Male Report co-author Wardell Pomeroy.[12]

The Ramsey affair is recounted differently by Wardell Pomeroy in his Kinsey biography than by Ramsey's former principal. According to Pomeroy, Ramsey's principal "knew about what he was doing and approved," but small-minded persons on the school board got Ramsey fired, implying he had moral problems. As Pomeroy tells it, Ramsey was something of a martyr, a victim of a "weasel-worded" attack reminiscent of the type of opposition Kinsey's Marriage Course at Indiana University had experienced (see Introduction).

In a telephone interview (May 1990) with the former Woodruff High principal, Eichel was told that the principal had only learned of Ramsey's sex studies from other teachers, who were appalled at what was going on. Ramsey was asked to stop his sex research, said he would, but did not, and was therefore fired by the school superintendent of the city.

Kinsey was very annoyed and wanted Ramsey to make a test case against the idea that the school board (and presumably not Kinsey) could decide what was "acceptable science."

Ramsey took no action, and Pomeroy concluded his account noting that "the grand design in Bloomington, to which the Peoria affair was only a sideshow, continued in an ever expanding fashion." Since no one knows anything about "aberrancy" at Woodruff Senior High in the 1940s, the results Ramsey contributed to the Kinsey research remain a mystery.[13]

Given the foregoing, some of it barely believable in a discussion about a famous research project, it will be highly instructive to read what the Kinsey team tried (successfully, for the most part) to tell the public they were doing with their statistics. They claimed that "some 'statistical sense' would seem to be a fundamental requirement for anyone attempting to investigate any species, including the human," as if *they* had such a sense (Male Report, p. 21). [At this point, readers may wish to review Hobbs and Lambert's critique—reproduced in chapter 1—of the Kinsey team's misuse of the accumulative incidence technique for tabulating human behavior.] They added, impressively:

> Satisfactory incidence figures on the homosexual cannot be obtained by any technique short of a carefully planned population survey. The data should cover every segment of the total population. *There is no other aspect of human sexual behavior where it is more fundamental that the sample be secured without any selection of cases which would*

12 See Dr. Kinsey and the Institute for Sex Research, pp. 83-86.
13 Perhaps one clue to the high "aberrancy" rate among Ramsey's Peoria subjects is the observation in Pomeroy's Kinsey biography that "a judge of the county court. . . . referred many cases of sex delinquency to him for help" (p. 83).

bias the results. . . . In order to secure data that have any relation to the reality, *it is imperative that the cases be derived from as careful a distribution and stratification of the sample as the public opinion polls employ, or as we have employed in this present study* [Male Report, p. 618; emphasis added].

This sounded scientific and correct, but it was not true. It was also not true that especially exhaustive validity testing had been done on the homosexual data (Male Report, p. 625).

The only worthwhile test was comparison with a 100% sample. This was applied only to a group that contributed a small weight to Kinsey's homosexuality statistics, but it showed homosexuality rates were higher than they should have been in Kinsey's partial sample. But all of this was academic. Although Kinsey claimed to have a substantial number of persons from 100% groups (Male Report, p. 95), 30 years after the Male Report was published, Paul Gebhard explained that "The term 100% [was] actually a misnomer. . . ."[14]

Hobbs and Lambert observed that the Kinsey authors seemed "anxious to compound any possible errors in almost any way which would increase the apparent incidence [of homosexuality]." The end result of all this was, as they pointed out, that Kinsey was able to conclude from a "small, atypical segment of the population (males who remain single) plus virtual absence from the sample of all Protestants, Catholics, and Jews who attend church with any degree of regularity, plus unusual definitions of 'homosexuality' and 'adult,' that over 6,000,000 males in the 1940s were 'predominantly homosexual'" (*American Journal of Psychiatry*, June 1948, p. 762).

A continuing result is that today we remain with some "givens" about sexual behavior. A *Time* magazine writer can boldly state, for example, without fear of contradiction, that "about 25 million Americans are gay" (*Time*, July 10, 1989, p. 56).

THE RUSSELL SAGE PROJECT

There has been ample opportunity for the Kinsey Institute to rerun the data and try and correct (or at least measure) the biases of the original Kinsey Report(s). This opportunity still exists today. But the correction has never been done—even while the Kinsey Institute has known that planning, funding, and policy making related to the current AIDS epidemic has been based on statistical data from the 1948 Kinsey report on male sexual behavior. There is, however, an intriguing story about the Institute's one known unsuccessful attempt to clean the data of sexually biased groups that were included in the "normal" population and to make a comparison with the early biased data of the original Kinsey Report.

Any attempt to clean the Kinsey data would have to take account of *known* sexually biased groups listed by Gebhard and Johnson in their 1979 book, *The Kinsey Data: Marginal Tabulations of the 1938-1963*

14   In Gebhard P. Johnson A: *The Kinsey Data: Marginal Tabulations of the 1938-1963 Interviews Conducted by the Institute for Sex Research*, W.B. Saunders Co., 1979, p. 31.

Interviews Conducted by the Institute for Sex Research (W.B. Saunders Company). Gebhard explained that "by known sexual bias, we mean a group which we knew to be substantially biased in some sexual way before we began interviewing its members" (p. 4). Examples included: "the Mattachine Society (a homosexual organization), the occupants of homes for unwed mothers, prostitutes employed by a famous madam, personal friends of individuals known to be sexually deviant, and patients in mental hospitals" (*ibid.*). It also would have to take account of prisoners, *who made up the majority of the non-college population* in the Kinsey Male Report.[15]

Cleaning these data would be a fascinating task. For example, Kinsey has told us that there were "several hundred male prostitutes" among his histories (Male Report, p. 216). Since, according to Kinsey, these persons "usually experienced orgasm" with their customers, they would be in his homosexuality statistics. Assuming a minimum of 200, this would be 3.8% of his total male sample or 4.7% of the sample from which he derived his homosexuality prevalence rates!

In 1963 (several years after Kinsey's death [1956]), the National Institute of Mental Health gave the Kinsey Institute a three-year grant to code and store the entire collection of sex histories (1938 to 1963) obtained by the original Kinsey-interview method. These were to be recorded on punch cards and tape in order to facilitate additional analysis of the data (Gebhard and Johnson, 1979, p. 2).

A logical next step was a publication on the complete data. John Gagnon, a project director at the Kinsey Institute, negotiated a grant with the Russell Sage Foundation in 1967. The grant was awarded in 1968 for the stated purpose of "Re-analysis of the Kinsey Data on Sexual Behavior."[16] It was Paul Gebhard, a Kinsey co-author and Kinsey's successor as director of the Institute, who finally published a report on the project (Gebhard and Johnson, 1979, p. 3). A major purpose of the grant was to compare the new and cleaned data with the data in the original Kinsey reports "so that the extent of prior error may be estimated and suitable qualifications and corrections made" (*ibid.*).

The grant description in the 1968-1969 *Annual Report of the Russell Sage Foundation* (p. 47) listed the principals in the grant as "John Gagnon of the State University of New York at Stony Brook and

15   In a personal conversation with John Gagnon (January 24, 1988), E. Eichel was told that "44% of all the prisoners" in the Kinsey male sample had *"Homosexual"* experience in prison. Since this 44% equalled "a third among the rest of the [non-college] population," the total prison population was approximately three quarters of the non-college population. Also, if *Time* magazine (August 24, 1953, p. 51) was correct in saying that 63% of Kinsey's sample was college-educated (ie, 37% was not), then a quarter or more of Kinsey's 5,300 male sample may have been prison inmates.

16   "Re-analysis of the Kinsey Data on Sexual Behavior" (grant description), *Russell Sage Foundation Annual Report, 1968-1969*, pp. 46-7. Russell Sage Foundation, 230 Park Avenue, New York, New York 10017.

William Simon of the Institute of Juvenile Research, Chicago, both *formerly* of the Institute for Sex Research at Indiana University" (emphasis added). It further stated that they were preparing a "Technical Report" to discuss "the biases resulting from sampling and interview techniques, and a comparison of the variances reported in the original volumes with those computed on the complete set of data" (*Russell Sage Foundation Annual Report, 1968-1969*, p. 46).

Apparently, after the grant had been awarded in March of 1968, Gagnon and Simon resigned from the Institute and were not invited back to complete the work.[17] However, according to Gebhard, "their new commitments prevented their continuing with the project. By then a large number of computer runs had been made but unfortunately, through an *oversight* these were made on the total rather than the 'cleaned' sample, and were consequently of no use" (Gebhard and Johnson, 1979, pp. 2, 3; emphasis added).

In spite of the fact that Gebhard had acknowledged that "the presentation obviously had to be in a form which would permit direct comparison with our first two volumes [the 1948 Male and 1953 Female Reports]" (*ibid.*), the final product consisted simply of a new data presentation. The data were not rendered in a form where a comparison would ever be possible with the first two Kinsey Reports (*ibid.*, p. 8). *The Russell Sage Foundation refused to publish the report*, and Gebhard found his own publisher—the same publishing house (Saunders) that had published the original Kinsey books.[18]

What then might have been the difference between the biased and the cleaned Kinsey statistics? Gebhard (with Alan Johnson, his data processor) provides a hint in *The Kinsey Data*. He states, "To have done a thorough comparison would have involved the equivalent of rewriting both 'Kinsey Reports' . . ." (p. 8.).

A clearer idea of what the difference between the cleaned and uncleaned data might have been was, in fact, provided by John Gagnon in his book *Human Sexualities*. Here Gagnon admits to a number of problems with the 1948 Kinsey Report that would have "inflated" the figures on homosexuality (pp. 253, 254). He notes (as was first pointed out by Albert Hobbs in his 1948 review) that "it took only one experience" at "any time" in an individual's life to be classified "homosexual" by Kinsey. Gagnon then goes on to describe how "even

---

17   E. Eichel attended a presentation by William Simon, "'Perversion': Pedophilia and Sadomasochism," presented at the 31st Annual Meeting of the Society for the Scientific Study of Sex, November 12, 1988 in San Francisco. In a personal conversation with Dr. Simon, Eichel was informed that Simon's role in the Russell Sage Foundation project was to make the comparison between the new and "cleaned" data and the data in the Kinsey Reports. Simon said he did not finish the project because he "was never invited back" to the Kinsey Institute.

18   The subject of "cleaning" the data was discussed in a personal conversation between E. Eichel and John Gagnon, January 24, 1988. When asked about the computer-run errors in attempting to compare Kinsey's biased 1948 data with the "cleaned" data, Gagnon said he had "no idea what happened." He had "left before the Gebhard and Johnson [1979] volume was ever published." The book was published "without [his] knowing about it" even though he had been "the person who invented the idea of doing it," Gebhard had done it "without ever discussing it" with him.

this rather modest version of homosexuality (once in a lifetime) was inflated":

> First, Kinsey had included in his total sample a considerable number of men [approximately 1,300] who had not gone beyond the twelfth grade, had been imprisoned [between 900 and 1,000 of these men], and who came from poverty-stricken and disorganized sectors of society, a number far greater than would have been included in any random sample. There was therefore an upward bias in the homosexuality figure. Second, interviewed in the study were men from groups nearly entirely homosexual in composition [*Human Sexualities*, p. 253; figures in brackets from Gagnon's footnote, p. 253].

Gagnon continues, "If we exclude these cases (the homosexual subgroups and the men with no college experience), there is a major drop in the [homosexuality] figures" (p. 253). He concludes, "We can estimate that there are probably something like three to four percent of the male population with exclusively homosexual preferences .... This is *not* anywhere near an estimate such as one in ten ..." (p. 254; author's emphasis).

Actually, as will become obvious from two male sexual behavior studies reviewed below—in one of which Gagnon was a co-author—Gagnon's modified figure of 3% to 4% for "exclusively homosexual preference" is still inflated.

CO-AUTHORS TROUBLED BY KINSEY DATA

In his book *The Kinsey Data*, Kinsey co-author Paul Gebhard described his concern about the homosexual bias he believed was in Kinsey's Male Report. According to Gebhard, "Individuals from improperly recorded biased sources could contaminate the large sample, conceivably to a serious extent." Sources with inadequate records as to possible bias could include "a homosexual community" (p. 28). Gebhard believed that "contamination was a fault in our first two publications [Male and Female Reports]" (*ibid.*). As Gebhard tells it in *The Kinsey Data*, Kinsey was more concerned with "building and defending the research" than he was with problems of bias. As he began to get input from new staff and critics, he became more aware of some of his sampling problems, but "unfortunately by then he was also hypersensitive and defensive as well as still a bit naive" (*ibid.*). Gebhard described trying to tell Kinsey that it was a mistake to have included prisoners in his male sample:

> I recall once suggesting that it might have been a mistake to have included prison inmates in the general population on which we based *Sexual Behavior in the Human Male*. I was promptly crushed by his response that 1) since I did not know the incidence of prison experience in the population—particularly at lower socioeconomic levels—how dare I suggest discarding everyone with prison experience, and 2) what right had I to assume that the lives of prisoners prior to incarceration were in any way atypical? Why should we "throw away" a lifetime of useful data simply because of one misdemeanor or felony? During the preparation of the volume on

females, Pomeroy, Martin, and I did conspire to compare prison with nonprison females and found a substantial difference in behavior. Much to Kinsey's credit when confronted with facts rather than suppositions, he agreed to omit prison females from almost all of the volume even though the omission made it impossible for him to present a picture of females with less than high-school education (Gebhard and Johnson, 1979, pp. 28, 29).

This retrospective from Paul Gebhard is especially interesting because Kinsey (and co-authors, including Gebhard) did not tell us this story in the 1953 Female Report. Instead they merely stated, deceptively it now appears, that "the record given in our volume on the male included a much larger sample of the grade school group [the group with high prisoner content] and *was probably more representative of that group of males*" (Female Report, p. 79; emphasis added).

"THE LONG, LOST SEX SURVEY"

In 1989, John Gagnon (with co-authors Robert Fay, Charles Turner and Albert Klassen) published the results of a 1970 Kinsey Institute study of the "prevalence of same-gender sexual contact" among a survey group of 1,450 men, aged 21 years or older (*Science* 243:338-348, 1989). Called "the long-lost sex survey" in a 1988 *Science* news story because it took so long to be published (disputes over priority of authorship have been cited—and denied—as the reason for delay), this study claims that "minimums of 20.3% of adult men in the United States in 1970 had sexual contact to orgasm with another man at some time in life; 6.7% had such contact after age 19; and between 1.6% and 2.0% had such contact within the previous year."

Although the authors acknowledge the non-randomness of Kinsey's earlier study (the reasons given—use of "institutional groups" such as "PTAs" and "disproportionately drawn from the Midwest and colleges"—deftly avoiding the *real* problem), they imply that their figures are not completely out of line with Kinsey's [37%] and that their 20.3% "might be taken as a lower bound" because of the "negative bias" that "societal intolerance" may have exerted. However, the 20.3% figure with "sexual contact to orgasm" is misleading because it turns out that only the interviewee's partner may have had the orgasm. By contrast, in Kinsey's 37% figure (but not other Kinsey figures, q.v.) the person interviewed was required to have achieved orgasm. So, in 1970, with a more liberal definition of homosexual contact, the Gagnon study turned up a prevalence of "some overt homosexual experience" of almost half that reported by Kinsey among 1940s men.

Completely ignoring the Maslow lesson, the authors of this new Kinsey study repeatedly argue that their figures are actually lower than they should be because of "the response biases that *one can reasonably assume . . . operate . . .*" (emphasis added). A closer look at the new Kinsey Institute study, and consideration of an even more recent study out of England, lead us to believe that the true rates of "exclusive homosexuality for life" (which Kinsey put at 4%) and "more or less exclusive homosexuality for at least three years between 16 and 55" (which Kinsey put at 10%) are far less than anyone has previously believed.

The 20.3% of 1970s adult men with a history of orgasmic sexual contact with another male is the figure from the new Kinsey study that has received attention. However, the more pertinent data from the authors' tables are that only 4%[19] of the men surveyed *reported* having had a homosexual experience at least once after the age of 20, and only 1.9% *reported* such experience "occasionally" or "fairly often"—for the rest (2.1%), contact was "once," "twice," or "rarely." It is also clear from the data that these percentages do not describe "exclusively homosexual" men. The majority of the men with adult same-gender contact were "currently or previously married." And, significantly, "the reporting of heterosexual contact with never married men [was] substantial."

Clearly this new Kinsey study points to an "exclusive lifetime homosexuality" figure for 1970 males well below the 4% Kinsey found in the 1940s.

As noted earlier, Albert Hobbs pointed out in his 1948 *American Journal of Psychiatry* review of Kinsey's Male Report that much of the "homosexuality" Kinsey was reporting referred to "an activity which may have occurred no more than once during a lifetime" and that "in the main the . . . phenomenon under observation [was] 'homosexual play' among preadolescents and adolescents rather than 'homosexuality' as a pattern of life." Data from the tables of this later Kinsey Institute report indicate the same process in operation. Of those men reported by Gagnon and his colleagues to have recorded same-sex contact on their survey questionnaires, for approximately 30% it was once, twice or rare—and it occurred before the age of 15. Whether once, twice, rare or occasional, 65% of these incidents had occurred by age 19.

A more recent survey of male sexual behavior, conducted in England and Wales between 1984 and 1987 among a randomly selected sample of 480 white males aged 15 to 49, indicated that "the proportion of men having had homosexual intercourse is lower than is sometimes believed" (*British Medical Journal* 298:1137-1142, 1989).

David Forman, principal author of this study and senior staff scientist at the Radcliffe Infirmary, Oxford, reported that his subjects were a randomly selected group whose "social class and marital state were broadly similar to those of the population of England and Wales." Importantly, there was "no prior indication that detailed questions on sexual history would be asked during the interview."

Forman found that only 1.7% of his sample had had homosexual intercourse, and less than half of these had had more than one partner. Of those with more than one homosexual partner, a majority had had more heterosexual than homosexual partners. It was concluded that "frequently cited figures such as 10% of men being more or less

---

19   The 6.7% quoted by the authors in their text is higher because it includes actual reports plus "assumptions" made for missing data.

exclusively homosexual cannot be regarded as applicable to the general population."

While the prevalence of "homosexuality" may be different in the U.S. and Great Britain, the public in both countries has believed occurrence rates to be much higher than they are. Certainly Kinsey's figures of 4% for exclusive lifetime homosexuality and 10% for more or less exclusive homosexuality (for at least three years between 16 and 55) for 1940s males look extravagant even by comparison to data from 1970s and 1980s (post-sexual-revolution) males.

Late-breaking news from the presentation of several sex surveys at the 1990 annual meeting of the American Association for the Advancement of Science in New Orleans seems to confirm a very low homosexuality rate in the U.S population. Revealing the results of two of these studies, University of Chicago sexual behavior researcher Tom Smith noted, "As Americans we've been perhaps a little more circumspect than popular media images lead us to believe" (*Newsday*, February 2, 1990).

In one of Smith's studies, titled "Adult Sexual Behavior in 1989: Number of Partners Frequency and Risk,"[20] conducted among a national full probability sample of the adult household population of the United States, it was found that "Overall . . . less than 1% [of the study population has been] exclusively homosexual" (p. 5).

GOING SOFT ON KINSEY

Although John Gagnon and co-authors, in the recent publication of the 1970 Kinsey Institute study, admitted to sample problems with the earlier male population used for Kinsey's Male Report, they carefully avoided pointing out the most serious deficiency. Here is what they said about Kinsey's male sample:

> Kinsey gathered most of his cases by recruiting networks of friends through contact persons who offered him entree to institutional groups (for example, faculty members who introduced Kinsey to their classes) and through similar contacts that led to less institutionalized collections of persons (for example, Parent Teachers Associations). The sample was disproportionately drawn from the Midwest and from college campuses (*Science* 243:338, 1989).

This pointedly avoids stating what the real problem with Kinsey's sample was—the inclusion of groups, such as prison inmates, sex offenders, prostitutes, etc., with a higher-than-normal level of unusual sexual behavior. This amounts to a deceptive whitewash of Kinsey's Male Report. Also, in their *Science* article, Gagnon and colleagues give a certain legitimacy to Kinsey's homosexuality figures by arguing that their 20.3% figure for homosexual contact represents a "lower bound" and that there are some similarities "overall" to Kinsey's 1948 data.

At an earlier, less sensitive time, John Gagnon has been much more direct about the prisoner content of Kinsey's male sample and the homosexuality data derived from it. But recently he was a principal in

---

20   A study by the National Opinion Research Center, University of Chicago, February 1989. Funded by the National Science Foundation.

the proposed $15 million government-funded Kinsey-type national survey on sexual behavior (see below) that was supposed to update Kinsey and define normal sexual behavior in the AIDS era. Highlighting, in the high visibility arena of *Science*, how Kinsey got his homosexuality figures may not have been considered appropriate.

Currently, the National Research Council of the National Academy of Sciences has called for a new Kinsey-type national survey on sexual behaviors "to slow the spread of AIDS . . ." (NRC advisory report on AIDS, p. 164). The proposed federally funded project has led to controversy concerning the purpose and validity of such a study. Considering that the early Kinsey data have proved predictably erroneous, it is of concern that philosophical disciples of Kinsey may be attempting to acquire new data to bolster an agenda of aberrant sex behaviors and alternate lifestyles. A stated goal of the study is to "update and build upon the studies by . . . Alfred Kinsey published in 1948 and 1953." In a familiar vein, it is claimed that "not only could the information help reduce disease, it also could define 'normal' sexual behavior . . ." ("Sex Surveys of Adults Teens to be Weapons in the War Against AIDS," Raleigh *News and Observer*, February 28, 1988).

Dr. Richard Green, long-time gay activist—and an M.D. who recently obtained a degree in law—stated that "he would expect a new survey to shed light on the relevance of sex laws, such as statutes that ban sodomy. For example, if anal intercourse is found to be practiced more by heterosexuals than homosexuals, using the sodomy statutes to prosecute gays would be discriminatory" ("Who's Having Sex? Data are Obsolete, Experts Say," by Jane E. Brody, *New York Times*, February 28, 1989).

[See chapter 7 for further discussion of the National Research Council's advisory report, *AIDS: Sexual Behavior and Intravenous Drug Use*.]

CHAPTER SEVEN

THE KINSEY GRAND SCHEME

Edward W. Eichel and Dr. J. Gordon Muir

Chapter Overview

The Kinsey Institute, in cooperation with the Society for the Scientific Study of Sex (SSSS)—specifically, its AIDS Task Force—and several other professional groups, is currently mobilizing to influence the direction of social policy and sexuality education in what is now the "AIDS Era."

The rationale for this action is that Kinsey-school sexologists need to be in a position to educate policymakers as to "what human sexuality really is like." Bruce Voeller, a coordinator of the SSSS AIDS Task Force, believes they are now in an excellent position to get the type of funding needed to "educate the world."

These and related developments are described below. They are, in effect, steps toward implementing what Kinsey co-author Wardell Pomeroy alluded to as the "Kinsey grand scheme"[1]—the development of a gay model of "sexual orientation" and sexual behavior for everyone. Sexual access to children is a long-term goal for some.

Appeals to anthropology for the legitimization of behaviors formerly considered aberrant are now part of both the gay and pedophile agendas. These agendas have other common aspects.

AIDS, SEX AND ANAL INTERCOURSE

In December of 1987, The Kinsey Institute for Research in Sex, Gender, and Reproduction (current name) held a special invitational

---

1   According to Pomeroy in his Kinsey biography (*Dr. Kinsey and the Institute for Sex Research*, Harper & Row, 1972) the "grand scheme" or "design" was in its "simplest terms" to find out what people were doing sexually. However, as has become apparent, it was actually to provide a statistical base for a new morality.

conference on "AIDS and Sex" to provide medically oriented researchers with what the Institute has termed a biobehavioral model of sex norms.[2]

This symposium—as the following details help to explain—was part of an ongoing effort to permit Kinsey-style ideologists in the sexology establishment to dictate that a gay model of human sexuality is really the "normal" one for everyone. In this view of sexuality, bisexuality is normal and anal intercourse is as natural and pleasurable for heterosexuals as vaginal intercourse. The special concerns of the AIDS era are being used as an effective cover for this type of promotion. To add credibility to such efforts, "initiatives" and "outreaches" have been established to include medical and family-oriented organizations in "coalitions" with sexologists, whose goals can thereby be cloaked in a measure of respectability. The narrative below offers some insights about the goals of the Kinsey conference and the events leading up to it.

At the November 1987 30th Annual Meeting of the Society for the Scientific Study of Sex, James W. Ramey, Ed.D., and Bruce Voeller, Ph.D., gave an update on the activities of the recently formed SSSS AIDS Task Force Committee.[3] Ramey, chairperson of the Task Force, has an extensive background of research in alternative lifestyles. He is co-author with Mary Calderone of *Talking with Your Child About Sex* (Random House, 1983; Ballantine Books paperback, 1984). Voeller, a microbiologist working on condom research in relation to AIDS, was one of the first coexecutive directors on the National Gay Task Force (NGTF). As a gay spokesperson, Voeller had written in the late seventies that gays "should put an end to . . . embarrassment about transcending monogamy," and had recommended "openly and honestly incorporating recreational sex into . . . relationships."[4] Together with his NGTF lesbian coexecutive director Jean O'Leary, he declared it "immoral to pretend to children that they don't have a variety of loving options . . . ."[5]

The goals of the AIDS Task Force were defined in an article in *The Society Newsletter* (September, 1987): "The Society is actively promoting development of research projects . . . which might further

---

2   The Fourth Kinsey Symposium, *AIDS and Sex: an Integrated Biomedical and Biobehavioral Approach*, sponsored by the Kinsey Institute for Research in Sex, Gender, and Reproduction, the National Institute of Allergy and Infectious Diseases, and the National Institute of Child Health and Human Development, convened at the Kinsey Institute, Indiana University, Bloomington, Indiana, December 5-8, 1987. Proceedings to be published by Oxford University Press.

3   "Report of the SSSS AIDS Task Force." Panel report by James W. Ramey, chairperson, and Bruce Voeller, presented at the 30th Annual Meeting of the Society for the Scientific Study of Sex, 1957-1987, *Three Decades of Sex Research and Beyond: Public Policy, Freedom of Inquiry, Scientific Advancements*, Atlanta, Georgia, November 6, 1987 (on audio cassette).

4   Bruce Voeller: "Stonewall Anniversary," *The Advocate*, July 12, 1979. Cited by Dennis Altman in *The Homosexualization of America* (Boston: Beacon, 1982), p. 176.

5   Jean O'Leary and Bruce Voeller: "Anita Bryant's Crusade," *New York Times*, June 7, 1977. Cited by Enrique T. Rueda in *The Homosexual Network: Private Lives and Public Policy*, Devin Adair, 1982, p. 99.

understanding of human sexual behavior . . . ."[6] The article continued: "This information is important because far too little non-clinical research is being funded despite the fact that much of the information necessary to combat AIDS is unknown (eg, how many heterosexuals practice receptive anal intercourse)." The newsletter related that "the Society's AIDS Task Force is preparing literature identifying social science research needs and making recommendations to legislators, governmental agencies, universities, and private agencies and foundations regarding the advancement of knowledge about sexual behavior and sexuality education."

The steps taken to mobilize a comprehensive AIDS initiative have been recounted in the AIDS Task Force Report presented at the SSSS conference in Atlanta (see footnote 3) and in *The Society Newsletter*. A first step was getting sister sexological organizations to create AIDS task force committees and send representatives to the SSSS Task Force. A second step was an outreach effort to recruit family-oriented organizations and services, which resulted in the development of a National Coalition on AIDS and the Family. A third step was the recruitment of medically oriented organizations and research institutes, which expanded the network into a consortium of professional organizations that includes the Kinsey Institute, the Sex Information and Education Council of the U.S. (SIECUS), the Planned Parenthood Federation, the National Council of Family Relations, Family Services of America, the American College of Pediatrics, and others.

In his Task Force Report presentation (November 6, 1987), Voeller announced that in a month he would be co-chairing "a special invitational conference at the Kinsey Institute [held December 5-8, 1987] with people from all over the world who are leading experts on AIDS— the heads of the CDC [Centers for Disease Control], some of the major European and African and Brazilian authorities and figures in AIDS research, and a whole segment of leading sex researchers: the 'old Kinsey guard' and the 'new Kinsey guard,' Bill Masters and his wife [Masters and Johnson], etc." Voeller explained that up until now, the clinical "AIDS researchers . . . have not had the privilege [of learning] and the [benefit of] knowledge of what human sexuality really is like."

In his summation, Voeller recalled how the Institute of Medicine in a 1986 report had "knock[ed] the Kinsey data saying it was statistically flawed . . . ." But, he related, "even they—from their relative color-blind position about sexuality—recognized that there was a need for more information."

Lauding the kind of changes brought about by support for AIDS education from Surgeon General C. Everett Koop, Voeller expressed his belief that at this point in time "the possibility of getting support, of doing research—of all kinds now—is at a place it's never been before." He continued: "And that's why we can use the clout we've got and address it to levering funds, levering support—and in that whole process educating the world."

6   "The Society's AIDS Task Force." In *The Society Newsletter*, a publication of the Society for the Scientific Study of Sex, September 1987, p. 4.

In the guise of assuming a leadership role in the AIDS crisis, the Kinsey Institute had included among its symposium speakers a very select group of people advocating the Kinseyan model of sexuality.

Former Institute staff member William Simon presented on the topic "Patterns of Oral-Genital Behavior" (symposium book of abstracts, p. 37). He observed that "oral-genital activity has moved (and continues to move) from the margins of 'perversion' to inclusion as part of conventional sex scripts." Simon interpreted "a preference/desire for oral-genital activity" to be "the result of an emerging preference for homoerotic experience." He added, "The increasing conventionalization of oral-genital activity may be seen as part of the evolving deconstruction of the cultural paradigm that emphasizes coitus as the dominant organizing and culminating sexual event."

A rough translation is that gay-oriented sexologists are at war with *sexual intercourse*. Intercourse is perceived as a threat to the objectives of the Kinseyan "gay" agenda. As long as coitus is regarded as *the* sex act it will interfere with the promotion of homosexual sex to heterosexuals. It also will get in the way of the agenda of pederast "boy lovers"—possibly the most prevalent type of pedophile[7]—who want to see sex with children legitimized.

At the Kinsey AIDS conference, Margaret Nichols, Ph.D., gave a presentation titled "Women and Acquired Immune Deficiency Syndrome (AIDS): Issues for Prevention." In her interpretation of studies and field reports, she suggested that "women are at risk [for AIDS] more from ongoing contact with one infected partner than from multiple sexual partners" (symposium book of abstracts, p. 34). This conclusion appears to be a contrivance to promote a promiscuous lifestyle. The more obvious conclusion would be that women are at greater risk from sex with potentially infected multiple partners than from one partner who is virus free.

In 1987, Dr. Nichols, who has become a spokesperson for women on AIDS, gave a presentation, under the auspices of the Human Sexuality Program at New York University and the Society for the Scientific Study of Sex, on the topic "Lesbian Sex Radical Movement: What Does It Mean for Female Sexuality?" According to the program announcement,[8] one of the objectives of the new movement is to redefine female sexuality by "expanding the boundaries and limits of what has traditionally been considered the female sexual experience." The Lesbian Sex Radical Movement has "borrowed some concepts from gay men" but appears not to want to borrow the message that the

---

7   The statement is often made by sexologists that there are more heterosexual than homosexual pedophiles (eg, see *SIECUS Report*, January 1980, p. 15). This appears to be an attempt to justify homosexual pedophilia. As pro-pedophile author and researcher Theo Sandfort put it, "The assumption [is] implicit that, should there prove to be just as much heterosexual as homosexual pedophilia, then homosexuals [do] not need to account for homosexual pedophilia in any special way" ("Pedophilia and the Gay Movement." *Journal of Homosexuality* 13(2/3):95, 1987.

8   See announcement for Margaret Nichols, "The Lesbian Sex Radical Movement: What does it mean for Female Sexuality?" Winter meeting, February 29, 1987, sponsored by The Human Sexuality Program, New York University and New York City Chapter, Society for the Scientific Study of Sex.

promiscuous, multiple-partner lifestyle has been a real ecological loser in the 1980s.

Nichols declared that Radical Sex Lesbians are "producing written, auditory and visual erotica, writing essays, and developing theories about female sadomasochistic sex, butch-femme sexual roles, group sex, casual sex and nonmonogamous relationships." At her NYU/SSSS lecture, Dr. Nichols presented a video demonstrating the technique of vaginal fisting.

A significant feature of the Kinsey Institute symposium, *AIDS and Sex*, was the coining and introduction of the term "Heterosexual Anal Intercourse [HAI]"—with some data on the behavior reported. (It was Bruce Voeller who had searched out researchers who might have data to show that some heterosexuals have tried anal intercourse.[9]) This appears to be an initial step in associating the heterosexual population with anal intercourse, thereby disenfranchising penile-vaginal intercourse as the natural heterosexual form of sexual relating. In his symposium paper "Heterosexual Anal Intercourse (HAI): Denial and Patterns of Exposure," David Bolling referred to that activity as "an increasingly prevalent and frequent sexual activity." Bolling then coined a second term, "active, *pleasurable* anal intercourse users (APAI)" (emphasis added). Bolling asserted in his paper that although anal intercourse was reported in his study mostly by women "not limited to one partner," the behavior "does not exclude other women . . . ."

There may be a legal strategy to this new research. As noted in the previous chapter, Dr. Richard Green, a gay activist and past president of the SSSS, told Jane Brody of *The New York Times* that if anal intercourse can be shown to be practiced more by heterosexuals than by homosexuals then prosecuting gays for sodomy would be discriminatory. [Note: Anal intercourse—aside from needle-sharing—is probably the highest-risk behavior associated with the spread of the AIDS virus.]

The categorization of anal sex as heterosexual is a logical strategy for Kinseyans. It denormalizes conventional sexual intercourse, which is regarded as natural and which is unique to male-female relating. This is part of a broader scheme to denormalize heterosexuality (see also chapter 4).

Does such a scheme seem unlikely? Consider that Kinsey and his followers have had a degree of success promoting the theory that everyone is really bisexual, not heterosexual.[10] This theory is based on the logic that since some heterosexuals have had incidents of same-sex experience in their lives—or possibly thought about it—it can be assumed that all heterosexuals are really bisexual (Male Report, pp. 638, 639).

9   Personal conversation between E. Eichel and Drs. David Bolling and Bruce Voeller at the 31st Annual Meeting of the SSSS (1988) in San Francisco.
10   The Kinsey bisexuality philosophy recently got some media attention in New Hampshire, where the Strafford County Prenatal and Family Planning Clinic introduced the sex education manual *Mutual Caring, Mutual Sharing: A Sexuality Education Unit for Adolescents*. In this manual, heterosexual children are referred to as "more accurately those . . . who believe that they are heterosexual." [See chapter 5.]

A logical next step for Kinsey disciples is to claim that if some heterosexuals have tried anal intercourse, then anal intercourse can be declared to be as normal for heterosexuals as penile-vaginal intercourse. The association of anal sex with heterosexuals serves to standardize a gay model of sexual behavior for heterosexuals. A grand coup would then be almost complete: the standardization of 1) a gay model of sexual orientation for everyone—with bisexuality considered the norm of sexual health—and 2) a gay model of sexual behavior for everyone— with anal intercourse considered as natural for heterosexuals as vaginal intercourse. The basic tenets of the real Kinsey "grand scheme" might then be established.

BEGINNING WITH HOMOSEXUALITY— A PERSONAL AGENDA

In his Kinsey biography, Wardell Pomeroy uses the expression "Kinsey's grand scheme" (or "grand design") several times. Pomeroy explains, "Our grand design, in simplest terms, was to try to find out . . . what people did sexually" (p. 4). But there is evidence that Kinsey selected individuals and groups for his studies that would enable him to get results he could use to promote specific sexual behavior and lifestyles. He knew exactly how to do this.

Kinsey had published a paper on the topic of homosexuality several years before he completed his famous Male and Female Reports. In this he previewed his agenda by advocating the normalcy of homosexuality and stressing that heterosexuality and homosexuality were not "mutually exclusive" ("Homosexuality: Criteria for a Hormonal Explanation of the Homosexual." *Journal of Clinical Endocrinology* 1:424-428, 1941). This rather obscure article indicates that *Kinsey had already begun the process of promoting bisexuality as the norm of sexual health seven years before publication of* Sexual Behavior in the Human Male.

To break down the stigma surrounding homosexuality, Kinsey, in his 1941 paper, called for an unbiased, objective, scientific study of homosexuality. He complained, "The best of published studies are based on the select homosexual population which is found within prisons, and it seems, heretofore, to have been impossible to discover the extent to which the phenomenon occurs in otherwise socially adjusted portions of the population" (*ibid.*, p. 425). Kinsey clearly *gave the impression* that he wanted to be the first researcher to study a truly random sample of males to assess the extent of homosexuality in the general population. In the event, he purposely and deceptively did the opposite. He went on to bias the Male Report with the inclusion of 1,000 or more prisoners.

After publication of the Male Report, when Kinsey's colleague Paul Gebhard suggested that "it might have been a mistake to include prison inmates in the general population on which we based *Sexual Behavior in the Human Male*," Gebhard was soundly, and hypocritically, rebuked by his boss for making "assumptions" about the lives of prisoners. Recounting this in his 1979 book *The Kinsey Data* (W. B. Saunders),

Gebhard explained that by this time Kinsey was more concerned with "building and defending the research" than he was with problems of bias.

In the book *Sex Offenders: An Analysis of Types* (Heinemann/London, 1965), Gebhard, Pomeroy and John Gagnon tell more of the real story of how Kinsey went about the study of homosexuality. They relate that Kinsey (who had complained about previous homosexuality studies being done on prisoners) looked upon the prison institutions "as a reservoir of potential interviewees, literally captive subjects" (p. 32). And so the Kinsey research made "no differentiation in [the] 1948 volume between persons with and without prison experience" (p. 33).

Gebhard was fully aware of what the inclusion of prisoners meant in a study designed to measure the prevalence of sexual behaviors. He wrote that the Kinsey Male volume included data on "persons who had been incarcerated in jails and prisons *where homosexual activity is relatively common . . .* " (*The Kinsey Data*, p. 8). Kinsey clearly also knew that he was building up a specialized collection of homosexual experiences from prisons—where heterosexual contacts were not even an option—in his data for the "normal" population.

When Gebhard questioned Kinsey about the inclusion of prisoners in the Male Report, he had also been told, "Why should we 'throw away' a lifetime of useful data simply because of one misdemeanor or felony?" For whatever reason, however—perhaps embarrassment at the blatancy of the bias they were bringing to their research—Gebhard and the other Kinsey co-authors managed to get their autocratic leader to exclude prisoners from their female sample. As Gebhard tells it, "During the preparation of the volume on females, Pomeroy, Martin, and I did conspire to compare prison with nonprison females and found a substantial difference in behavior." Finally, Kinsey "agreed to omit prison females from *almost* all of the volume . . ." (*The Kinsey Data*, pp. 28, 29).

The overwhelming conclusion is that Kinsey knowingly presented a criminally biased model of sexual behavior to the world as "normal." The atypical sexual behavior of prisoners and other biased groups was used to convince people that the normal population engaged in a higher percentage of aberrant sexual behavior (particularly homosexual relations) than was actually the case. Far from being an objective scientist, Kinsey intentionally weighted his data, attempted to obscure the bias and promoted a preset agenda.

ON TO PEDOPHILIA

From the standpoint that Kinsey's research was biased and reflected a personal agenda, it is worthwhile to question his philosophy and personal sex history. Kinsey, who so radically impacted upon ideas about the nature of human sexuality, challenged traditional concepts of normality. He argued that sexual differences—in orientation—were simply points on a continuum; the differences were a matter of degree, as opposed to being differences that could be defined as abnormalities or pathologies (Male Report, p. 639). Simply stated—Kinsey believed there was no such thing as sexual perversion; and it is clear he considered adult relations with children as a normal sexual activity.

In discussing variances of sexual behavior, Kinsey surmised, "Normal and abnormal, one sometimes suspects, are terms which a particular author employs with reference to his own position on that curve" (Male Report, pp. 199, 201). Logically, on the same basic premise, one can speculate that Kinsey's sexual orientation and behavior may have influenced *his* own viewpoint and affected *his* objectivity as a scientist.

Although the details of Kinsey's personal sex history exist, and are presumably in the archives of the Kinsey Institute, these have never been revealed, though some hints may have been dropped. Historian Paul Robinson, writing in the *Atlantic Monthly* (May 1972), expressed his own view:

I suspect that Kinsey's great project originated in the discovery of his own sexual ambiguities.

Robinson went on to propose that the story of Kinsey and a close friend, described in Pomeroy's biography, "suggests that Kinsey may have discovered in himself the homosexual tendencies he would later ascribe to a large proportion of the population."

Kinsey's credibility as an objective scientist, however, is much more compromised by what he apparently did (and did not do) in his research, and by his sweeping generalizations, than by opinions about his own history.

It is quite clear, for example, that, without any factual foundation upon which to base his case, Kinsey was advocating pedophilia. In chapter 2, Kinsey's view of the possible socio-sexual benefit of adult sexual contact with preadolescent females was reviewed. Kinsey made these claims in spite of the fact that 80% of the sexually molested girls that he reported on "had been emotionally upset or frightened by their contacts with adults . . . ." He acknowledged that some girls "had been seriously disturbed," and further reported a "clear-cut case of serious injury" and instances of "vaginal bleeding." Kinsey nonetheless concluded, "It is difficult to understand why a child, except for its cultural conditioning, should be disturbed at having its genitalia touched . . . or disturbed at even more *specific* sexual contacts" (Female Report, p. 121; emphasis added). Kinsey also reported, among other things, that young boys needed the help of older persons to discover sexually effective masturbatory techniques (chapter 1).

The pedophile mentality conveyed in Kinsey's reporting is also evident in the manipulative strategy he employed in the interviewing of young boys. Kinsey relates, "When the interviewer tussles with the four-year old boy, he may ask him whether he similarly tussles with the other boys in the neighborhood, and rapidly follows up with questions concerning tussling with the girls, whether he plays with any girls, whether he likes girls, whether he kisses girls" (Male Report, p. 58).

Kinsey's biographers have described behaviors in Kinsey's sex history that are remarkably consistent with character traits presented in the profile *Child Molesters: A Behavioral Analysis*, published by the

National Center for Missing and Exploited Children (in cooperation with the Federal Bureau of Investigation).[11] Kinsey's background indicates that he placed himself in professional and nonprofessional positions where he had access to young boys, such as Y.M.C.A. camp counselor, boys' club leader, and Boy Scout leader—activities he kept up "during his college and graduate years, and even after his marriage."[12] As a sex researcher, Kinsey structured his research in a manner that made sexual experimentation with children a legitimate part of his scientific endeavor. And he used the research results to promote the acceptance of pedophilia.

In addition to his interest in sex experiments with children, Kinsey was an avid collector of pornography[13] (and maker of sex films)—an elemental feature of the pedophile syndrome.

In the final analysis, was Kinsey objectively researching the nature of human sexuality in his child sex experiments—or was he attempting to establish the idea that children should start sexual activity early under the guidance of adult "partners"? Certainly, if the partner idea ever caught on, the conditioning of children away from normal heterosexual development would be in progress; Kinsey himself stated that a disposition toward homosexuality or bisexuality "depends in part upon the circumstance of early experience" (Male Report, p. 204). Clearly this suggests the possibility of manipulating—rather than facilitating—the process of psychosexual development. Pomeroy may have hinted at the answer to the question concerning Kinsey's motivation and goals when he acknowledged that Kinsey's "very faults"—"his dogmatic and aggressive nature"—"made it possible for him to get his grand design in motion . . ." (Pomeroy, 1972, p. 472).

In the interest of promoting a new scheme of human sexuality, it appears that Kinsey initiated a two-part strategy. First, he advocated the establishment of *bisexuality* as the balanced sexual orientation for normal, uninhibited people. In effect, the objective was to get heterosexuals to have homosexual experience. This was the basic step in obliterating the heterosexual norm of sexuality, with the traditional protective family structure, values and conventional sexual behavior (heterosexual intercourse) implied. This would open the way for the second and more difficult step—the ultimate goal of "cross-generational sex" (sex with children).

PEDOPHILIA—THE EMERGING "ORIENTATION"

Although difficult to achieve, the goal of making adult-child sexual relations acceptable is looking more possible than ever. Even Kinsey

11   *Child Molesters: A Behavioral Analysis for Law Enforcement Officers Investigating Cases of Child Sexual Exploitation*, by Kenneth V. Lanning, FBI Behavioral Science Unit, February 1986.

12   Christenson CV, *Kinsey: A Biography*, Indiana University Press, 1971, pp. 13, 14, 23.

13   Kinsey began an erotica collection—including drawings and writing from prison inmates and material confiscated by police departments. According to Wardell Pomeroy's biography of Kinsey, this grew into "the largest collection of erotica in the world . . . presumed to be more extensive than the legendary Vatican collection." The Kinsey collection is housed in the Kinsey Institute, but the "Vatican collection," it now appears, was a figment of Kinsey's imagination (see *Fidelity* magazine, April 1989).

might be surprised if he could know of the academic and intellectual validation that is being attempted for the practice of pedophilia. An effort is clearly underway to "respectabilize" this behavior formerly regarded as deviant. The first requirement for this process was establishing that children were sexual beings. Academic sexology largely accepts that Kinsey did this. The second requirement is to have pedophilia regarded as an "orientation," just as Kinsey's scale enabled homosexuality to be so perceived. This second requirement is now being met, according to the publication *Behavior Today* (incorporating the former *Sexuality Today*), a weekly newsletter for mental health, family relations and sexuality professionals:

> A new sexological theory often begins with a softly spoken comment heard by a few who then initiate discussion and, over the years, begin to write and research on the idea.
>
> At the SSSS 31st Annual Conference, Dr. Sharon Satterfield made a soft three-sentence comment within her three-hour presentation on "Child Sexual Abuse." *Dr. Satterfield, a nationally recognized expert on sex offenders and the sexual abuse of children, stated that pedophilia—a condition where adults are sexually attracted to pre-pubescent children—may be a sexual orientation rather than a sexual deviation. She then raised the question as to whether pedophiles may have rights. While no one, including Dr. Satterfield, believes that pedophiles should be allowed to victimize children, three days (and hundreds of papers) after her presentation, people were still talking about the idea of pedophilia as a sexual orientation.*
>
> Several individuals were already drawing parallels between homosexuality and pedophilia: common early childhood "onset" and the immutability of the orientation as well as the social attitudes to both "orientations." As more and more clinicians keep reporting failure at helping pedophiles change their sexual desires, just as they have found that they cannot help homosexuals become straight, we may have to look more closely at what is for many a very uncomfortable theory that pedophiles may always have as their primary sexual orientation an erotic to pre-pubescent children. *In the final analysis the difference between sexual orientation and deviance may not be a scientific judgment, but a reflection of what society finds acceptable or repugnant* [*Behavior Today*, December 5, 1988, p. 5; emphasis added].

The classification of pedophilia as a normal sexual orientation is not the final step in a Kinseyesque agenda. Another sex theorist has attempted to advance the status of the pedophile to that of Good Samaritan, dedicated to helping children learn about, and develop, their sexuality. In other words, pedophiles could be viewed as natural helpers of children, with special gifts—much as John Money views homosexuals as special people (see chapter 4).

In her article "Intergenerational Sexual Contact: A Continuum Model of Participants and Experience" (*Journal of Sex Education & Therapy* 15(1):3-12, 1989), Joan A. Nelson, Ed.D., advocates a model of adult-child sexuality in which sex acts with children are to be viewed as acceptable and even essential to the healthy development of the child. She minimizes the harmful effect of what has generally been perceived as child sexual abuse; and she emphasizes the harmful effect of "society's condemnation" of adult-child sex—an approach straight out of the pages of Kinsey *et al.*

Dr. Nelson provides a new vocabulary that is designed to change the normal viewpoint about sex with children. She is aware of the Kinseyan strategy of changing words to influence how people think— and, ultimately, to influence behavior. Nelson recommends that both the adult and the child engaging in a sex act be mutually referred to as *participants*—paralleling Kinsey's use of the term "partners"—rather than as child molester and victim, respectively. Sex acts with children are to be referred to simply as *sexual experience*—an "inclusive, non-condemnatory" term, rather than as "*abuse, victimization, molestation, assault,* and *exploitation.*" Nelson further advocates that the general area of adult-child sex is to be covered by the neutral-sounding term *intergenerational sex.* (She has also used the equally innocuous-sounding description "cross generational sex" in an earlier article, "Incest: Self-Report Findings From a Nonclinical Sample" [*Journal of Sex Research* 22(4):463-477, 1986].)

Finally, Nelson suggests a new classification of sex offender in place of the term *pedophile.* She recommends that the pedophile be referred to as a *visionary.* She makes the distinction that the "visionary" type "participates in sexual contact not for her or his own gratification, but in response to a child's attempt to acquire practical knowledge." Nelson points out that the "visionary" is also an "advocate" of "children's right to work," and "to vote," etc. The visionaries "believe the troubles that characterize our times are rooted in childhood sexual repression that prohibits age-free expression of sexual affection."

Nelson builds her case that adult sex with children can be beneficial to the child. She points out that the "visionaries" of the pedophile movement cite Kinsey (1953) in suggesting "that early sexual experience is often positively correlated with greater adult sexual and interpersonal satisfaction."[14] She continues to press the same basic Kinsey line, citing a contemporary sexologist, Domeena C. Renshaw, M.D., on the topic of incest: "There may . . . be a strong sense of [the victim's] self-satisfaction at having emerged and adapted well in spite of, *or even because of,* the incest experience"[15] (emphasis added).

Pedophilia and Incest appear to be following in the footsteps of Homosexuality. Quoting sex research historian Edward Brecher, James Ramey wrote in 1979 that "after the homosexual taboo began to break down, incest as the last social taboo would soon follow suit." According to Ramey, "we are roughly in the same position today

14   In a March 1980 *Psychology Today* article, "The Pro-Incest Lobby," essayist and critic Benjamin DeMott notes that Joan Nelson describes herself as having experienced as a child" an ongoing incestuous relationship which seemed . . . the happiest period of my life."

15   Renshaw DC, *Incest*, Little, Brown, 1982.

regarding incest as we were a hundred years ago with respect to our fear of masturbation" (*SIECUS Report*, May 1979, p. 1).

Clearly pedophilia is a potential orientation for the future. Many of its academic sympathizers are still in the woodwork (see also chapter 4 and Appendix C ["The Last Taboo"]), but pioneering spirits are following the same subtle path that is accomplishing the normalization of homosexuality. One milestone to watch for will be the appearance of the word "pedophobia." We haven't quite got that far yet, but expressions like "age-free affection" and similar euphemisms are beginning to appear from the lips and pens of academic sexologists.

MELANESIAN STUDIES—ANTHROPOLOGICAL SUPPORT FOR BISEXUALITY/PEDOPHILIA

The Kinsey "grand scheme" is just now finding its way to the cutting edge of the U.S. government's initiative against AIDS, with a little help from selective anthropological data from primitive tribes. In 1989 the National Research Council published an advisory report, *AIDS: Sexual Behavior and Intravenous Drug Use*.[16] The section of the report that deals with "Sexual Behavior and AIDS" lists the lead author as John H. Gagnon, former project director at the Kinsey Institute. In the section on "Anthropology's Perspective on Human Sexual Behavior," discussion centers on the fact that in "perhaps 10-26% of all Melanesian groups" homosexual experience is "not a deviant form of cultural behavior" (p. 160). (However, neither was ritualistic cannibalism in some groups, but the report does not cover this; see below.)

The reader is further informed that

Among the Sambia of Papua, New Guinea, for example, homosexual practices begin at ages 7-10, when all young boys are taken from their mothers to be initiated into the male cult. For some 10-15 years, they engage in erotic practices, first as fellator, ingesting the semen of an older bachelor, and then as fellated or semen donor. . . . The pattern of same-gender sexual activity and avoidance of women continues until marriage, after which young men may follow "bisexual" behaviors for some years [pp. 160, 161].

The purpose of this information is to show that human sexuality is "astonishingly plastic and variable in its expression" (p. 160), which implies a range of normal sexual behaviors, adult-child sex included. Gagnon's source here is Gilbert Herdt's book *Ritualized Homosexuality in Melanesia* (University of California Press, 1984). Herdt, it should be noted, is editor of the book *Gay and Lesbian Youth* (Harrington Park Press, 1989), which suggests a specialized point of view. Herdt's work is also quoted in support of the view that heterosexuality is not the norm and that "sexual behavior is primarily a sex act, and the sex of the partner is of secondary consideration."[17]

Gagnon, for his part, has previously expressed the view that there are various sexualities. These are based upon learning experience; none

---

16   Charles F. Turner, Heather G. Miller, Lincoln E. Moses (eds.), National Academy Press, Washington, D.C., 1989.

17   See, for example, Coleman *et al.*, *Journal of Sex Research* 26(4):525, 1989.

are to be considered unnatural (*Journal of Sex Research* 23[1]:120, 1987). Gagnon has also written in his 1977 book *Human Sexualities* (Scott Foresman & Co.), "we may have to change the ways in which [children] learn about sex. We may have to become more directive, more informative, more positive—we may have to promote sexual activity—if we want to change the current processes of sexual learning and their outcome" (p. 381).

The NRC document is consistent with the Kinsey two-point agenda. Bisexuality and adult-child sex are implied to be an advance over the "cultural restrictions" of the modern Western world. In this report—supposedly relevant to AIDS prevention—it is stated that "descriptions of the cultural life of the Sambia and other 'homosexual' groups in New Guinea challenge Westerners to reevaluate standard generalizations about adolescent and sexual development" (p. 161). In case this might seem a bit extreme, the reader is assured in the preamble that "the members of the committee responsible for the report were chosen for their special competences and with regard for appropriate balance."

Appealing to the cultural practices of Melanesian groups and arguing the normalcy of homosexual sexual activities from certain tribal customs is particularly ironic at this time. Recently AIDS virus infection has been compared to another slow virus infection, kuru, that devastated the Fore tribe in New Guinea. In this case the mode of spread was by ritualistic cannibalism. British venereologist Dr. John Seale compared the spread of the two diseases:

> They are both caused by viruses of types that were not known to infect humans before epidemics gradually unfolded. They first became manifest in communities in which *aberrant social behavior* had become elaborate cults within minority groups—cults which historically most societies have abhorred [*Journal of the Royal Society of Medicine* 80:200, 1987; emphasis added].

In contrast to Gagnon's observations about Melanesian culture, Seale's were highly relevant to the spread of AIDS. Seale's analogies—and the indignant response they elicited—concerning kuru, AIDS and behavior are summarized below because they tell us something about the non-science of "cultural relativism."

Seale described the "ominous similarities" between AIDS virus infection and kuru: they are slow virus infections (ie, with prolonged asymptomatic incubation periods) resulting from the practice of "aberrant social behavior" within minority groups, and both are "calamitous" to the societies affected. Probably only very recently have these viruses crossed the species barrier from animal to human. Kuru came first in 1957 and provided a lesson that "modern medicine subsequently totally ignored . . . the potential for catastrophe from new, epidemic, slow-virus diseases arising in humans indulging in biologically deviant behavior, or caused by medical practices [eg, blood, tissue exchange]."

The deviant behavior in the case of kuru was ritual cannibalism of deceased relatives. Transmission of the virus occurred "while the brain was extracted, squeezed by hand into a pulp and pushed into bamboo cylinders to be cooked." In the case of AIDS virus transmission, the initial deviant behavior was the preference among some homosexual men "for traumatic interference with each other's lower intestinal tracts as a group activity." This was later compounded by needle-sharing activities in "shooting galleries." In the case of kuru, the aberrant activities have ceased and the disease is dying out. Simple lesson, but it has caused offense.

In the case of AIDS, "the ultimate virological nightmare," the approach is different. As Seale puts it, "Infection is said to be an entirely private matter for the individual, which should be concealed from the rest of the community. Society's only defense to halt the epidemic is declared to be education—for those engaged in aberrant social behavior—on how to modify the techniques of their lifestyle without actually forsaking it. This, in reality, would merely slightly reduce the high speed with which the deviant behavior disseminates the virus." Seale adds, hilariously (except it is not a laughing matter), that "a similar approach to the prevention of kuru would have been for the Australian authorities to have distributed free rubber gloves and pressure-cookers to the villagers. Educational lectures on safe cannibalism would have been funded by Canberra. The cannibal lobby would have insisted that kuru was a civil rights issue, and that nothing should be done to curtail the newly liberated lifestyle of an historically oppressed minority."

As if there indeed were a "cannibal lobby," a group from the UCLA School of Public Health responded to Seale with a discussion paper on "biocultural considerations" concerning "kuru AIDS and *unfamiliar* social behavior" (*Journal of the Royal Society of Medicine* 82:95, 1989; emphasis added). Seale's approach was declared "indefensible," lacking a "sense of cultural relativism." These authors claimed (with a straight face?), "the lesson to be learned from the response to kuru must surely be one of cultural sensitivity—not the sweeping condemnation of people *whose mores might appear anomalous.*" They added, for those without a sense of cultural relativism, that "longstanding practices almost invariably have some adaptive advantages that an untrained observer [such as Dr. Seale] would be likely to overlook."

The UCLA authors' article was replete with required jargon, such as "popular stereotypes," "societal prejudice," "anthropological imperatives," and concluded, among other things, that "the absence of an anthropological perspective precludes meaningful understanding of AIDS and gives rise to unfortunate social consequences—foremost of which is a tendency to blame victims of disease."

Anthropology has been enlisted both in the service of a gay agenda and a pedophile agenda. In his article "Bisexuality, Homosexuality, and Heterosexuality: Society, Law, and Medicine," the well-known Johns Hopkins sexologist John Money appears to advocate bisexuality as the norm of sexual health. He applies the term "obligative heterosexuality" to individuals who are exclusively heterosexual, implying that exclusive heterosexuality is a quasi-pathology—a cultural artifact of repressive societies. Money claims that "condemnation of homosexuality induces impairment of all sexuality rather than an increase of heterosexuality." He supports his case for bisexuality with anthropological findings on the Batak society of Lake Toba in Sumatra (*Journal of Homosexuality* 2(3):231, 1977).

Joan Nelson, who described the new "visionary" concept of pedophilia in her article "Intergenerational Sexual Conduct: A Continuum Model of Participants and Experiences" (referenced earlier), notes that "visionaries cite anthropological findings on primitive tribes" in support of their role, which, apart from sexual contact with children, includes "[teaching] practical sex education along with other teachings about health, safety, and nature."

For the vast majority, who have not had anthropological training and who still hold to the "19th century" concept of a heterosexual norm, it might be worth noting the trend in some anthropology studies (or in their analysis) to "democratize" and "universalize" aberrant sex acts. Psychologist and sex researcher C. A. Tripp, a friend and colleague of the late Alfred Kinsey, wrote in his 1975 book *The Homosexual Matrix* (McGraw-Hill) that anthropology was one branch of science where homosexuals may be able to "extend the parameters of [the] field":

> [A] few of the contributions made by the field-anthropologist who happens to be homosexual are exceptional—not because his work is better or worse than that of anybody else, but simply because of his slightly different standpoint. In the first place, his basic life-style sometimes makes it easier for him to pick up and travel and to spend protracted periods of time in Timbuktu. He appears to be especially sensitized to sexual and to homosexual elements in a foreign milieu, and is often remarkably adept at making his informants feel at ease in discussing such matters [p. 277].

Apparently, an objective of gay activism, according to John Gagnon in the NRC report on AIDS, has been the "development of gay caucuses within professional and scientific societies" (p. 126). This movement of homosexuals into the scientific community has occurred in areas relevant to sexuality and vulnerable to sexual politics:

> It is possible to identify a number of research programs begun in the early 1970s that differed substantially from earlier studies. They were often associated with specific *reform agendas* and openly included gay men and lesbians as full scientific participants. This is *one of the most crucial changes in the landscape of research on same-gender sexuality*: people who would have been only the subjects of research and barred from participation as researchers because of their "biases" became valued members of research programs [Gagnon, NRC AIDS Report, p. 127; emphasis added].

Elsewhere, in his article "Disease and Desire," Gagnon wrote, "In this new research climate, gay scientists and intellectuals began a *research agenda* in sociology, psychology, history, and even psychoanalysis" (*Daedalus: The Journal of the American Academy of Arts and Sciences*, Summer 1989, p. 53; emphasis added). Anthropology clearly can be added to this list. As *Time* magazine noted in regard to efforts to legitimize parent-child sex, "Some try to give the argument a bit of serious academic coloration, ransacking anthropological literature for a tribe or two that allows incest . . . " (*Time*, April 14, 1980, p. 72).

Superficial forays into anthropology—some even achieving recognition and fame—are nothing new. In some cases they can be seen in retrospect as efforts to find role models for an ideology. Margaret Mead was recently shown to have been guilty of this in her celebrated work among the Samoans. Famous for its attack on conventional sexual mores, Mead's Samoan research (published as the best seller *Coming of Age in Samoa*) was quite devastatingly exposed by New Zealand anthropologist Derek Freeman as an attempt to impose her ideology on the evidence.[18]

Enlisting science in the service of sexual agendas should be no surprise to anyone. Vern Bullough, a historian of the gay movement, has put it very bluntly with regard to homosexuality: "Politics and science go hand in hand. In the end it is Gay activism which determines what researchers say about gay people" (*Washington Blade*, December 18, 1987, p. 19).

(Bullough recently provided a foreword for Dutch pedophile Edward Brongersma's book *Loving Boys: A Multidisciplinary Study of Sexual Relations Between Adults and Minor Males, Volume I* [Global Academic Publications, 1986]. In this he wrote that pedophilia is "a subject that too often has been ignored or subjected to hysterical statements." See chapter 4.)

THE GAY AGENDA AND PEDOPHILIA

From some of the foregoing it will be obvious that the agendas of gays and pedophiles are closely connected. There is a commonality of research sources used for "scientific" support, an overlap of objectives and a similarity of language, cliches and tactics, particularly in the pursuit of "rights." In addition, a number of activists share both agendas.

Compounding the problem is the fact that Alfred Kinsey, who laid the foundations for the modern gay movement, implied a whole spectrum of non-traditional and abnormal sexual behaviors under the term homosexual. As John Gagnon has pointed out, "For 'homosexual,' Kinsey could have substituted any form of sexual activity. . . . He regarded it all as part of biological potential and mammalian heritage" (*Human Nature*, October 1978). Also, Kinsey's view of human sexuality involved a continuum from heterosexual to homosexual and a parallel continuum from birth to death (see chapter 1). He did not believe in distinct categories of sexuality or in trying to force facts about behavior into "separate pigeon-holes" (Male Report p. 639).

The association of two agendas has been a problem for some in the gay movement who have resented the attempt by pedophiles to piggyback on adult homosexual and lesbian issues. Lesbian columnist Nancy Walker has said in response to North American Man/Boy Love

18   See *Margaret Mead and Samoa: The Making and Unmaking of an Anthropological Myth*, by Derek Freeman, Harvard University Press, 1983.

Association (NAMBLA) founder David Thorstad's claim that he is "fighting for the rights of children to control their own bodies": "Let Thorstad and his confreres at least say what the real issue is: that they want to [copulate with] children. Prepubescent children are not taboo because this is a sex-negative society, but because they can be physically hurt and may be psychologically injured as well by sexual intimacy with adults" (*Time*, September 7, 1981).

The problem of pedophiles in the gay movement is complex, however, because pedophiles have not always identified their sexual preference and agenda. And there is evidence that advocates of adult-child sex have clandestinely originated some of the basic strategies of gay activism. In fact, pedophiles may have been leaders in the gay movement.

Dutch social psychologist and pro-pedophilia lecturer Theo Sandfort, who has been a guest speaker at New York University's Human Sexuality Program summer seminar in Holland, has given some insight on the strategy of pedophiles. In his 1987 article titled "Pedophilia and the Gay Movement" (*Journal of Homosexuality* 13(2/3):89, 1987), Sandfort describes how in The Netherlands pedophiles have been an influential force in the gay movement. From time to time they surface, and pressure is put on homosexuals and lesbians to include pedophilia and "broaden the idea of the gay identity."

Many members of the homosexual and lesbian community are not naive about the exploitive activities of pedophiles and have resisted the pressure to tie in a child-sex agenda to unrelated social causes. At a gay rights march in April of 1980, NAMBLA leader Thorstad's appearance "caused the National Organization for Women and the Coalition for Lesbian and Gay Rights to pull out . . . " (*Village Voice*, August 20-26, 1980).

Regardless of current tensions between proponents of pedophile and strictly gay agendas, Kinsey is the philosophical father of both. His 1940s research remains the "scientific" foundation on which these overlapping movements rest.

BEYOND THE KINSEY GRAND SCHEME

While adult-child sex is identified as a major objective of the Kinsey "grand scheme," arriving at such a goal will not be easy. For those who subscribe to both gay and pedophile agendas—and they are in influential positions in academic sexology—there is a challenging road ahead. But the challenge is being met with a subtle and comprehensive campaign affecting society's most-prized belief systems, professions and institutions. We are fully aware that the following alleged elements of this campaign may sound like science fiction, even though we have already seen most of them in the sex education and sexology literature:

- Encourage gay-activist movements, and establish homosexuality as a normal sexual orientation.

• Declare pedophilia a sexual orientation and add adult-child sex to the agenda.

• Promote widespread promiscuity to create a sexual anarchy, where so many are implicated that the distinction of pedophilia might seem insignificant.

• Promote the sexual rights of children, to open the way for pedophilia.

• Attack religion to undermine the Judeo-Christian concept of sin and eliminate the distinction between right and wrong.

• Attack psychoanalysis to eliminate psychoanalytical concepts that associate aberrant sexual behaviors with mental illness. Dissociate sex from pathology.

• Lobby the judicial system to reform sex laws so that aberrant sexual behavior is not considered criminal. Legalize aberrant sex acts to eliminate punishment for sex crimes.

• Promote hostility between the sexes. Align feminists with gay activists in a campaign against heterosexuality *per se*.

• Exploit childhood rebellion to alienate children from parents. Separate children from the protective traditional family structure.

• Redefine *Family* to break the heterosexual model of a nuclear family with a mother and father.

What chance of success does such an agenda have? Probably not much. When mainstream Americans learn to recognize the components of such a campaign, however cunningly disguised the elements are inside "AIDS education" programs, "initiatives" to dispel "homophobia," and the like, they are likely to make short shrift of them.

CHAPTER EIGHT

CONCLUSIONS

ENGINEERING HUMAN SEXUALITY

Dr. J. Gordon Muir and Edward W. Eichel

It will be clear to most readers that Kinsey reached the following three general conclusions about human sexuality:

1. The normal expression of human sexuality is bisexuality. That this capacity is not realized in many people is because of "cultural restraints" and "societal inhibitions," which are assumed to be negative influences.

2. Sexual contact with adults would be a normal part of growing up for children in a less inhibited society. This adult-child sexual relationship helps to socialize children and assists the development of full sexual potential in adulthood.

3. Promiscuity and diversity of sexual expression correlate with sexual health.

Neither Kinsey nor his coworkers spelled out their conclusions as clearly as stated here. But they are discernible as a common thread woven through the Male and Female Reports and in subsequent works by Kinsey co-authors. These conclusions are, however, succinctly summed up by Kinsey in his statement in the Female Report that "it is . . . difficult to explain why each and every individual is not involved in every type of sexual activity" (p. 451). Actually, Kinsey does provide an explanation of sorts. He considered that the "human animal" developed "[e]exclusive preferences and patterns of behavior, heterosexual or homosexual . . . only with experience, or as a result of social pressures (Female Report, pp. 450, 451).

In the penultimate chapter of his Male Report, titled "Animal Contacts," Kinsey relates that all "six types of [human] sexual activity" (masturbation, nocturnal emissions, petting, heterosexual intercourse, homosexual contacts and animal contacts) only "*seem* to fall into categories that are as far apart as right and wrong, licit and illicit, normal and abnormal, acceptable and unacceptable in our social organization. In actuality, they all prove to originate in the relatively simple mechanisms which provide for erotic response when there are sufficient physical or psychic stimuli." He added, "the scientific data which are accumulating make it appear that, *if circumstances had been propitious, most individuals might have become conditioned in any direction*, even into activities which they now consider quite unacceptable" (Male Report, p. 678; emphasis added).

Although Kinsey claimed in his Male Report that he was only trying "to accumulate an *objectively determined body of fact* about sex which *strictly avoids social or moral interpretations*" (p. 5), he did the exact opposite. Just as he did the exact opposite of what in 1941 he claimed in a medical journal he was doing on the study of homosexuality. The best studies up to that time were flawed, he said, because they were based on the "select" population that is "found within prisons"!

Nowhere are Kinsey's interpretations more obvious than in his comparisons of human and animal behavior. Behaviors historically condemned by society are described as normal and justified by "normal mammalian practices." On the other hand, behaviors conforming to traditional mores and involving controls not found in "lower animals" are described as moralistic "rationalizations." However, if historical precedent can be found to justify socially condemned behavior, that is different.

The animal analogies did not escape the attention of all reviewers of that time. Writing of the Female Report, sociologist Bernard Barber of Bernard College noted "the biologistic overtone, and confusion on the relationship between the biological, psychological, and social aspects of sexual behavior [that] pervade this volume." The well-known author, lecturer and theologian, Reinhold Niebuhr, referred to "the crude physiological naturalism" that governed Kinsey's research, "into which he was betrayed by ignorance." Albert Hobbs probably best illustrated the fallacy of Kinsey's "crude naturalism" in his 1948 review in *The American Journal of Psychiatry*. He observed that "examples of behavior which is abnormal, if 'normal' is derived from behavior of infrahuman mammals, are speech, abstract thought, writing, driving automobiles, wearing clothes, eating cooked food, and making studies of sexual behavior"!

Of course Kinsey's research was not totally the product of ignorance. It is clear from the first two chapters of this book that an agenda was also involved that is revealed in Kinsey's background, his attitude to conventional morality, his selection of coworkers, his sampling procedures, his secrecy over methods, and in many statements by Kinsey himself and subsequently by coworkers and Kinsey Institute employees.

With regard to child sexuality, Kinsey was the first and remains the only sex researcher who has demonstrated experimentally the "orgasmic potential" of human infants and children. This experimental evidence, it is claimed, is also sufficient to debunk Freud's view that there was a sexually latent or dormant period in adolescence. If children are not sexually active in their adolescent years, according to Kinsey, this "results from parental or social repressions of the growing child" (Male Report, p. 180). Kinsey's research provided the "scientific" foundation for the belief that children benefit from becoming sexually active at an early age—with the help of adult "partners."

These conclusions fitted a preconceived bias that has been expressed many times and in many ways by Kinsey and his coworkers. It seems reasonable that this bias was rooted in Kinsey's own sexuality. And it may be, as sexual historian Paul Robinson pointed out in a review of Wardell Pomeroy's book, *Dr. Kinsey and the Institute for Sex Research*, "that Kinsey may have discovered in himself the homosexual tendencies he would later ascribe to a large portion of the population" (*Atlantic Monthly*, May 1972, p. 99).

It is certainly clear to us that Kinsey set out to find what he wanted to find. He even chose his coworkers only after carefully checking their sexual backgrounds. As Pomeroy put it, he was hired on the basis of his personal sex history because he "had not picked up all the taboos, and the inhibitions and the guilts that . . . [his] colleagues had . . . (see Introduction).

The ultimate purpose of the Kinsey Reports was to prove a theory and establish a new morality.

Shortly after publication of the Male Report, Kinsey noted in a letter to Alan Gregg of the Rockefeller Foundation:

[T]here are inevitably persons who object—that we have no right to publish and distribute *results which threaten our moral system* as much as this book does [In Pomeroy WB: *Dr. Kinsey and the Institute for Sex Research*, Harper & Row, 1972, p. 289; emphasis added].

The books did threaten the moral system that then existed. As noted earlier, Paul Robinson wrote of the Male Report, "the fundamental categories of his analysis clearly worked to undermine the traditional sexual order" (*The Modernization of Sex*, Harper & Row, 1976, p. 58). For better or worse, they did more than anything else to change it by setting in motion—as observed later in *Esquire* magazine —"the first wave of the sexual revolution." The Reports became a self-fulfilling prophecy that is still in mid-course; for, clearly, Kinsey's full sexual agenda has not yet been realized in our society.

What has been achieved by Kinsey and coworkers thus far has been on the basis of presenting statistics to the American public purporting to demonstrate the wide range of sexual behaviors that average people were engaged in. Of course, as we now learn, this revelation of "normal" sexuality was from information solicited from a largely unconventional sample of the population. The "revelation" *was* false but *is* becoming true. The teaching of many of Kinsey's findings as fact is helping to establish them as such.

The predictions of beneficial societal effects from the Kinsey studies also have proved false. Kinsey spoke of the faith of the man in the street that "the whole of the social organization will ultimately benefit from the accumulation of scientifically established data" such as the Kinsey authors were presenting (Male Report, P. 4). The implication of his research was that once the Judeo-Christian codes restraining sexual behavior were eliminated ideal sexual adjustment and happiness would be more nearly attainable. But it did not work out that way.

There is still a long way to go in achieving the full Kinsey vision, particularly with regard to getting across the concept of cross-generational sex (adult sex with children), but, as we have seen, this notion is beginning to trickle down into the sex education system from the highest echelons of academic sexology. And there are no institutions today with degree-granting human sexuality programs where the Kinsey philosophy of sexuality is not accepted and taught. This then establishes the future of sex education.

The real Kinsey "grand scheme" is continuing to evolve. Little, it would appear, has been left to chance. The sex education establishment is now in place to engineer the direction of sexual attitudes and behaviors in coming generations. What Mary Calderone referred to in 1968 as a need for a new design of "production line" to develop a society as sophisticated sexually as it is technologically has been met. AIDS education has been the giant spur that recently has accelerated this process forward. This has led to perhaps one of the greatest hypocrisies of our time—the pretence of providing safe-sex instruction to children while in reality advancing an agenda that encourages them to be sexually active, including indulging in high-risk lifestyles and behaviors.

Deceptive use of the word "Family" by persons and programs that are effectively destroying it, is another of the great hypocrisies of the past 40 years. It's rather like the use of the term "Democracy" by nations like East Germany (German *Democratic* Republic). As Amherst professor Benjamin DeMott wrote in *Psychology Today* (March 1980) concerning the campaign to modify the incest taboo, "the emergence of the permissivists as *concerned friends of the family*—a strange turn of events—will surely be partly responsible" (emphasis added).

Along the same lines, we have SIECUS co-founder Lester Kirkendall, an emeritus professor of *Family* Life, writing in a 1984 *SIECUS Report* that his desire is to help "stabilize marriage and the family," but who is also on record the following year in the *Journal of Sex Education* as looking to the day when cross-generational sex will be legitimate and "the emphasis on . . . normality and abnormality will be much diminished . . . ."

When the concept of Family is undermined—and already the family is almost destroyed in some segments of society—then the whole human ecology is threatened. However, the specifically human ecology has been dissociated from the usual spectrum of ecological concerns and remedial action seems well-nigh impossible. One reason for this is that whereas it is easy for the media and the usual army of celebrities to get aroused by ecological threats like Alar or malathion, it is very difficult to be activist about something in which one is part of the problem.

One of the most seriously distorted aspects of Kinsey's sex research was that he sought out a population that would provide the data to support his preset agenda. The results stunned and fooled the heterosexual public. But perhaps the greater victims were homosexuals. Just as Kinsey's interview sample of heterosexuals was unconventional, so was his sample of homosexuals.

The homosexual interviewees would have been predominantly the activists and the promiscuous, recruited in such places as prisons and gay bars, and through contacts of similar persuasion. Perhaps more than any other group, non-promiscuous homosexuals, and those not wishing to reveal their orientation, would be absent or scarce in Kinsey's sample. And thus, in addition to false numbers, a false picture of homosexuality also was presented that has contributed to a whole generation of gays adopting promiscuity as part of their identity, assuming that it represented sexual liberation.

There is no scientifically acceptable research foundation for Kinsey's conclusions. Only a form of a scientific foundation exists, in Kinsey's vague, veiled and deceptive presentation of his own research—a presentation which belies what actually happened.

In view of Kinsey's grossly and knowingly unrepresentative interviewee populations, his use of data from illegal sexual experimentation on children, his history of deception in other endeavors, his predetermined bias and selection of like-minded co-researchers, his unethical and deceptive omission of data injurious to his own hypotheses, and his lucky coincidence in finding out about human sexuality exactly what he wanted to find out, we believe Kinsey's research to be worse than worthless—we believe the evidence overwhelmingly points to fraud.

Fraud is further supported by the failure of Kinsey's data to stand up in the real world. AIDS projections based on Kinsey's estimates of the homosexual population are beginning to look out of step with the facts. And recent, and more credible, sexual behavior surveys have produced vastly more conservative findings on national sexual behavior—40 years into the Sexual Revolution.

The Sexual Revolution has been, nevertheless, real and devastating, and Kinsey helped to start it by putting large numbers on various types of sexual activity and having these activities thereby "respectabilized."

Herein lies a warning for the future. Some of the people who were involved with Kinsey and his Institute want to continue bean counting. Wardell Pomeroy wants "new data" on such things as "simple nose counting of various types of sexual behavior."[1] Considering the conduct and the impact of the first Kinsey-Pomeroy nose-counting study, one thing should be abundantly clear: Neither the Kinsey Institute nor any disciple of Kinsey's should be allowed near such a project if public money is involved.

Fraud is a serious charge. It calls for reevaluation of the greatest single human sexuality research project ever undertaken and an assessment of the damage it may have caused to society. And since Kinsey co-authors Pomeroy and Gebhard are still well-known and influential sexologists, and the Kinsey Institute presumably still houses all Kinsey's original data, it calls for a response from these sources.

There is more to be said on this subject. In a sense this book is a primer, a series opener. It is now a time for accountability, and for those who will defend what Kinsey and his followers have done to step forward and be heard by a more informed public.

---

1   Pomeroy W, Schaefer LC. Impact of published surveys and research on public concepts of human sexuality. In Forleo R, Pasini W (eds.): *Medical Sexology*, PSG Publishing Co., 1980.

APPENDIX A

Extract from Dr. Maslow's Letter to a Colleague, April 29, 1970

(Reproduced by Permission of Mrs. Bertha Maslow)

About Kinsey "doing me dirt," this is the story: Kinsey, in his pre-pontifical days while he was still able to learn, was making the rounds of all the people who had done research with sex—damned few there were. I liked him then, and we spent a great deal of time together, working over the proposed interview and bull-sessioning generally. Also, in my innocence he taught me a great deal. For instance, I remember his taking me to 42nd Street to actually point out the hustlers, whom I had passed a thousand times without even noticing.

But when I warned him about "volunteer error" he disagreed with me and was sure that his random selection would be okay. So what we did was to cook up a joint crucial test. I put the heat on all my five classes at Brooklyn College and made a real effort to get them all to sign up to be interviewed by Kinsey. We had my dominance test scores for all of them and then Kinsey gave me the names of the students who actually showed up for the interviews. As I expected, the volunteer error was proven and the whole basis for Kinsey's statistics was proven to be shaky. But then he refused to publish it and refused even to mention it in his books, or to mention anything else that I had written. All my work was excluded from his bibliography. So after a couple of years I just went ahead and published it myself.

Whatever contacts I had with him in his last years were not cordial. He seemed to have changed in character.

APPENDIX B

Dr. Paul Gebhard's Letter to Dr. Judith Reisman Regarding Kinsey Research Subjects and Data (March 11, 1981)

In February 1981, Dr. Judith Reisman wrote to the Kinsey Institute (addressing her letter to Dr. John Gagnon). She asked several pointed questions, particularly with reference to the illegal experiments on infants and children from which Kinsey and team had derived their landmark conclusions on childhood sexual response. Reisman received a reply from Dr. Paul Gebhard, then director of the Institute, which shed some light on how the "scientific" child sex abuse had been conducted. Gebhard's letter, however, is more notable for the questions he avoided answering. Reisman's questions (abbreviated) and Gebhard's letter of response are reproduced below.

Reisman's Questions:

1. "Who were the 'technically trained' individuals [who had sexual contacts with younger boys and who observed preadolescent orgasms (Male Report, p. 177)] who kept diaries and records for the Kinsey team? What was their training . . . and where was it obtained? What were their ages, backgrounds? Was their sexual orientation heterosexual or homosexual? Were these [persons] males, and were they pedophiles, parents . . . if parents did they engage in an incestuous activity with the children . . . as subjects? That is, was a familial [sexual] relationship part of the research design?"

2. "Has there been a follow-up into . . . adult life [of the 317 boys, aged 5 months to adolescence, whom the trained observers studied in sexual activities]? If so, where have the results been published? Table 34 [Male Report, p. 180] notes a 5-month boy 'capable' of 3 orgasms in '?' minutes, as well as [a 4-year-old] 'capable' of '26 climaxes in 24 hours.' How were these [and the other] 'orgasms' brought about, in precise methodological terms? Was this with parental permission, participation? Upon what basis were the 'adult males who have had sexual contacts with young boys' [determined to be] reliable interpreters of the boys' experiences?"

3. "Why is there no mention of homosexual incest in the [Male Report], and why is [the word *incest*] not [used] nor indexed in the [Female Report]? On this point, why were the sexual histories of the 915 incarcerated [white] females and the 934 black females excluded from the final report? We are just now aware of the relationship between anti-social behaviors such as alcoholism and prostitution and early sexual abuse. Did Kinsey's work uncover such relationships within the incarcerated and black populations?"

4. "What is meant by 'such breaks [between female preadolescent and adolescent sexual activity] . . . do not occur in lower mammalian females, they do not occur among most of the primitive groups on which sexual data are available' [Female Report, p. 116]? Among lower mammalian females, estrus dictates the point at which intercourse will occur. Has the Kinsey group information to the contrary? To which primitive groups did the Report refer? Precisely what differences did these groups exhibit, and what was the role of the female in the power structure of the group?"

5. "Page 103 in the [Female Report] notes 'physiologic changes [in both female and male infants] . . . as young as 4 months of age.' How were the responses determined? Were the methods of Masters and Johnson used for measurement of orgasm? . . . Please be specific in the response to this question. Who observed the responses [and what was] the background of the observer(s)? Are these people available for interview? Could you kindly supply the names and addresses of those observers?"

Gebhard's reply:

Dr. Gagnon left the Institute a dozen years ago and so I am responding to your February 8 letter addressed to him. You pose more questions than I could fully answer in anything less than a monograph, but perhaps my brief reply will be satisfactory.

Since sexual experimentation with human infants and children is illegal, we have had to depend upon other sources of data. Some of these were parents, mostly college educated, who observed their children and kept notes for us. A few were nursery school owners or teachers. Others were homosexual males interested in older, but still prepubertal, children. One was a man who had numerous sexual contacts with male and female infants and children and, being of a scientific bent, kept detailed records of each encounter. Some of these sources have added to their written or verbal reports photographs and, in a few instances, cinema. We have never attempted any follow-up studies because it was either impossible or too expensive. The techniques involved were self-masturbation by the child, child-child sex play, and adult-child contacts—chiefly manual or oral.

We omitted incest, except for one brief mention, because we felt we had too few cases: 47 white females and 96 white males, and most of the incest was with siblings. We have turned our incest data over to Warren Farrell to supplement his larger study which I think is still unpublished.

We have not yet done any analyses (except for some study of pregnancy, birth and abortion) of our female prison sample, but someday I hope to do so.

We have done little with our Black case histories because they are so diverse and atypical that a distorted picture might emerge. Only the Black college-educated males and females could be truly labeled a sample. Their data are published in Gebhard and Johnson, *The Kinsey Data*: . . . Philadelphia, W.B. Saunders Co., 1979. This volume also gives our incest data in table 279.

As to non-human mammals, prepubertal sexual activity is common in males, but rare in females below the primate level. Female primates seem partly emancipated from hormonal control and do display some prepubertal sexual activity.

The anthropological data we gleaned from the ethnographic literature and from several compendia such as Ford and Beach, Karsch-Haack, etc, and this Human Area Relations Files.

Comment:

Several key questions remain unanswered, and some new ones arise:

1. Who were the "technically trained persons" who conducted illegal sexual experiments on infants and children?

2. If a principal source was parents who "kept notes for us," then presumably they were trained ahead of time since they all kept notes on precisely the same things. Who did the training?

3. For those children where the experimenters were not parents, who provided the informed consent?

4. It is suggested that teachers and nursery school owners may have been involved in sexual experimentation with children. What schools were these? Are they still around today?

5. It remains unexplained how "physiologic changes" and "specifically sexual responses" in infants were determined to be occurring.

6. The question about how to be in touch with some of these experimenters was ignored.

7. Gebhard says, "We have not yet done any analyses (except for some study of pregnancy, birth and abortion) of our female prison sample . . . ." In the Female Report, of which Gebhard was a co-author, it is written: "Because the sexual histories which we have of white females who had served prison sentences (915 cases) prove, upon analysis, to differ as a group from the histories of the females who have not become involved with the law, their inclusion in the present volume would have seriously distorted the calculations on the total sample" (p. 22). On which occasion was Gebhard telling the truth?

8. Gebhard says, "We omitted incest, except for one brief mention, because we had too few cases." In December 1977, Philip Nobile wrote in *Penthouse* that Gebhard was "releasing Kinsey's startling incest material" for incorporation in a new book by Warren Farrell. Which is correct—"too few cases" or "startling material"?

9. The question on homosexual incest remains unanswered.

It is inexcusable that a principal in a major "scientific" project, regarded as the most significant ever in the area of human sexuality, would so respond to legitimate and important questions on methodology and data. The Kinsey Institute has a clear duty to address these and other issues.

APPENDIX C

ATTACKING THE LAST TABOO

(*Time* Magazine, April 14, 1980. Copyright 1980, Time Inc. Reprinted by permission)

Sex researchers love to shock the public. Trouble is, the public is becoming more and more difficult to shock, and researchers are running out of myths to attack. Perhaps that accounts for the latest—and what may be the most reprehensible yet—trend in the field: well-known researchers and a few allies in academe are conducting a campaign to undermine the strongest and most universal of sexual proscriptions, the taboo against incest.

Most of the chipping away at the taboo is still cautious and limited. Says John Money of John Hopkins, one of the best-known sex researchers in the nation: "A childhood sexual experience, such as being the partner of a relative or of an older person, need not necessarily affect the child adversely." Money and Co-Author Gertrude Williams complain in their forthcoming book *Traumatic Abuse and Neglect of Children* about the public attitude that "no matter how benign, any adult-child interaction that may be construed as even remotely sexual, qualifies, a priori, as traumatic and abusive." One who commits incest, say the authors, is like "a religious deviant in a one-religious society"—thus neatly planting the notion that opposition to incest is quite like religious intolerance.

Wardell Pomeroy, co-author of the original Kinsey reports on males and females, is far more blunt. "It is time to admit that incest need not be a perversion or a symptom of mental illness," he says. "Incest between . . . children and adults . . . can sometimes be beneficial." Indeed the new pro-incest literature is filled with the stupefying idea that opposition to incest reflects an uptight resistance to easy affection and warmth among family members. Writes Anthropologist Seymour Parker of the University of Utah cautiously: "It is questionable if the costs (of the incest taboo) in guilt and uneasy distancing between intimates are necessary or desirable. What are the benefits of linking a mist of discomfort to the spontaneous warmth of the affectionate kiss and touch between family members?"

The SIECUS Report, the publication of the Sex Information and Education Council of the United States and an unfailing indicator of fads and fashions in the sex research world, published a major article attacking the incest taboo. Though the journal's editor, Mary Calderone, and her colleagues ran an ingenuous editorial denying that the article was advocating anything, the piece in fact depicted the taboo as mindless prejudice. Wrote the author, James W. Ramey: "We are roughly in the same position today regarding incest as we were a hundred years ago with respect to our fears of masturbation." Ramey, a researcher who has worked with many of the leading sex investigators, says the incest taboo owes something to "a peculiarly American problem—the withdrawal of all touching contact." With a little more touching in the home, he thinks, the nation might not be facing "the present rash of feverish adolescent sexual activity outside the home."

As in any propaganda campaign, the words and terms used to describe incest are beginning to change. The phrase "child abuse" is distinguished from "consensual incest" involving a parent, and "abusive incest" is different from "positive incest." Some try to give the argument a bit of serious academic coloration, ransacking anthropological literature for a tribe or two that allows incest, or arguing that the incest taboo is dying of its own irrelevance. Rutgers Anthropologist Yehudi Cohen offers a simplified pseudo-historical argument: the taboo is a holdover of a primitive need to form personal alliances and trade agreements beyond the family. Since that is no longer necessary, he says, "human history suggests that the incest taboo may indeed be obsolete." Joan Nelson, a Californian who holds an M.A. in psychology from Antioch, has a special interest in the subject. She has launched the Institute for the Study of Sexual Behavior, and has passed out questionnaires looking for "good or bad" incestuous experiences.

For whatever reason, public interest in incest as a subject seems to have increased. Hollywood provides a good index; one survey shows there were six movies about incest in the 1920s, 79 in the '60s. The numbers are still growing. Recent films on the subject include *Chinatown, Luna* and the made-for-TV *Flesh and Blood.* But probing a sensitive subject for better understanding is one thing, justifying incest is quite another.

How did the lobby against the taboo come about? One strain of its philosophy springs from the fringes of the children's rights movement, which insists that small children be granted all the rights of adults. Some have taken that to mean the right to be sexually active with any partner at all. Says Larry Constantine, an assistant clinical professor in psychiatry at Tufts, one such self-styled sexual radical: "Children have the right to express themselves sexually, even with members of their own family."

But most of the pro-incest thought rises logically enough from the premises of the sex-research establishment: all forms of consensual sexuality are good, or at least neutral; problems arise not from sex, but from guilt, fear and repression. That kind of faith is bound to lead its believers in crusades against all sexual prohibitions, including incest.

Traditional academics have tended to look down on sex researchers as pushy, ham-handed amateurs, and the arguments for incest will do little to change that view. The literature shows absolutely no attention to psychological realities: that often an adolescent and surely a small child can hardly produce anything like informed consent to an adult it depends on for life and guidance; or that the lifting of the incest barrier would invite the routine exploitation of children by disturbed parents. The sex researchers may get the shocked public reaction they expect, but their arguments are truly too simpleminded to earn it. Critic Benjamin DeMott, professor of English at Amherst, feels that outrage is not the proper response to what might be called the proincest lobby. Says he: "These voices cry out loudest for pity."

APPENDIX D

PROJECT 10: WHAT SCHOOLS TEACH CHILDREN ABOUT GAY SEX

(Manley Witten, *Valley Magazine*, August 1988. Copyright, 1988, *Valley Magazine* [World of Communications, Inc.] Reprinted by permission).

A controversial program sponsored by the Los Angeles Unified School District pits parents and legislators against principals and board members in a battle likely to have nationwide impact. At issue is whether morality and life-style should be taught at home or in the school.

February 24, 1988, began like any other Wednesday at San Fernando High School. Before day's end, however, one incident became the thunderbolt that jolted parents into an electrifying confrontation with the Los Angeles Unified School District Board of Education.

Elizabeth Ramos, 16, arrived that day prepared to take a test in her fourth-period history class. Instead, the test was postponed and her 11th-grade class was brought into the library. There, according to a number of students, they heard Virginia Uribe, a lesbian teacher, tell them she practices "safe sex," that it is OK for them to have sexual feelings for other people of the same sex and, based on research, that 10 percent of them probably are gay.

They say she also gave telephone numbers for students to obtain additional information on gay and lesbian life-styles.

Students say when they voiced disagreement, some based on their religious beliefs, Uribe kept changing the subject.

Like others in her class, Elizabeth has no interest in gay life-styles, but she was forced to attend.

Unknowingly, Elizabeth was thrust into Project 10.

Project 10 is a school-sponsored program, which therefore uses taxpayer dollars, to counsel students by offering "emotional support, information, resources and referral to young people *who identify themselves* as lesbian, gay or bisexual or *who want* accurate information . . . ," according to literature distributed by the LAUSD (italics added for emphasis).

Extensive interviews by *Valley Magazine* indicate that parental consent was not obtained for any of the 150 students who heard Uribe speak that day.

Project 10 opponents allege that this lack of parental consent is a violation of California Education Code Section 51550, which provides in part that, "No government board of a public elementary or secondary school may require pupils to attend any class in which human reproductive organs and functions and processes are described, illustrated or discussed, whether such class be part of a course designated 'sex education' or 'family life education' or by some similar term, or part of any other course which pupils are required to attend.

"If classes are offered in public elementary and secondary schools in which human reproductive organs and their functions and processes are described, illustrated or discussed, the parent or guardian of each pupil enrolled in such class shall first be notified in writing of the class. . . .

"Opportunity shall be provided to each parent or guardian to request in writing that his child not attend the class."

Some teachers and administrators question whether this section applies to Uribe's presentation at San Fernando High School. Uribe herself claims she does not think obtaining parental consent is needed legally, but she has no objection to it.

Sexually explicit materials made available to students through Project 10—and only recently discontinued after public protests before the school board—have included the book *One Teenager in 10: Testimony by Gay and Lesbian Youth* [Warner Books, New York, 1983].

The following is a portion of a graphic chapter that is excerpted from the book: "I am a sixteen-year-old lesbian. I have been a lesbian since I was twelve. I had known my dance teacher for three years before I was asked to give a special dance presentation in another city. . . . 'I want to make love to you. Let's go to bed,' (my teacher said). . . . She positioned me on the bed, with my head on a pillow and my legs spread as wide as she could get them .
. . . Before long she was getting her face closer to me and kissing me; using her mouth and tongue on my c . . ., giving me a feeling I had never felt before
. . . . We continued that night, all weekend and for almost three years until I had to move with my family. I became a lesbian and a woman that weekend!
. . . Since I moved, my teacher and I talk occasionally on the phone, and we write each other. . . . My present lover and I have been together for almost a year. . . . She is fifteen and will be in the ninth grade next year."

Critics also contend that the lack of notice has deprived parents of the opportunity to avail themselves of protections afforded them under Education Code Section 51240. This section states: "Whenever any part of the instruction in health, family life education and sex education conflicts with the religious training and beliefs of the parent or guardian of any pupil, the pupil, on written request of the parent or guardian, shall be excused from the part of the training which conflicts with such religious training and beliefs.

"As used in this section, 'religious training and beliefs' includes personal moral convictions."

In April, about 1,500 parents and students rallied outside San Fernando High School to protest Uribe's visit and Project 10. Many carried signs reading, "Let parents teach values and schools teach 3Rs" and "Books not condoms."

One of many speakers, Bishop Armando Ochoa, said Project 10 is inconsistent with the role of the school because "it's not an effort for compassionate counseling to troubled youths, but a camouflage for people to be homosexual."

The bishop, representing the Archdiocese of Los Angeles, said the school board imposes Project 10 without consulting parents, thereby creating an adversary role with the community it should serve. Parents are concerned with quality teachers in the classroom and not social engineering, he said.

Critics of Project 10 interviewed by *Valley Magazine* list six major reasons for opposition in addition to lack of parental consent.

They claim:

* The reference to 10 percent of the population being homosexual is false;

* Project 10 advocates homosexuality as a viable life-style and recruits students into homosexuality;
* It violates the right to privacy between parent and child;
* It abridges students' free exercise of religion;
* Encouraging homosexual life-styles increases student exposure to the fatal dangers of contracting AIDS;
* And, at least until recently, it utilized sexually explicit material.

In June, 90 people spoke before the school board's Educational Development and Student Life Committee at the first public hearing on Project 10 since it began four years ago. The committee continues to support Project 10 and, according to Uribe, held the hearing because someone found an "obscure board rule" that calls for a public hearing if it is requested.

"I didn't do anything different at San Fernando that I do any other place," says Uribe, who has been a science teacher at Fairfax High School in Los Angeles for more than 30 years. "I spoke on the civil rights of gay and lesbian kids."

Uribe says she has visited about 40 schools and she has been given board approval to visit all the 121 junior and senior high schools in the district.

Many parents say schools should teach academics and not "social engineering."

"I think we should boycott the school," says Elizabeth's mother, Lupe Ramos, adding that the school district loses funds based on the number of students absent. "We teach our children something, the school teaches them something else, and they're getting all confused. 'Which way do I go?' At that age they are very rebellious against parents. The school is using students, a captive audience, as pawns for their liberal way of thinking. We have to go back to morality in schools, starting with the dress code."

She said she wrote a letter to the San Fernando High School principal asking to discuss the incident, but she is still waiting for a response.

"I've lost my trust in the school system and the administration of the Board of Education," she says. "At one point, whatever the school said, that would be fine with me. Now, I read everything with scrutiny, read between the lines and up and down.

"The school asks for my consent to take the students to the museum of science, but (when Uribe spoke) they didn't even let us know."

"I don't understand why they had to drag 90 percent of the students who aren't gay to hear Uribe," says Salvador Paniague, whose daughter, Michelle, heard Uribe speak. "Why mandate the 90 percent because 10 percent are gay?"

"I couldn't believe that the school had allowed such a thing to take place," says his wife, Evelyn. "Of all things, not to contact us and let us give permission like they do in sex classes. (Students) shouldn't have been pulled out. I work for a public school and that doesn't happen at all without the parents' consent."

"Students started debating with (Uribe)," says Michelle. "They were telling her it was wrong, but she didn't want to hear what we had to say. I don't know of any students who agreed with her. When she talked about an encounter with her previous lover, everyone was saying it was gross. One student told her, 'God made Adam and Eve, not Adam and Steve.'"

Uribe's talk "made me sick," says Elizabeth. "We couldn't believe how the school could let someone like this come and talk to us."

"I would rather have taken the history test," she says.

Many parents were upset because they had not been notified in advance of Uribe's visit.

San Fernando High School Principal Bart Kricorian was not available for comment, despite four calls by *Valley Magazine* requesting his response to Uribe's visit to the school.

Uribe says she only visits schools when invited.

"If I had done my homework, I would have known (what to expect at San Fernando High School)," says Uribe, who describes her background as including a counseling credential, master's degree in psychology and doctorate in counseling psychology. "People were very hostile. There are a group of people in the area representing various philosophies of education who have coalesced and are hostile to sexual education in school, period. Some feel school should be reading, writing and arithmetic, with no social issues. . . . Without the leadership (of fundamental Christian groups), students wouldn't have been upset.

"I've spoken all over the city to hundreds and hundreds of people since the program has been going and haven't had five complaints."

In the Valley, there are complaints.

"Schools can't be turned into the battleground to change or mold our children into accepting a life-style that is contrary to my belief as a parent," says the Rev. Tim Emerick of Luz de Cristo in Van Nuys. His son, Juan, who was taken from his economics class to hear Uribe speak, says he kept thinking, "What does this have to do with economics?"

"I don't feel that the school should be a forum for homosexuals." Juan said at the June hearing. "These are family issues that involve family values. . . . If these kids need help they should get the help with parents' knowledge and consent or they should get help outside, separately from the school."

Tim Emerick said more than 1,500 signed petitions opposing Project 10 have been sent to the school board.

"The petitions made very clear that we will remember you (the board) at election time," he says. "Your constituency is against this, you're for it, and we'll remember on Election Day."

The school board is seemingly pleased with Project 10, having honored Uribe in March.

Spearheading opposition to Project 10 is the Rev. Lou Sheldon, Chairman of the Traditional Values Coalition, a statewide registered lobby of 5,000 churches plus individuals.

"First, Project 10 is a recruitment program," Sheldon says. "No balanced program is offered. (Students') religious upbringing is set aside. They are given the gay youth newsletter and other gay affirming material. They are encouraged to go to the Gay and Lesbian Community Services Center.

"Second, the parent/child relationship is being violated—flagrantly violated—when you have the state and school district becoming an adversary against parent/child privacy rights and tearing down those rights. The parent does not even know their child is being counseled into homosexuality until the counselor prepares the student to tell the parent. 'Coming Out to Your Parents' is a pamphlet distributed through Project 10.

"Third, you have the school district (establishing religion by) saying, 'We have the right moral answer concerning homosexuality even though that answer transcends your answer.'

"Fourth, the board is violating the students' and our First Amendment rights concerning free exercise of religion. Their spokespeople belittle, demean and insult anyone who is opposed to Project 10.

"Lastly, the program is based on lies. Even the name, Project 10, is propaganda, trying to make people believe that 10 percent of all people are homosexual . . . . (Two Kinsey Institute officials) say that 4 percent of the males and closer to 1 percent of the females act in a homosexual manner most of their lifetime."

Uribe bases the 10 percent on research by Alfred Kinsey.

Page 651 of Kinsey's *Sexual Behavior in the Human Male*, published in 1948, says "10 percent of the males (in the sample) are more or less exclusively homosexual for at least three years). . . . Four percent of the white males are exclusively homosexual throughout their lives, after the onset of adolescence."

"People are not born homosexual," Sheldon continues. "Various factors in their life lend to their choosing the homosexual life-style. . . . There are many groups across America, such as Exodus International, who have helped thousands of people to escape from the homosexual life-style."

Rick and Cathy Mills, formerly of Van Nuys and now living in Knoxville, Tenn., say they are proof that people who once were homosexual can become heterosexual. They say before they met and were married, each had been homosexual and then independently left that life-style. They say they have counseled nearly 200 people who didn't want to be homosexual anymore.

At the June public hearing, Karen Blakeney said she represents thousands of ex-gays in the United States.

"Project 10 promotes the viewpoint that one is born inherently gay," she says. "But the burden of proof concerning that viewpoint still lies with those who propose it. Scientifically, it has not been proven that there is any genetic code that predisposes anyone to a gay orientation. Psychologically, there is evidence, however, that one's life experiences do have a profound effect on how we view our sexuality."

Ruth Rich, instruction specialist for health education for the school district, says the official position regarding sexual education is abstinence.

"No one wants youngsters to be involved in early sexual activity," Rich says. "It is not in their best interests. . . . We want students to grow to maturity without sexual involvement. We want them to be good decision-makers."

She says students should be taught not to label themselves or others unnecessarily and to develop self-esteem for who they are.

"Most students are not sexually active and if they are, we tell them of the risk of pregnancy and disease," she says.

Sheldon claims by sending students to the Gay and Lesbian Community Services Center, Uribe encourages minors to find potential sex partners. Uribe counters that when heterosexual kids go to a dance, they meet potential sex partners. She says it is erroneous for people to think gays seek to have sex right away with other gays they meet, adding that if schools provided a support system for gays they wouldn't have to go elsewhere.

Project 10 comes across as "very humanitarian," Sheldon says. . . . "(On the surface) it's an altruistic, community-based on-site program, aimed at a minority that has historically been excluded. It's information-oriented and uses appropriate resources. It's innocuous."

"But," he adds, "it's atomic if you read between the lines."

Project 10 began at Fairfax High School in 1984, when a gay student who transferred from another school was harassed by other students, Uribe says. The harassment led to fighting, the student went to another school, where it happened again, and he dropped out.

"When this happened, I didn't know what to do," Uribe says. "I talked to another kid who was gay to set up an informal rap at lunchtime. This kid and other kids looked at me like I was crazy. No one had ever talked to them about this." She spoke to Fairfax Principal Warren Steinberg, who was supportive of the need for a "safe room," where gay and lesbian students could come to discuss their feelings with Uribe.

Uribe organized a support group comprising community members, including parents, students and clergy.

"Within a month, 25 kids were coming once a week . . . talking about their experiences in school, about harassment," Uribe says. This became the pilot program for Project 10.

Uribe received approval last fall to take the project district-wide. The board never voted on the project, although it was approved by a committee. The board says programs not requiring additional funds do not need board approval.

Gabe Kruks, director of youth services for the Gay and Lesbian Community Services in Los Angeles, offers support for Project 10.

"It is crucial for Project 10 to exist," he says. "(The aspect of recruiting) is ridiculous. There is no advocacy. You can't make someone gay or straight. . . . Project 10 can help prevent suicides (and suicide attempts, which are higher statistically among gay youths). . . . Project 10 affects the whole school—on the lower level it addresses and sex education;homophobia and on a higher level provides education on all issues affecting gays."

Asked about the impact of the homosexual life-style on traditional family values, Kruks offers these statistics:

Half of all marriages end in divorce. A study in Los Angeles County in 1983 showed 52,000 incidents of sexual and physical abuse of children. In certain categories of abuse cases, 95 percent are family-related.

"Traditional family values are divorce (and child abuse)," he says.

An assistant principal in one LAUSD secondary school, who spoke on the condition that his name not be used, says he refused to disseminate a packet of materials for Project 10 that Uribe distributed.

"It's not a decision junior high people can make without their parents," he says. "This should come from the home." He says about a dozen of the more than 100 counselors Uribe addressed last year agree with him, but they're afraid to speak out for fear of retribution. He says he is intimidated by board members because he likes the school he is in and doesn't want a different assignment.

Kruks says *One Teenager in 10*, of all books available, probably has the most positive and profound impact for kids and parents.

"It is not inappropriate," he says. "We're either going to have censorship or not."

Mort Tenner, administrative consultant in the Office of School Operations, says he was asked to investigate allegations that some materials available through Project 10 were pornographic. His report, presented to the board this year, indicated *"One Teenager in 10,"* has no place whatsoever in the school, he says.

He also says, *Changing Bodies, Changing Lives* [Random House, New York, 1980], which was available to students, is approved for use by health teachers but not for student instruction.

Tenner says the district superintendent notified Uribe to remove both books.

Uribe claims that she did not use *Changing Bodies, Changing Lives.* Tenner indicated it was previously available at the Fairfax High School library.

This book has been referred to by critics as a how-to manual that graphically and explicitly describes in the simplest terms the various techniques that homosexuals utilize to engage in a variety of gay and lesbian sex acts.

Tenner also says the operations staff will present recommendations in September on whether parental consent will be required for Project 10, adding that it is a logical extension of what is done for health courses when sexual reproduction is discussed. He said while speakers are cleared by school principals, it is wise to let parents know the subject matter in advance.

He says the recommendation will be announced at the first meeting of school principals next month.

State Assembly woman Marian La Follette, R-Northridge, has garnered the support of the Republican Caucus not to approve any measure that calls for new monies for the Los Angeles Unified School District until Project 10 is stopped.

"Parents could accomplish so much if they would speak out," she says. "I know they're frustrated but we cannot acquiesce and roll over and say it's useless. We must be aware of the kinds of programs the school board is sponsoring and supporting. We must make our pleasure or displeasure known to principals of schools as well as the board. Pressure and vigilance are needed. . . . The board is convinced that this is a proper program."

A member of the Assembly Education Committee, La Follette says it is important for the school board to recognize a group of parents and pupils who are, first, heterosexual and, secondly, not prepared to discuss this subject in school.

"Parents should be the ones to teach life-styles," La Follette says, adding it's not just Christians who oppose Project 10. "A lot of people are appalled at what the school board does but are not as vocal as some. A large group of people leaves battles to others."

La Follette, who is working to divide the board into several smaller ones to better serve the various communities within Los Angeles County, says it is important for the board to recognize that pupils are not prepared to discuss sexuality in school.

"Young people have lots of problems with sex. The teen years are a big question. Young people who are homosexual have counselors available to respond to their needs and concerns. That is an objective of the Project 10 outreach."

But, she says, Project 10 also places "an avowed lesbian in the position of promoting homosexuality."

At the June hearing before the Educational Development and Student Life Committee, Steve Afriat, a gay who is a member of the board of Head Start in the Valley, told the panel he hopes Project 10 is expanded "in every single high school in the Los Angeles Unified School District, because those children are everywhere." He called Project 10 a "sanctuary for gay and lesbian students (who have nowhere to turn)."

The media also have taken Project 10 to task. The Valley's *Daily News* editorialized in June that the program is "practically an invitation to a lawsuit: Uribe is not highly credentialed, is perceived by many to be biased, and counsels students under little supervision. . . . We believe the responsibility for the program's poor reception rests squarely on the shoulders of the school board."

"Schools make my job (as a parent) tough," Lupe Ramos says. "We teach our children to live right, morally and ethically, and give them self-respect. The school system—not the academics, but the sex education, projects like this one—really makes it tough for parents."

"Sex is not dirty, people make it dirty," Ramos says she tells her daughter. "(It's) the most beautiful thing a man and woman can share to show love, but only after they're married. . . . Those of us who want to preserve our culture, preserve family values, we're being stepped on by the school system. . . . In this country it's hard to live by that culture. I'm glad my mother and father were old-fashioned because if not I probably would be patting Virginia Uribe on the back. But I'm not, I'm sticking with my values. It boils down to moral and family values."

BOOKS REFERENCED

Altman D. (1982). *The Homosexualization of America.* Boston: Beacon Press.

Bayer R. (1981). *Homosexuality and American Psychiatry: The Politics of Diagnosis.* New York: Basic Books.

Bayer R. (1989). *Private Acts, Social Consequences: AIDS and the Politics of Public Health.* New York: The Free Press.

Bell AP, Weinberg MS. (1978). *Homosexualities: A Study of Diversity Among Men and Women.* New York: Simon and Schuster.

Bell R. (1980). *Changing Bodies, Changing Lives: A Book for Teens on Sex and Relationships.* New York: Random House.

Brecher R, Brecher E. (Eds.). (1967). *An Analysis of Human Sexual Response.* London: Andre Deutsch.

Breasted M. (1970). *Oh! Sex Education.* New York: Praeger.

Brongersma E. (1986). *Loving Boys (Volume I): A Multidisciplinary Study of Sexual Relations Between Adult and Minor Males.* Elmhurst, NY: Global Academic Publishers.

Brown L. (Ed.). (1981). *Sex Education in the Eighties.* New York: Plenum Publishing Corp.

Burgess AW, Groth AN, Holmstrom LL, Sgroi SM. (Eds.). (1978). *Sexual Assault of Children and Adolescents.* Lexington, MA: Lexington Books.

Christenson CV. (1971). *Kinsey: A Biography.* Bloomington, IN: Indiana University Press.

Cochran W, Mosteller F, Tukey J, Jenkins W. (1954). *Statistical Problems of the Kinsey Report.* Washington, DC: The American Statistical Association.

Cory DW. (1951). *The Homosexual in America.* New York: Greenberg.

Crooks R, Baur K. (1983). *Our Sexuality* (2nd ed.). Menlo Park, CA: The Benjamin/Cummings Publishing Company.

D'Emilio J, Freedman EB. (1988). *Intimate Matters: A History of Sexuality in America.* New York: Harper & Row.

Densen-Gerber J, Benward J. (1976). *Incest as a Causative Factor in Anti-Social Behavior: An Exploratory Study.* New York: Odyssey Institute.

Dickman I. (1982). *Winning the Battle for Sex Education.* New York: SIECUS.

Durant W, Durant A. (1968). *The Lessons of History.* New York: Simon and Schuster.

Faden RR, Beauchamp TL. (1986). *A History and Theory of Informed Consent.* New York: Oxford University Press.

Finkelhor D. (1979). *Sexually Victimized Children.* New York: Free Press.

Forleo R, Pasini W. (Eds.). (1980). *Medical Sexology: The Third International Congress.* Littleton, MA: PSG Publishing Company.

Freeman D. (1983). *Margaret Mead and Samoa: The Making and Unmaking of an Anthropological Myth.* Cambridge, MA: Harvard University Press.

Freud S. (1962). *Three Essays on the Theory of Sexuality.* (Strachey J, ed. and trans.). New York: Basic Books.

Gagnon JH. (1977). *Human Sexualities.* Glenview, IL: Scott, Foresman & Co.

Gagnon JH, Simon W. (1973). *Sexual Conduct: The Social Sources of Human Sexuality.* Chicago: Aldine Publishing Co.

Gebhard P, Gagnon J, Pomeroy W, Christenson C. (1965). *Sex Offenders: An Analysis of Types.* New York: Harper & Row.

Gebhard P, Johnson A. (1979). *The Kinsey Data: Marginal Tabulations of the 1938-1963 Interviews Conducted by the Institute for Sex Research.* Philadelphia: W.B. Saunders Company.

Geddes DP. (Ed.) (1954). *An Analysis of the Kinsey Reports on Sexual Behavior in the Human Male and Female.* New York: Mentor Books.

Herman J, Hirschman L. (1981). *Father-Daughter Incest.* Cambridge, MA: Harvard University Press.

Himelhoch J, Fava SF. (Eds.) (1955). *Sexual Behavior in American Society: An Appraisal of the First Two Kinsey Reports.* New York: W.W. Norton & Company.

Hoch PH, Zubin J. (Eds.) (1949). *Psychosexual Development in Health and Disease.* New York: Grune & Stratton.

Hoffman E. (1988). *The Right to be Human: A Biography of Abraham Maslow.* New York: Tarcher/St. Martin.

Hunt M. (1974). *Sexual Behavior in the 1970s.* Chicago: Playboy Press.

Karlen A. (1971). *Sexuality and Homosexuality.* New York: W.W. Norton & Co.

Kelly G. (1986). *Learning About Sex: The Contemporary Guide for Young Adults.* Hauppage, NY: Barron.

Kinsey AC, Pomeroy WB, Martin CE. (1948). *Sexual Behavior in the Human Male.* Philadelphia: W.B. Saunders Company.

Kinsey AC, Pomeroy WB, Martin CE, Gebhard PH. (1953). *Sexual Behavior in the Human Female.* Philadelphia: W.B. Saunders Company.

Lanning KV. (1986). *Child Molesters: A Behavioral Analysis.* Washington, DC: National Center for Missing & Exploited Children.

Legman G. (1964). *The Horn Book: Studies in Erotic Folklore and Bibliography.* New Hyde Park, NY: University Books.

Linedecker C. (1981). *Children in Chains.* New York: Everest House.

Mack JD. (1981). *Vivienne: The Life and Suicide of an Adolescent Girl.* Boston: Little, Brown.

Mark A, Mark VH. (1981). *The Pied Pipers of Sex.* Plainfield, NJ: Haven Books.

Masters WH, Johnson VE. (1966). *Human Sexual Response.* Boston: Little, Brown.

Masters WH, Johnson VE, Kolodny RC. (1977). *Ethical Issues in Sex Therapy and Research.* Boston: Little, Brown.

Masters WH, Johnson VE. (1979). *Homosexuality in Perspective.* Boston: Little, Brown.

McGrady PM. (1972). *The Love Doctors.* New York: Macmillan.

McNaron T, Morgan Y. (Eds.). (1982). *Voices of the Night: Women Speaking Out About Incest.* Pittsburgh, PA: Cleis Press.

Mead M. (1971). *Coming of Age in Samoa.* New York: William Morrow & Co.

Montgomery KC. (1989). *Target: Prime Time.* New York: Oxford University Press.

Moore TV. (1943). *The Nature and Treatment of Mental Disorders.* New York: Grune & Stratton.

O'Brien S. (1983). *Child Pornography.* Dubuque, IA: Kendall-Hunt.

O'Carroll T. (1980). *Pedophilia: The Radical Case.* Boston: Alyson Publications.

Pomeroy WB. (1968). *Boys and Sex.* New York: Pelican Books.

Pomeroy WB. (1969). *Girls and Sex.* New York: Pelican Books.

Pomeroy WB. (1972). *Dr. Kinsey and the Institute for Sex Research.* New York: Harper & Row.

Pomeroy W, Flax C, Wheeler C. (1982). *Taking a Sex History: Interviewing and Recording.* New York: The Free Press.

Renshaw DC. (1982). *Incest.* Boston: Little, Brown.

Robinson P. (1976). *The Modernization of Sex.* New York: Harper & Row.

Rothenberg RE. (Ed.). (1981). *The Plain-Language Law Dictionary.* New York: Penguin.

Rueda ET. (1982). *The Homosexual Network: Private Lives and Public Policy.* Old Greenwich, CT: Devin Adair.

Sandfort RT. (1982). *The Sexual Aspect of Pedophile Relations.* Amsterdam: Pan/Spartacus.

Schlafly P. (Ed.). (1985). *Child Abuse in the Classroom.* Wilmore, KY: Crossway Books.

Shelp EE. (Ed.). (1987). *Sexuality and Medicine, Volume II: Ethical Viewpoints in Transition.* Boston: D. Reidel Publishing Co.

Sgroi S. (Ed.). (1982). *Handbook of Clinical Intervention in Child Sexual Abuse.* Lexington, MA: Lexington Books.

Socarides CW. (1977). *Beyond Sexual Freedom.* New York: Quadrangle Books.

Strong B, DeVault C. (1986). *The Marriage and the Family Experience.* Anaheim: West Publishing Co.

Tripp CA. (1975). *The Homosexual Matrix.* New York: McGraw-Hill.

Wallerstein J. (1989). *Second Chances: Men Women and Children a Decade after Divorce.* Ticknor & Fields.

Weyr T. (1978). *Reaching for Paradise: The Playboy Vision of America.* New York: Times Books.

Yankelovich D. (1981). *New Rules: Searching for Self-Fulfillment in a World Turned Upside Down.* New York: Random House.

Zimbardo PG, Ebbeson EB, Maslach C. (1977). *Influencing Attitudes and Changing Behavior.* Reading, MA: Addison-Wesley.

INDEX